SOLOMON GOLDMAN

A RABBI'S RABBI

Dr. Goldman in 1946

SOLOMON GOLDMAN

A RABBI'S RABBI

By Jacob J. Weinstein, D.D., D.H.L.

Rabbi Emeritus
KAM Temple, Chicago, Illinois

KTAV PUBLISHING HOUSE, INC.

NEW YORK

1973

Library of Congress Cataloging in Publication Data

Weinstein, Jacob Joseph, 1902–
    Solomon Goldman: a rabbi's rabbi.
    Bibliography: p.
    1. Goldman, Solomon, 1893–1953. 2. Zionism—United
States. 3. Judaism—United States.
BM755.G58W45   296.6'1'0924 [B]   72–10301
ISBN 0–87068–196–6

TABLE OF CONTENTS

In Acknowledgement

This book and the completion and publication of "From Slavery to Freedom," the University of Chicago Edition of "The Ten Commandments," edited by Maurice Samuel, the placing of crucial papers and correspondence in various libraries and Archives was made possible by the Goldman Memorial Foundation. The author gratefully dedicates this volume to the members of the Foundation Committee, Mr. David Jacker, Mr. Harry Kulp, Mrs. Alice Goldman, Mrs. Joseph Epstein and Mrs. Albert Zemel. The Committee and the Author record here their profound thanks to the many friends and disciples of Solomon Goldman who established the Foundation to honor his memory.

Introduction

When the Goldman Memorial Committee approached me to undertake the task, first, of reading the vast correspondence and memoirs of Solomon Goldman and, then, of acting as a kind of literary executor to determine what disposition might be made of his papers and unpublished writings (evaluate them and, if the material merited, write a biographical study), I found the invitation compelling on several grounds. I was, first of all, indebted to Goldman for the inspiration of his early writings, *A Rabbi Takes Stock* and the *Jew and the Universe*, both of which I read before I ever met him. The admiration which his writings evoked in me was deepened by more intimate association during my rabbinate in Chicago between 1939 and 1953. Though Goldman was a rabbi of a Conservative Congregation, and I of the oldest Reform Congregation in Illinois, there were no theological or denominational barriers between us. Goldman was a true disciple of his teacher, Solomon Schechter, who first used the phrase Catholic Israel to define a Judaism which always managed to rise above parochial pulls and denominational devices. Goldman was an iconoclast when it came to labels. He was so intent on seeing and hearing the essential Jew that he quickly brushed aside the peripheral badge.

Goldman became my exemplar and model. He established a system of priorities which I could respect even when I could not emulate them. When I became too deeply involved in social issues, he reminded me of a rabbi's first obligation to Torah study. As I enlarged the tent of my activities, he gently urged me to drive my stakes deeper. He encouraged me to withstand the pressures of my congregation to popularize and package the grains of wisdom gleaned at the Seminary and spend the rest of my time on pastoral glad-handing and back-slapping. He insisted that the study of Hebrew had to be the backbone of our religious school curriculum, and the passion for Zion-Israel rebuilt and Hebrew regained—the first commitment of the American Jew. He encouraged me, as he did all my Reform colleagues in Chicago, to restore peoplehood to Judaism and clothe the abstract thesis of monotheistic theology with the living flesh of our people's long and varied experience in time and space. Above all, he gave me a constant example of a dedicated man who could see human pettiness and rascality without becoming cynical, who could be passionately partisan without bigotry, who could compromise on occasion without jettisoning vital principal, who could hold fast to ultimate purpose even while incontinent necessity pressed hard on him. Cowed as I was by wealth, tarred by the *shtetl's* allergy to worldly success, I learned from Goldman that rich men were often softies and were flattered at being asked for large gifts once they got over the initial shock.

So this book is offered as a labor of love from a disciple and a colleague. If I am charged with crossing denominational lines to pay this tribute to a Conservative rabbi, I can plead that my subject was not a respecter of walls, that, as he prayed for the restoration of a Jerusalem built without walls, so he labored to lower and bridge the denominational barriers which the accidents of history, the random pace of evolutionary growth, had imposed on the Jewish people committed to the one God of Israel.

The ecumenical value of a Reform rabbi writing the life story of a Conservative leader is but a graceful plus to the more important motive for this book, which is to offer to a bewildered and often disillusioned rabbinate of today the example of a rabbi who overcame equally discouraging circumstances and equally pernicious doubts. It is true that the rabbinate is not suffering the seismic shock now so pervasive in the Catholic priesthood as belatedly it enters the twentieth century, since fortunately, Judaism did not impose celibacy on the clergy and allowed considerable leniency toward the command to multiply and fructify, and remained loyal, in its fashion, to the prophetic imperative to make justice the foundation stone of the good society on earth. Nevertheless, the synagogue faces an agonizing reappraisal of its role, and the rabbi an even more agonizing evaluation of his function, in a world where the very stars tremble as man rides dune buggies on the moon but persists in the murderous madness of war and in the slow but certain poisoning and devitalization of the good earth.

Our problem is not so much to recruit students for the rabbinate as to persuade them to assume the care of a congregation when they receive ordination. An ever growing percentage of the graduates prefer to enter other forms of communal work, or a Hillel foundation, or a chaplaincy or teaching position. More practicing rabbis are leaving the synagogue to try their hand at business or counseling, or Jewish communal service. A rabbi, at best, must be a generalist, and the trend of industry and the professions is towards specialization. Too often, the rabbi is a jack of all trades and master of none. The administrative burden of a congregational rabbi is often antithetic to the need for study and meditation. The young people who are the lifeline to the future (and Judaism has always been continuity oriented) consider the synagogue a part of the establishment and, to that extent, taboo. The fact is that religion is a sometime thing with most Jews, and the synagogue has moved from the center of the average Jew's concern to the periphery. The great blanket of despair woven by anarchic technology, political impotence in the face of war, the alienation of man from meaningful vocation, from the warm fellowship of primary groups, finds the traditional answers of the pulpit inadequate, and the traditional consolations of the prayer book often as shoddy as Job's comforters.

And yet, one begins to detect a backlash from despair and disillusion, a reaching out for faith and the certainty which religion once gave its devotees. Especially among the young does one find a searching for personality in the universe, for order and compassion in nature, for mythopoeic rituals to celebrate the seasons of life. The Zen fans, the Hare Krishna roving bands, the Jesus freaks have their counterpart in the Jewish youth who find in Hasidism a satisfying answer to their hunger for an unstructured faith that can be joyous, communal, ecstatic, and rooted in specific tradition. These young are very wary of returning to the synagogue as it is now constituted. They will have to find their own groupings and their own type of communal management. They need help and will accept it from the elders of the established synagogues if it is offered freely, openly, and without strings. Many of the dissidents are especially turned on by Israel. There they find radical experiment with social organization, a return to nature, an end to split loyalties and ambivalence of identification. In a strange and wonderful way, Hasidism, as a religion of the wise heart, and Zionism, as a return to historic selfhood, are the two avenues through which our alienated youth may return to the household of Israel.

The rabbi who wishes to aid in that return will be well advised to ponder the life and works of the subject of this book. For here he will find a man who, through dint of disciplined scholarship, had that finely tuned integrity which comes to a rabbi who knows that he is rabbi—a teacher—in fact as well as in name. He will encounter a rabbi who was able to manage a large institution and bend it to his purposes because he imposed upon it the same priorities he bound upon himself. He will meet a man who eagerly recognized the centrality of Israel in Judaism and ethnic loyalty as the key to Jewish identity. He will find a man who insisted that we abandon the convenient hypocrisy of the Sunday school and give to Jewish education the time and instrumentation that a 3000-year-old world culture needs and deserves—a school equal to the best of our secular schools. He will rejoice in a leader who would not surrender to the anti-defamationist traders in scare techniques nor to the philantropists who used their contributions as much to mask their gentile hearts as to cover the nakedness of their poor brethren. He will discover a rabbi who was bold enough to believe that the best way he could serve America was to keep alive the Jewish Biblical, Talmudic and *shtetl* values that they might become part of the American heritage. Lastly, he will take heart from his confrontation with

the cluster of contradictions that assail him on every side by witness-
ing with what grace, humor, and skill, this rabbi's rabbi wove and
fused together in viable strength and harmony the antinomies of
particularism and Universalism, individualism and collectivism,
Israel and Diaspora, reason and intuition, family and the world,
justice and compassion.

I wish to acknowledge with heartfelt thanks the assistance given
to me by Maurice Samuel, Dr. Louis Finklestein, Dr. Mordecai
Kaplan, Judge Louis Levinthal, Rabbi David Graubart, Robert
Szold, Dr. Samuel Beck, who through close association with Rabbi
Goldman were able to help me evaluate the record more intelli-
gently. To the members of the Goldman Memorial Committee,
Harry Kulp, David Jacker, Mrs. Solomon Goldman, Naomi Goldman Zemel, and Gayola Goldman Epstein, I am even more grateful
for our report sessions over a period of two years, which we recalled
with poignant delight the impact on our lives of a gallant husband
and father and an excitingly affectionate friend and teacher.

To Mrs. Norman Groffman, Mrs. Samuel Block, Mrs. Morton
Grodzins, and Mrs. Gay Smith my thanks for the many hours of
typing, revising and retyping the manuscript. A special note of
thanks is due to Ruth Glushanok whose keen editorial eye detected
the flabby permissiveness often imposed by professional speakers on
the written word.

PART I:
A RABBI'S RABBI

Chapter 1

Early Beginnings

SOLOMON GOLDMAN was born on 19 August 1893, at Kozin in the province of Volhynia in Russian Poland. Volhynia was part of the Pale of Settlement, that vast compound into which the various Russian and Polish governments herded the Jews using them as small traders and artisans to give flexibility to a rural economy and, unhappily, as scapegoats to deflect the ripened discontent of their peasantry when hard liquor and Orthodox Christianity lost their sedative powers. He was born to Abraham Abba and Jeanette Grossman, each of whom boasted a long ancestral line of rabbinic students and scholars. Solomon relished the family legend that his grandfather on his mother's side, Rabbi Joshua Grossman of Kishineff, slept for forty years with a stone as his pillow in mourning for the destruction of the *Bet ha-Mikdash*, the Temple on Zion, and in the hope that he might have the merit to contribute a stone for its rebuilding.

Volhynia today is becoming *Judenrein* as the result of the harsh decrees of Poland's Communist regime subservient to its Russian master. Polish archives will not preserve the records of its Rabbi Joshuas. Solomon Goldman loved to linger on *shtetl* lore to frustrate the Poles' intention to condemn his ancestors to oblivion. Jeanette Grossman prayed that Solomon would be the twelfth rabbi in the line of her descent to add *yichus*—ancestral prestige—to the family tree, bring comfort to the folk Israel and hasten the redemption.

Abba and Jeanette were among the fortunate thousands of East European Jews who migrated to America at the turn of the century. They came to New York and found a place to live in Brownsville, a section of Brooklyn. The record is sketchy for the next ten years, but it reveals that Solomon inherited a sizable allotment of the intellectual energy which his people had generated like radium in peat bogs in the Pale of Settlement. At the age of twelve, Solomon worked as a buttonhole-maker in a pants sweatshop and, at thirteen, he was tutoring less gifted youngsters in both English and Hebrew studies. He was not conscious that he was living in two cultures or making a contribution to cultural pluralism; learning was one as God was one. He went through the public schools of Brooklyn like a hot knife through butter. He studied the Tanach and the Talmud first with Uncle Mendel and various *melamdim,* and then at the Yitzchak Elchanan Yeshivah. It was here that he met Louis Finklestein, and a friendship began which was to endure all his life and which was to prove crucial in a large part of his life's activities. The restless dynamism of the young Solomon led him, while still a student, to become the principal of the Young Judea training school for leaders, founder of the Graetzians, a Jewish history-study society, and coeditor, with Louis Finkelstein, of the *Jewish Forum.*

When his searching mind found too many barriers at Yitzchak Elchanan Yeshivah, he entered the Jewish Theological Seminary in 1912 despite Uncle Mendel's dire warning that he would be corrupted by the "Professors" at that unorthodox place. He entered with Louis Finkelstein and David Aaronson, and in one of the letters Solomon wrote to Louis Finkelstein there is a vivid description of the examination of the candidates by Professor Louis Ginzberg. They were much in awe of the man who was to become the greatest scholar in American Israel. They were entranced by the gracious manner with which he bore the mighty weight of his learning, the kindly patience with which he listened to their bravura answers, the subtle manner in which he encouraged them to venture into the deeper waters of the Talmud, and the delicate chivalry with which he bailed them out when the mountainous waves of *halakha* proved too much for the frail craft of their learning. Solomon became a favorite student of Professor Ginzberg and won from him the accolade: "You are a strong and skillful swimmer in the sea of Talmud."

A great power of concentration, an extraordinary *sprachgefühl* (feeling for language), a most retentive memory, and an insatiable curiosity made it possible for Solomon to pursue his studies at the Seminary, take courses at New York University, attend lectures at Columbia, especially those of John Dewey and Charles G. Shaw, and follow a personally tailored curriculum on his own in Greek, French, German, and geometry. On top of all this, he found time to tutor boys for Bar Mitzvah and for entrance examinations. David Aaronson recalls that in the summertime, when the windows were open, crowds of youngsters would gather to hear Solomon expound the Sidra or the Haftarah and to marvel at the cleverness of his commentaries and the passion of his eloquence.

When he was still two years from ordination, Solomon received a most unusual commendation from Dr. Solomon Schechter, the chancellor of the Seminary, and one of the most luminous minds in the entire history of Jewish scholarship. It came in a letter written on 12 May 1915, and was addressed to the secretary of congregation Petach Tikvah, in Brooklyn.

I have your letter of May 4 in which you ask me to recommend to you a Rabbi for your Congregation Petach Tivah.

As a rule, it is not the policy of the Seminary to recommend men to pulpits unless they have completed their full course of study, and for this reason I have been waiting with my reply in order to find the proper men for you among those who are going to graduate this year, or who have already graduated in the past. But it has come to my knowledge since, that one of our Senior students, Mr. Solomon Goldman, has been doing such excellent work in your Congregation up till now, and has proven himself so useful and so earnest in his activities for your community, that I feel justified in making an exception in his case, and recommend him to you for the position. He is indeed one of our best students, highly promising in every respect, both as regards scholarship and ability as preacher, teacher and social worker. Of course, it will take him another two years before he will receive his authorization of the Seminary as Rabbi, but I trust the relation which exists between him and your community will only prove a stimulus to him in his studies and will enable him all the more to equip himself with the necessary experience. I have every confidence that he will make himself worthy of any position he may hold.

Wishing you success in your good work in the cause of Judaism, I am,

Very truly yours,
Solomon Schechter
President

Solomon Goldman received his ordination in June of 1918 and as well, married Alice, the daughter of Emanuel and Rose Lipkowitz. Rabbi David Aaronson, in congratulating Solomon on the publication of the first volume of the *Book of Human Destiny* series, recalls the first date that Solomon had with Alice and the beatific look of adoration in his eyes as he sat next to her on the subway for the long trip back from Coney Island. It was a marriage blessed by heaven, for Alice was to sustain him through all the many crises of his turbulent career and make a home that was both an adjunct to the synagogue and a haven from the intolerable pressures of his multifaceted career. Of necessity, she had to be a surrogate father during the early years of Geulah and Naomi when the problems of Judaism and the Jews pulled the rabbi away from home for weeks at a time. She kept the home sound and serene and helped to involve the girls in their father's work as they grew older and bring them to an acceptance, with a minimum of rebellion, of their difficult role as exemplars in a fish bowl, and as daughters who had to share their father's paternal care and warmth with the myriad sons and daughters of the congregation.

Now we move to that part of the record that tells of the eleven years which Rabbi Goldman spent in Cleveland, Ohio. His brilliant achievements at Anshe Emet and on the world Jewish scene tend to eclipse these eleven years, but they were formative years and give clear evidence of the qualities which made him one of the three outstanding rabbis of the twentieth century. The four years which he spent at B'nai Jeshuran from 1918 to 1922, were years in which Rabbi Goldman gathered his forces, learned the elements of good administration of a synagogue, experimented with various types of pulpit discourse, examined the rather skimpy material available as textbooks for religious-school classes, and, above all, felt the width and the depth of the gap between the profession of Orthodox and/or Traditional Judaism and its practice.[1]

Here, in his first congregation, Goldman became painfully aware of how little the training he received at the seminary helped him to establish criteria, standards, and guidelines to help the immigrant Jew in his groping efforts to apply the heldover memories of his old-country *Yiddishkeit* to the new conditions of American life in big cities. He became even more painfully aware that the patterns of adjustment which proved tolerable for the Yiddish-speaking immigrant generation were not meaningful for their American-born children. He could very well appreciate the embarrassment and awkwardness of these children when they came to services with their parents on the major holy days and sat restive and fidgety during the long, and to them, unintelligible portions of the service. At B'nai Jeshuran he came to the difficult conclusion that an effective Hebrew education program was beyond the congregation's resources in money and manpower, and that only through establishing a citywide system of Hebrew schools could some portion of the young be saved to Judaism. He therefore joined with the distinguished Hebraist A. H. Friedland in forging the elaborate network of Talmud Torahs in the city of Cleveland. The friendship begun here was to grow in respect and affection with later years.

By 1922, Goldman realized that B'nai Jeshuran could not become the synagogue which he envisioned as viable for America. He accepted the leadership of the Jewish Center which was a merger of two traditional synagogues, Anshe Emet and Beth Tephiloh. Here he found more adequate facilities and a more responsive lay leadership for his wide-ranging, ambitious plans. In a very short time it became apparent that there he could speak about Judaism or religion without compromising his convictions. He showed he was

---

1. "Traditional" is a term which has come into use in the past few decades to designate a style of Jewish observance somewhere between Orthodoxy and Conservatism—but since these terms are stretchable, "Traditional" too is elastic.)

aware of the intellectual and social climate of American life and of
the secular conditioning of the young folk who came not so much
to worship as to be persuaded that they ought to worship, not so
much to identify with the Jewish people as to be convinced that
they ought to be so identified. Goldman directed himself to this
challenge with unbounded zeal and consummate skill. What he
could not accomplish with a textual sermon, he attempted with a
kind of oratorical essay, a form compact with close reasoning and
apt reference to philosophical and sociological sources interspersed
with telling analogies and choice Midrashim. Perceiving that he
might be thought to be a special pleader, he brought to the Sunday
Forum Lecture Series Harry Elmer Barnes, M. C. Otto, Eustace
Hayden, Oswald Villard, John Erskine, John Dewey, James Harvey
Robinson, Horace Kallen, Morris R. Cohen. He brought poets Carl
Sandburg, Maxwell Bodenheim, Louis Untermeyer. He introduced
the congregation to Stephen Wise and demonstrated that this Re-
former was not a "goy." He shared his own great enthusiasm for
Mordecai Kaplan with those in the congregation who were groping for a philosophy of Judaism that would not be so sectarian as to
be parochial nor so universal as to be unidentifiable as Jewish. Observers on the scene noticed that there was a decided diminution in
the migration of East European Jews to the Reform Temples, that, in
fact, there was a choice group of young college men from Reform
homes who were regular attendants at these services. There was even
a sprinkling of non-Jews who discovered that this rabbi and the men
he brought to the Center offered the keenest intellectual stimulation
to be found in Cleveland.

Goldman might have become smug and considered his mission
achieved as the 2,500-capacity auditorium of the Center filled up
with eager worshipers on Friday night and with thoughtful listen-
ers on Sunday morning. But he learned early that there is a vast
difference between listening and understanding, between passive
absorption and that active interplay of minds which is the best cru-
cible of mature wisdom. He decided to select the more responsive
of the young people and invite them to his home for concentrated
study. He respected the intelligence of the group by letting them
select the fields of inquiry most germane to their interests. He en-

couraged the widest possible discussion, but he insisted that the
discussants do the reading that might convert mere opinion into
factual judgment. They later called themselves the "Deot" group
—the knowledge seekers. Goldman selected his Forum speakers
largely with an eye to their suitability for this group. He arranged
with the speakers that they would spend a long afternoon or evening
leading the group in discussion of a previously selected topic. Thus,
in addition to the persons mentioned above, the Deot group held
stimulating sessions with Bialik, Tchernichowsky, Chaim Greenberg,
Norman Thomas, Peter Witt, Upton Sinclair, Owen Lovejoy. The
group represented many points of view: assimilationists, Zionists,
Reform, Conservative, and Orthodox Jews, atheists, agnostics, Hu-
manists, Philosophical Anarchists, Socialists, Republicans, and Democrats. They were held together by the rabbi who played many parts
—midwife, mediator, provocateur, ringmaster—but never forgot that
his essential role was that of rabbi and that his ultimate goal was the
cultivation of intelligent lay leadership for the Jewish people.[2]

During his four years at B'nai Jeshuran, Goldman remained a
local figure. Even his offer to go on a speaking tour for the Jewish
Theological Seminary was not accepted on the ground that he was
not well-known enough. It required less than two years at the Jewish Center to project Goldman onto the national scene as one who
deserved a place in the councils of the mighty. In the fall of 1925,
David A. Brown, national chairman of the National Committee of
the United Jewish Campaign, invited Goldman to serve on the
National Committee to raise the unprecedented sum of $15,000,000
for the relief of the Jews of Eastern Europe. Goldman replied to
David A. Brown refusing this invitation on the ground that he could
not make peace with the soil of Russia and, more important, that
this money could be better spent transporting several thousand families of Jews to Palestine. He urged that since the Jews had not
followed up the promise of the Balfour Declaration, every opportunity must now be seized to buy the land and bring the people to
the land so a national Jewish home might be secured. Mr. Brown

---

2. See letter of David Hertz to Mrs. Alice Goldman, February 6, 1966, Appendix II,
pp. 270–277.

turned this letter over to Mr. Louis Marshall, the acknowledged
leader of the American Jewish Committee, president of Temple
Emanu-el and the one with most ready access to the economic and
political decisionmakers in America. Mr. Marshall wrote a scathing
four-page letter to Rabbi Goldman charging him with being callous
to the suffering of his fellow Jews, obviously willing to let them
agonize in despair because of his addiction to a particular "ism," "an
iridescent dream at best." He took Goldman severely to task for setting his opinion against that of the selected and elected leadership
of American Jewry who, at the Philadelphia Conference, had received authentic reports of the condition of the Jews in Russia,
Poland, Romania, Yugoslavia, etc., etc., had studied all the alterna-
tives and had, in their sober and collective wisdom, decided upon
the $15,000,000 campaign. The great Marshall was implying that it
was colossal *chutzpah* on top of callousness for Goldman to set his
opinion against the judgment of his betters. With the shrewd skill
of a master advocate, Marshall went on to demolish the argument for
Palestine. It would cost 8 billion dollars, he estimated, to buy and
restore the land and transport the Jews. "Had Goldman forgotten,"
he asked, "how hard it was to raise even one million for the Jewish
Theological Seminary?" Since the Jews of Russia had not jumped
at the chance to come to America notwithstanding the pogroms and
despite the permissive immigration laws, how much less would they
be inclined to go to Palestine? Then the wily Marshall reminded
Goldman that if he persuaded Jews not to give to East European
relief, they would be more readily persuaded not to give to Palestine.
The thing to do was to have courage to ask for both. Let the Zionists
cooperate and they would find that the pocket they breached for
Europe would be more open for Palestine. He ends with this paragraph so revealing of the touch of arrogance with which power taints
even the best of us:

> In conclusion let me say that, though I would regret the fact of your denying
> yourself to your brethren in Eastern Europe, this campaign will proceed. The
> majority of the Jews in the United States still believe in Holy Writ and in
> its commands that we shall not withdraw our hands from our brethren who
> are needy nor place a stumbling block in their path. They are unwilling to
> give these admonitions a narrow, parochial, partisan connotation, and I there-

fore feel justified in prophesying that the fund which we are seeking to collect will be subscribed.[3]

This exchange might have humbled a less secure man. For Goldman it was a revelation of the German Jews' deep resistance to Zionism, of their pathetic faith that the Joint Distribution Committee could, by making the Jew more productive as a worker and an industrialist, create a permanent haven in East European lands. It made him keenly aware of how classical Reform Judaism, as exemplified in Temple Emanu-el, had drastically attenuated the national and ethnic bond in the mystique of Judaism. It made him apprehensive of the influence the Marshall-Warburg-Schiff Jews might have on his alma mater, the Jewish Theological Seminary, a fear which was to precipitate a long and sometimes bitter dialogue with his classmate and closest friend, Dr. Louis Finkelstein. It made him more anxious than ever to tap the resources of the East European Jew. He had seen the affluence that had come to many of the immigrant peddlers on Eastern Parkway, Brooklyn, and now he saw the same economic strength that had come to many in Cleveland. He believed that if they could be trained to give in accordance with their means, the problem of the synagogue and Jewish education in America could be solved, and Palestine could become the national home. As he wrote in 1927 to Judge Julian Mack:

> I wonder whether you are aware of the fact that on Eastern Parkway, President Street, etc., in Brooklyn, there are Jews of untold wealth. There are from three to five hundred men in that community who could give all the money that Palestine needs. They are nearer to the cause and more easily approached. We have never concentrated on these people.

Judge Mack was not convinced. He replied on this point:

> Frankly, these rich Jews of East European birth are, in my judgement, the most hopeless lot. The richer they grow the more ashamed they seem to become both of their birth and their Orthodoxy; too many of them are ready to hide both; what they want is the honor of leadership—not the obligations of service. . . . I am glad if any method can be devised to get them to give

---

3. See the correspondence between Marshall and Goldman, pp. 223–227.

in larger amounts. I should however be most happy if I am doing them an injustice, and if they would, with their excellent business ability, really be induced to give time and thought in loyal service to the cause itself.[4]

Another by-product of Goldman's coming to national prominence was to lead to an internal crisis and to a court trial which was much more significant to the Orthodox Jewish community than the famous Monkey Trial in Tennessee which made Darwin, Darrow, and Bryan household words. In the vast reaches of the Center which now numbered some 1,500 families, a Hebrew school of several thousand, and still more thousands of Jews who used its gymnasium and other recreational facilities, there remained a hard core of more Orthodox Jews, especially those who had been prominent in the Beth Tephilo congregation before its merger with Anshe Emet. They had been thrilled at first to see the vast public response to Rabbi Goldman, and had hoped that he would convert the heathen to what they believed was the only Torah-true Judaism, their own kind of Orthodoxy. They looked upon the youth leaders, the college-trained faculty of the religious school, the visiting guests in the pulpit and the Sunday Forum as missionaries for their brand of Orthodoxy. It became apparent to them during Goldman's first year, that what they called Orthodoxy and what Goldman called traditional Judaism were two radically different religions. Those who were genuinely motivated by loyalty to Orthodoxy were joined by some who resented the new leadership which Goldman was bringing into the Center. They had recourse to an old set of by-laws adopted in 1917, which gave any group of five members the power to veto any amendments or changes in ritual made at a meeting expressly called for the purpose of making such changes. The by-laws had never been operative and were, in fact, unknown to many of the members. When Goldman refused to make adequate concessions to the dissidents, they took their case to the Bet Din, the Rabbinical Court of the Union of Orthodox Rabbis of the United States headquartered in New York. Goldman was summoned to the Bet Din to answer the charges made against him. The rabbi refused to recognize the

---

4. See the full correspondence between Goldman, Judge Mack and Stephen Wise, pp. 228–234.

authority of the Bet Din because he contended the Jewish Center was a member of the United Synagogue, the lay body of the Conservative Movement, and had called its most recent rabbis from the Rabbinical Assembly, the association of Conservative rabbis. In this he was sustained by the overwhelming majority of his Board. The thirteen dissidents, now advised by officials of the Union of Orthodox Rabbis, took their case to the Court of Common Pleas of Cuyahoga County, Ohio. They charged Rabbi Goldman and thirty members of the Board with:

> . . . violation of the Constitution and By-Laws which establishes the congregation as an orthodox or traditional congregation, by which is meant a religious doctrine which recognizes the absolute authority of the Five Books of Moses as being the inspired word of God as well as the Talmud and the Torah Codes and which also recognizes the sacred character of those ceremonial observances which through the centuries have become identified with Orthodox Judaism.

The petitioners charged that since the installation of the defendant Goldman as rabbi, the leadership has been opposed and hostile to the doctrines of Orthodox or Traditional Judaism and all the ritual and ceremonial observances appertaining thereto and has failed and refused to observe the trust imposed upon the church property in the following particulars.

The charges listed here are the most vivid of a total of thirty-eight complaints:

> By permitting Goldman to announce publicly many times and against the protests of the plaintiffs that the Five Books of Moses were not inspired by God, and were not written by Moses and that the Decalogue or Ten Commandments were not given or revealed by God to Moses at Sinai . . .[5]

> By permitting the Rabbi to forbid the Priests (Cohanim) to pronounce the priestly blessing during the holiday services.

> By permitting the Rabbi to ridicule in his sermons the great religious figures of Israel.

---

5. In his exhaustive debunking of the Higher Criticism in the three volumes of the *Book of Human Destiny*, Goldman concludes that Mosaic authorship can neither be proven or disproven. See pp. 175.

By forbidding the mourners in the congregation to say Kaddish individually in a voice audible to the congregation.

By permitting eating without saying grace or covering the head.

By permitting the kissing of brides by the Rabbi during marriage ceremonies.

By permitting the Rabbi to carry books openly through the streets on the Sabbath while on the way to service.

By omission of that part of the Sabbath Services beginning with *Pitum Haktores* having reference to the composition of the incense. . . .

By permitting the Rabbi to urge the congregation from the pulpit on Rosh Hashanah to read the book known as "The Mind in the Making" by James Harvey Robinson, which publication is hostile to and a denial of Orthodox Judaism.

By permitting the Rabbi to be absent regularly from daily morning services.

By permitting the Rabbi to partake of meals at public hotels and restaurants and at public affairs without inquiring concerning Kashrut. . . .

By permitting the Rabbi and Forum Committee to make of the Forum a hot-bed of radicalism by inviting speakers widely known for their radical tendencies to preach their views to young men and women on Sunday mornings. . . .

In view of this behavior the plaintiffs demand that the Constitution adopted by the congregation in November, 1924 be set aside in favor of the original Constitution of 1917 and that the congregational properties be returned to those in the congregation who will dedicate them to the cause of Orthodox or Traditional Judaism.

In his reply, Rabbi Goldman gave the court a masterful lecture on the history of Judaism and the development of the various divisions in Judaism as well as answered the specific charges brought against him. The crucial part of his response is as follows:

Defendant denies that the term "traditional" is synonymous with "Orthodox," as applied to Judaism, Defendant avers that there has been no governing body of Jewish churches for the past eighteen hundred years, but that each congregation makes up a separate entity, responsible alone to itself and without control by any other organization. Among the Jews, the word "traditional" is used in connection with Jewish law, and in Judaism from time immemorial there has been recognized the existence of both a written law and a traditional law. The written law is embodied in the Pentateuch—

the Five Books of Moses. The traditional law was handed down from generation to generation orally, until committed to writing in the year 200 A.D. For
at least the last thousand years no Jew has challenged the binding effect of
the traditional law. Prior to 1,000 years ago, at various stages in Jewish
history, traditional law was challenged—it being considered the fabrication
of the Rabbis. But now all experts upon Judaism will agree that the oral law
is of genuine and gradual development. The word "Orthodox" in the
Christian church has been used to designate rigidity and inflexibility in
creed and was never applied to ritual or practice. In the Jewish religion on
the other hand there has never been a rigid definition of creed and the term
"Orthodox" has not had a meaning in the Jewish religion until the last
century and then it has been and is used in connection with ritual or practice.

There are three so-called groups of Jewish churches all of which have
sprung up within the past one hundred years, but none of which are gov-
erned by any central organization, nor do all of the members of any one
observe uniformity of ritual and practice. These three groups are known as
the Reformed, Conservative, and Orthodox. All of them designate themselves as traditional. The Jewish Reformed churches eliminate the traditional prayer book; omit all reference to Zion in their rituals; eliminate the
Hebrew language and the men remove their hats at service.[6] They are
indifferent to the observance of Jewish customs and traditions outside of the
synagogue; they do not recognize the dietary laws, do not require Jewish
divorce and eliminate the second day of Jewish holidays. The Conservative
Jewish churches retain with but slight modification the traditional prayer
book, retain references to Zion, retain the Hebrew language, insist upon the
observance of dietary laws, the Jewish divorce and the second day of holidays.
Orthodox Jews insist upon the rigid observance of Jewish customs and practices outside of the synagogue as well as within. They insist upon eating with
covered heads; in the ceremony of washing their hands before a meal and in
the ceremony of grace before and after meals. The ritual forbids shaving.
The Rabbis of the defendant congregation are shaven, as are the members
and even the plaintiffs in this action. The synagogue of this congregation
never has had the central platform which is usual in Orthodox churches. The
members of the church, including the plaintiffs, eat with uncovered heads,
and many of the members, including some of the plaintiffs, do not observe
the ceremony of washing hands or grace before or after meals.

---

6. Rabbi Goldman reveals partisan bias here. He is describing all Reform temples
in terms of a few ducal temples in the North and some in the South which became
the private chapels of assimilationist families. The vast majority of Reform synagogues did not eliminate Hebrew from the services, nor all references to Zion. There
were several who permitted the wearing of hats and one made the use of the *kipah*
mandatory.

There are three Rabbinical seminaries in America. The Hebrew Union College trains Rabbis for the Reformed temples; the Jewish Theological seminary for Conservative congregations, and the Talmudic College for Orthodox congregations. The organization of Conservative churches is known as the United Synagogue of America. The defendant congregation has had two Rabbis, both of whom were graduates of the seminary training Rabbis for Conservative congregations and it has at all times belonged to the United Synagogue of America. Its official stationery has at all times—even long prior to the employment of its present Rabbi—and since—publicly stated its said affiliation with the said Conservative organization. This congregation applied to said Conservative organization for a recommendation prior to the selection of its present Rabbi; said organization recommended said Rabbi who was then known by the defendant congregation to be the Rabbi of another Conservative congregation.

The customs, ritual and practices of the defendant congregation have been largely in conformity with those of other Conservative synagogues. During the regime of its first Rabbi and since its present one, it has had a late Friday evening service, in conformity with other Conservative churches, as distinguished from Orthodox churches.[7]

The court held with Rabbi Goldman and his thirty-one trustees. The case was actually the first heresy trial of a rabbi held in an American court. The Yiddish, and especially the Orthodox press gave it headline attention. The Cleveland Orthodox zealots were made to wish that they had picked on Rabbi Wolsey instead.[8] They had not bargained with Goldman's ability to meet them on their own ground. He met the arguments of the Halachists brought by the Union of Orthodox Rabbis with pertinent quotations from the Talmud and the Codes and revealed their own shallow understanding of *halakha*. By the end of the court hearings, the Orthodox Rabbis wished fervently that the Isaac Elchanan Yeshivah had been able to keep Solomon in the fold, or failing that, that he might have gone to the Reform temple and preached his heresies to the "goyim" —the Reformers.

---

7. It is not clear why the term church is used to designate synagogues. It seems so alien to Goldman's convictions. It may have been suggested by the attorney that the Judge would be more comfortable with this term.

8. Rabbi Louis Wolsey, Rabbi of the first Reform Temple in Cleveland, an ardent non-Zionist and advocate of so-called classical Reform, reform based on the Pittsburgh Platform of 1875.

Rabbi Stephen Wise chortled with glee and wrote Goldman:

> So you are to be the Yiddischer Bishop Brown. I am sorry that I cannot get in the fight with you. It ought to be lots of fun, and I will pay you the compliment of telling you that I am rather sorry for your opponents. I think they are going to be very sorry that they tackled the thing at all before you get through with them.

The trial and its outcome cleared the air. Goldman threw himself into building the Center and helping Dr. A. H. Friedland create an effective Hebrew school system. Dr. Samuel Beck, then editor of the *Center Forum* magazine and a member of the Deot group, recalls that Goldman singlehandedly brought back a large number of young Jewish intellectuals. He made them teachers in his religious school. Many of them later became prominent in their professions in law, medicine, engineering. Others became judges and political leaders or powerful business executives.[9] The high sense of responsibility which characterizes the Cleveland community in all civic and philanthropic endeavors is in some measure due to Solomon Goldman's work in Cleveland from 1918 to 1929.

The Cleveland Jewish Center under Goldman's leadership became the largest, most active Jewish-oriented institution of its kind in the country. The rabbi was respected not merely because he represented so large and thriving a community but for his own extraordinary gifts. His name was recognized and honored in the high places of national Jewish organizations. It is hard to understand why, in 1929, he decided to accept the invitation of a delegation representing the Anshe Emet Congregation on Chicago's north side. Perhaps he felt that the strenuous work of converting a reluctant Orthodox group into positive Conservative Jews had left many scars. There is evidence that he was grievously disappointed in the strange hostility shown him by Rabbi Abba Hillel Silver when Goldman was being considered for a lectureship at Western Reserve University. The record does not give us much help in determining his

---

9. Dr. Beck, a distinguished member of the University of Chicago Psychology Department, recalled after a lapse of forty-five years, the names of Morris Berick, Ralph David Herz, Myron Guren and Leonard Levi as but a few of the Deot members who were later to become prominent.

motives. For whatever reasons, he did make the fateful decision to leave Cleveland for Chicago in the late spring of 1929, arriving in Chicago in July to prepare the ground to assume the rabbinate of Anshe Emet.

This congregation had been in existence almost sixty years. It had had a checkered career since its humble Orthodox beginnings. Its mode of worship changed as its leadership changed. Sometimes the leader was a refugee rabbi, or a popular cantor, or an ambitious layman who could read the siddur. By 1929, it had come on evil days. Its membership had fallen to some ninety actual dues payers, and only with the help of a few families that had become affluent and still had a sentimental attachment to the synagogue could they raise the $25,000 annual budget, even though the synagogue was in a neighborhood that was attracting the more ambitious and wealthy Jewish families from Chicago's west side.

Rabbi Goldman came prepared not only with extensive files of sermons and lectures but with well-drawn-up charts of administrative procedures. He was never one to assume that an idealist, or a poet, or a scholar had necessarily to be a *schlemiel* when it came to practical matters. *Pirke Abot* had long anticipated American pragmatism when it reminded us that where there is no meal, there can be no Torah. The organizational outlines which Goldman presented to the officers of Anshe Emet contain such items as a minute breakdown of the membership and the streets they lived on as the necessary prelude for a membership drive. They contain a breakdown of the dues paid by each member, and all the other sources of revenue, with shrewd suggestions as to how these might be increased. There is a carefully considered chart of staff personnel with detailed job descriptions for each member. There are cards neatly designed and attractively worded which are to be placed above the collection boxes. There are prepared directives as to how the switchboard operator is to address callers, politely discover the purpose of the call, and where and to whom to refer the call. There is a model of a congregational bulletin, with a statement of priorities for the material it should contain. There is a dummy of a synagogue calendar listing the time and place of the services, the meetings, the school rooms and the conditions on which they are available to the membership and to the community. It was often said of Brigham Young that had he not chosen to head the Mormon Church he could have become another Andrew Carnegie. Solomon Goldman may have often shown impatience with pedantry, with nit-pickers, with those who love to stew in trivia, but he always had a high regard for the necessities of planning and organization. He believed that the more important the cause, the more important the instruments which afford it hands and feet.

The results of this careful planning soon became apparent. In spite of the fact that the first High Holy Days at Anshe Emet came just before the black days of the Depression, the congregation became alive. Indifferent members became concerned and brought unaffiliated friends to hear their new rabbi. A typical letter is one received from a visitor on 19 October 1929:

> My dear Mr. Goldman:
>
> Words cannot express the feeling I enjoyed in being privileged to listen to your most interesting services during the High Holydays, through the kindness of my friend. . . .
>
> I would be happy indeed to become a member of your congregation and would be indebted to you accordingly if you would be kind enough to mail me an application.

At the annual meeting of the congregation on 14 May 1930, President Isidor Cohen could report that the membership had doubled since the High Holy Days and that the income had increased from $21,000 of the year before to $60,309.12 as of 1 May.

Rabbi Goldman made this statement at that meeting:

> It is too soon to pause to evaluate the effectiveness and permanence of our work. Spiritual and cultural efforts must be given a span of time. The human mind and the human heart cannot be permanently affected in a short time.
>
> I would be guilty of extreme pessimism if I did not express my gratification at the response we met with this year. It was a source of great joy to discover that one can be heard in as tumultuous a city as the city of Chicago. When I decided to come here and be with you, it was my fear that no voice could be heard above the din in this huge metropolis. I was happy to find that my fear was unwarranted. I believe that we have made a slight beginning.

Indeed that voice would be heard above the din! It was the instrument of an encyclopedic mind and an understanding heart. The place of Rabbi Goldman in the annals of Jewish history will largely depend on his written works. The pen is mightier than the sword. "And all the rest which the Lord did for Israel, is it not written in the book of wars?" Thus the Bible testifies that immortality depends on the record. The record in the volumes which came from his pen will, as long as libraries endure, preserve a part of the mind and heart of Solomon Goldman for a time beyond time. How much richer would that testament be if there were added to these books a faithful tape recording of the many sermons and lectures which were not committed to writing? If that tape, in addition, were accompanied by television, one could have a fair simulacrum of the living experience. He had the advantage of a noble mien. The wayward crown of sparkling silver hair hovered precariously over a brow aglow with intellectual energy. His voice without affectation or stentorian projection was mellow like a clear spring in a lush pasture and insinuated itself into the heart of the listener. But that same voice could change its timbre in the flash of an eye and thunder in wrath and beat like a hammer on an unawakened conscience, or peal out like the *Tekiah Gedolah* on Rosh Hashanah. He was at his best when he drew on the vast storehouse of our literature. He had so often refined the material in the alembic of his mind, that it came out pure silver. He had an engaging manner of assuming that his audience, being Jewish, would know the particular talmudic or midrashic reference, or would immediately recognize it once it was mentioned. He was like the royal *mazkir* (reminder) recalling to the king what only the day's preoccupation with urgent affairs had temporarily eclipsed. He had the crucial gift of opening the pores of the heart to clear the pathway to the mind. There were occasions, of course, when he could lay about him like Samson smiting the Philistines with the jaw-bone of the ass. But this was on rare occasions, and he considered it the chastisement of love. Once when a generous supporter took the rabbi's condemnation of vulgar wealth as personal, Goldman insisted that he was flaying the sin and not the sinner, and that his hostility toward the sin could in no way diminish his love for the sinner.

What Goldman did with his material was even more remarkable. He could tell well-known biblical tales with that special nuance which is the grace of those who have mastered the original Hebrew. He had a unique way of informing the data with the impact of personal relevance and a sense of immediacy. He could bring Isaiah, Rashi, Rambam, Elijah Gaon, the Besht, and Solomon Schechter into your presence, and have them cast the light of their learning on the problem of authority and freedom as it related to your son's resistance to your admonition that he not smoke on Shabbat. He swung his learning like a trinket on his wrist, never exchanging the oil of gladness for the spirit of heaviness. The elan of his soul proved equal to the towering weight of his erudition. The natural juices of his vitality had digested his learning and made it bone of his bone, flesh of his flesh. He conveyed more than information, more than knowledge, more than wisdom. He evoked echo-auguries of dimly remembered moments of truth. He brought to the surface yearnings that coursed from heart to viscera and back again. He communicated ecstasy and agony, and you became quietly aware that you were being joined to your neighbors in a spiritual initiation. You felt that you were part of a congregation that had become a fellowship through the testing and healing and binding of this man's words. Maybe that is what we mean when we say that such and such a man has "charisma."

Goldman knew that the pulpit was his stronghold, that it gave him power over people, but he never considered this power as an end in itself. He considered his oratory as an invitation to more effective learning in the adult education classes which he made a vital part of the synagogue program. He always conducted these classes himself. The outline of a course he gave in the fall of 1934 and the spring of 1935 on the history of the Jews under the Romans reveals the immense amount of reading and research he did in preparation for these courses. Reference material from Josephus, Philo, Livy, and the Talmud, which was not easily available, he mimeographed, while he left to the students the initiative to consult Graetz, Marx, Margolis, and the *Jewish Encyclopedia*. This was concentrated, detailed, involved material for men and women who never had, or had long forgotten, the discipline of graduate study.

Goldman's uncanny ability to reveal the gold seams in the quarry of history held the students to the quest. They felt repaid when the classwork gave them a richer background to appreciate the more popular lectures and became confirmed addicts when the pain of grubbing and correlating turned into the deep-down pleasure of intellectual discovery with the teacher as a powerful exemplar.

The pulpit charisma proved useful in another way. Men and women who were touched by the eloquence and power of his words came to offer themselves as workers for the temple. Goldman early discovered that a few hours spent with competent and willing persons was worth every bit as much as hours spent on a sermon or an article. He developed a keen eye and ear for detecting leadership potential. He had the master touch of conveying personal interest and concern without subservience or backslapping. The few minutes he spent in personal conversation always seemed longer because he appeared leisurely no matter how long the waiting list. His warmth of greeting and his solicitous questions made one feel that he had nothing on his mind and no other care than the welfare of this one congregant. While he often called attention to the fact that Judaism had wisely refrained from making God into a person, and no one was better aware of the risks and dangers of personality cults, he nevertheless shrewdly understood that a warm and reverent feeling for Rabbi Goldman could be made into a constructive preparation for devotion to Anshe Emet, to the Jewish community, to the national home, to a better world.

With the aid of hundreds of lay leaders, men, women, youth, Solomon Goldman made of that struggling little ninety-member *shul* a community within a community, a radiating powerhouse serving America somewhat in the manner Achad Ha'am predicted a restored Israel might serve the Diaspora. The synagogue at Pine and Grace became a beehive of activity from morning till midnight, seven days a week, every day of the year. Nothing human was alien to its program. There was a chapel for daily morning and afternoon services, conducted by laymen who were competent *ba'aley korim* (readers of the service); there were morning study groups and classes, art and dramatic classes; there was a class sponsored by Rabbi Goldman to prepare the women to preside at meetings that included voice and

posture training, the writing of proper greetings, introductions, closing statements, parliamentary procedure, skills in conducting discussion groups; there were Boy and Girl Scout meetings, youth groups,
the youth synagogue, choral groups and, for some years, even an
Anshe Emet orchestra under professional direction. There were Hebrew classes four days a week, the youth synagogue on Saturday and
the one-day religious school on Sunday. Not only was the immediate
neighborhood aware of the comings and goings at Anshe Emet, but
the buses which brought the children from distant parts of the city
brought the name of Anshe Emet to all parts of Chicago and its suburbs.

Activity for its own sake is an acceptable offering in America. But
Goldman would not have it so for Anshe Emet. These manifold
activities must justify themselves, he said time and again, in contributing to a stronger Jewish identity, a firmer commitment to the
synagogue, the Jewish people and the welfare of the larger community. Jewish centers, Jewish clubs, and neighborhood houses
might properly be satisfied with activity for its own sake, but a synagogue could not do so without being false to the essence of its being.
The synagogue could feel justified in its existence only if it inspired
men and women to become active in all the various ways in which
cooperative and collective society improves the common lot and
helps prepare an environment that evokes the best impulses and
fulfills the finest aspirations of the human being. So Anshe Emet
folk were found in numbers larger than their proportion to the
population in helping-hand societies, among the solicitors for Red
Cross, Salvation Army Crusade, Boys' Town, and even more in the
ranks of those who raised money for the Community Chest, Sinai
Hospital, Jewish Welfare Fund, the United Palestine Appeal and a
myriad other Jewish and civic causes; Hadassah, Zionist Organization of America, Histadrut, Mizrachi, B'nai B'rith, Council of Jewish Women, Hillel, Menorah—all found Anshe Emet members
responsive to their call and, very often, found that their officers came
from the ranks of Anshe Emet. It became an unwritten practice for
many civic and philanthropic organizations to have Anshe Emet
members on their boards as conduits to the synagogue's reservoir of
social responsibility and concern. Under Solomon Goldman's leadership the congregation developed an image of itself as a synagogue

whose members were committed by virtue of that membership to be responsive to any call upon their humanity.

All that has been said so far of Anshe Emet might be said to a lesser degree of other synagogues. But there were two aspects of the Anshe Emet character and program that were unique. Both were reflections of the philosophy and character of its rabbi. Anshe Emet became the haven and rendezvous of the Hebrew and Yiddish writers and scholars of the Jewish world. Like Mendele Mocher Seforim, Goldman was often so busy helping other authors and publishers get out their works that he could not complete his own. The editors and publishers of *Bitzaron, Gilyanot,* and *Gazit* received regular subventions from Rabbi Goldman year after year. This money came from a special fund in which Rabbi Goldman placed all his honoraria for lectures, articles, royalties and rabbinic services. Few Hebrew or Yiddish authors published or even began to write their book without the blessing and support of the rabbi. From June to November of 1946 for instance, the following writers, editors, journalists, and scholars received financial help, technical counsel, or other kinds of support and encouragement from the Rabbi: Judah Goldin, J. Abromski, Mordecai Avada, Dr. Meyer Waxman, Menachem Ribalow, Prof. A. S. Yahuda, Rabbi George Abelson, Mr. Telphir, Dr. Simon Bernstein, Isaac Lamdan, Mr. Stybel, Jacob Klatzkin, Aaron Kaminker, Professor Torczyner, Dr. Isenstadt, Dr. Rosenfeld, Professor Hugo Bergman, Professor Schalit, Eliezer Greenberg, Samuel Burshtyn, David Pinski, Ben Yehudah, Saul S. Spiro, Boraisha.[10]

Goldman calculated that in less than four years he had expended some $40,000 to assist Hebrew and Yiddish authors in bringing their work to light. His especially close relationship with Ephraim Lisitzky and Simon Halkin was more one of scholarly collaboration than that of patron. The profound expressions of gratitude of these two fine poets reveal that Rabbi Goldman was much more valued by them for

---

10. In the supplement on pp. 278 ff, we have reproduced the communications which Rabbi Goldman sent to these individuals through the good offices of his dear friend Dr. Samuel Feigen, the orientalist. Goldman was so pressed for time that he had to give up the practice of dictating his answers in Hebrew and resorted to this method of correspondence with his Hebrew and Yiddish friends.

his crucial effect on their thinking and feeling. Goldman made it a practice that when any Hebrew or Yiddish man of letters came to Chicago, he would have him as a guest at the Friday-night services or at his home or in his study and introduce the guest to congenial groups. He encouraged the guest to read from his work and often translated these excerpts for the benefit of those not familiar with the language. These Oneg Shabbats and literary soirées became a kind of two-way passage even before the State of Israel was established. The poets and scholars came to know why Rabbi Goldman was not a forsaker of the *galut,* why he had confidence in the survival of a vigorous Judaism in America, and Anshe Emet members came to realize that in spite of the arduous demands of life in Palestine, the Hebrew word was flourishing and more books were read per capita in Tel Aviv than in any other city of the world.

The second way in which Anshe Emet, at the urging of Rabbi Goldman, was an innovator and pioneer in Conservative and Reform Judaism was in the establishment of a day school which was planned to cover the elementary grades. Goldman undertook this step in 1945 with a certain amount of trepidation. He was a staunch patriot. He deeply resented the phrases, *a klog zu Columbus* and *America ganef.* He loved America. He considered it quite appropriate that the interior of the synagogue should have panels in glass and canvas devoted to Washington, Jefferson, and Lincoln side by side with those devoted to Moses, Isaiah, and Jeremiah. He dreamed the dream of Walt Whitman—of America as a nation of nations. Still he had dramatic evidence in Chicago that ethnic groups like the Irish, the Poles, the Italians and Germans were holding back from the natural process of acculturation, that, in their desire to preserve certain pockets of economic and political influence, they were throwing sand in the delicate machinery of representative democracy. This was especially true of the Catholic religious body which not only offered a protective umbrella over a considerable segment of the ethnic groups but, in its parochial-school system, was implanting certain habits of mind, certain dogmatic and authoritarian principles that were sometimes at variance with democratic ideals. He was most hesitant about adding another possible obstacle to the democratic process, another competitor to the public-school system—still the best antidote to the divisive memories of the separate ethnic groups and the separatist tendencies encouraged by political opportunists. Goldman was keenly aware of these risks. But he was even more aware of the failure of the religious schools, the Sunday schools, even when supplemented by a three-day or a four-day Hebrew school, to convey adequately an effective knowledge of the four thousand years of Jewish history and the vast literature which recorded the faith, the culture, the civilization of the Jewish people in their four-millenia march through historic time. He was persuaded that only a schooling of prestige and resources comparable to our secular schooling could succeed at this task, and he persuaded himself that the proper organization of a curriculum, a careful selection and preparation of textbooks, a conscientious training of teaching personnel who would understand the interplay and the mutual supportiveness of the Judaic and Western cultural tradition could overcome the danger of conflict in the value systems of the two traditions.[11]

Happily, Goldman could take comfort in the realization that he had labored courageously and skillfully in removing the most serious roadblock to a program combining Jewish and secular education, namely the authoritarian mind-set which is an almost inevitable consequence of the dogma of the complete and absolute truth of the revelation of Torah to Moses on Sinai. Goldman was unable to persuade either the Jewish Theological Seminary[12] or the Rabbinical

---

11. It is interesting to note that twenty-five years after the inauguration of Anshe Emet Day School, Rabbi Louis I. Newman of the Rodfei Sholom congregation in New York is the first rabbi of the Reform wing to establish a day school. He too has long been convinced that the Sunday school was a sorry palliative even at its best, and in spite of the addition of two or three afternoon sessions for Hebrew classes. While it may be true that some of the supporters of the Rodfei Sholom Day School see it as an escape from some of the less pleasant by-products of integrated schools, the majority no doubt are motivated by a more positive concern for meaningful Jewish survival and have come to accept the solution which Goldman pioneered thirty years ago. It may also be of some historic value to record that KAM Congregation conducted a day school from the late 1860s to 1890 where Hebrew language instruction and Jewish history was mingled with the three R's—Reading, Writing and Arithmetic. The school was legally chartered to prepare students for high school. The motivation here was mainly inspired by the poor condition of the elementary schools in post–Civil War Chicago.

12. See Chapter IV for a more detailed discussion of this endeavor in his long and sometimes furious correspondence with Dr. Louis Finkelstein.

Assembly to take the authority, or delegate it to proper commissions, to bring the *halakhah* on Jewish observances up to date, or to establish clear and simple guidelines to help Jews honor their tradition while responding to the inevitable pressures of the cultural climate of their environment. He had been an enthusiastic ally of Dr. Mordecai Kaplan in the Reconstructionist attempt to meet this challenge, but found that Reconstructionism was too bogged down in philosophical and theological profundities to be of much practical assistance.[13]

In the late forties, just after the establishment of the State of Israel, Goldman undertook to write a series for his synagogue bulletin which would be a kind of modern *Shulhan Arukh* for the members of his congregation and for any other Jews who were seeking not so much an authoritarian code of law with sanctions as a moral and religious set of guidelines. His introduction to this series illustrates not only the motivation of this quest but his zestful delight in dragooning Conservative Judaism and forcing it to get off dead center and to let go of its canny opportunism in allowing its elastic position to be defined by the opposite pulls of Orthodoxy and Reform:

There is much that I am tempted to say by way of introducing this column, which is to become a more or less regular feature of the Anshe Emet Bulletin. I should, for example, like to raise the question of the origin of Jewish mores and folkways and break a lance in the age-old debate whether or not every jot and tittle of Biblical and rabbinic laws and ceremonies were revealed to Moses on Mount Sinai, whether or not the expression *Torah min-ha-Shamayim* is more than a habit of speech in the mouths of many occupants of pulpits. It were interesting to inquire whether the Halachah was ever conceived of as evolving and subject to amendment or whether it was always viewed as Sinaitic, static and immutable. It were enlightening to take the vast tomes of Codes and Responsa and trace out the lines of departure that distinguish those among them which were published only yesterday from those that were indited a thousand years ago. It would or should dissipate misty speculations on the development of the Halachah if, for example, we dealt critically with the question as to what there was that Abaye prohibited which Rabbi Isaac Elhanan Spector permitted and vice versa. It would be adding a valuable

---

13. See Chapter II for some of the incidents of his collaboration with Kaplan.

chapter to the study of the psychology of religion to review the legal fictions that have accumulated in the past two thousand years as a result of the heroic efforts made by men of giant intellect to breach the solid bastions of the law. Such a study might perhaps help us understand why it was that the thousands of pages that have been devoted to the investigation of the laws of marriage and divorce have brought the woman of today, whose husband has disappeared or who brazenly refuses to give her a *get* (divorce) little more relief than was the portion of her sister in misery a century or two ago. Or why her status with regard to marriage and divorce is no different from what it was in the days when it was first recorded that "a wife *** a Canaanitish slave *** large cattle *** landed property can be acquired or bought, . . ." or from the time when the exact meaning of the word "take" in the verse reading "if a man takes a wife" was derived from the accidental fact that the same word is also employed in the account of the purchase of the Cave of Machpelah.

It should certainly not be sowing to the wind to plumb the minds of those who, though they maintain that the *Shulchan Aruch* is the definitive and authoritative codification of the divinely revealed law, have for purpose of edification, instruction, propaganda, and education narrowed, in recent years, its amplitude to a hairsbreadth of rules of diet and the Sabbath. It should not be a wasteful effort to account for the silent composure with which they have greeted or perhaps even encouraged the violation of such Shulchan Aruch prohibitions or injunctions as the following:

Not to put on one's undershirt (or remove one's pyjamas) in a sitting up position.
Not to put on the left shoe before the right.
Not to walk erect.
Not to pour, on the Sabbath, hot coffee or tea into a cup containing sugar.
Not to allow one's wife to apply rouge on that day.

Above all, as a "Conservative" Rabbi, I am most tempted to unriddle the conundrum of "Why Conservative Judaism?" What is it after? To what end has it separated itself from Orthodox Judaism? If, at the end of half a century, or is it a century? it has found it imprudent, inexpedient or inconsistent with the Halachah to approve the mixed pew and has been compelled to look upon Congregations and Rabbis who have introduced the practice as violators of the law, then why should not these congregations and Rabbis rejoin their Orthodox brethren and "live in sin" with them?

All these riddles are challenging and intriguing, but we must fight them off. For despite the fact that practically all of them have been the subject of endless discussion, "traditional" Judaism has stood still, and Jews, certainly those among them who have lived in the Western world, have floundered for so long a time in indecision and confusion, that they have persistently honored the whole complex of Jewish ceremonial in the breach rather than observance. Indeed they neither honor it nor are they contemptuous of it. They just do not take it into account. It is not a part of their consciousness. It never enters their calculations.

They will deny their children a Jewish education altogether or keep them out of school two-thirds of the school year; they will have no Bible in their home; they will get rid of every Hebrew book they inherit as if it were so much rubbish; they will not buy one Jewish book a year and will not read one in ten years; they will not usher in the Sabbath with Kiddush or ever pray; they will start out for their vacation on the eve of the Sabbath or a festival; week after week they will have rabbis solemnize the marriage of their children and serve shrimps with unconcern. Were all this cleared away, or were its relation to Jewish observance properly evaluated, we should then see how little our weighty dissertations and ideological disputations have contributed to the development of a Jewish mode of living in the United States or elsewhere in the Western world.

Aside from that my present purpose is humble and restricted. I shall attempt with the co-operation of a number of intelligent, studious-minded, patient, and courageous men and women to throw a few planks over the chasm that divides the ceremonial practices of those of us who move within the orbit of the Anshe Emet from what are presumed to be our professions.

We neither said to our people that the sanctity of the Sabbath is of a character that for its sake the American Jewish Community must resolve itself to an inferior economic position, to forego prestige and influence, to be in no position to help in the upbuilding of Palestine or provide relief in Europe and elsewhere. Nor did we tell our people that such a sacrifice no community could make, and that since they were compelled to work in order to live, to build Talmud Torahs and Yeshivot, to redeem the land of Palestine, and "ransom the captives," and since the Lord had brought them to this land of opportunity "to save the lives of many peoples," the laws of gainful employment were set aside till such time as, through our persistent and consecrated efforts, the five day week would become the law of the land. We did neither the one nor the other. And since almost everybody had to work on the Sabbath, everybody was ipso facto an idolater. That idolaters would not be "observers of Mizvot" we could have learned from the homilies on a certain chapter in the Book of Exodus, or by way of common sense. Our gripes and murmurs and harangues have been ludicrous, distasteful, and offensive.

Second, we have fallen into the habit of wholesale non-observance because there has been no sifting of the ceremonies and customs, no weeding out of the obsolete, unintelligible, and time-worn, and no attempt made at distinguishing those of greater importance from those of lesser importance. If carrying a handkerchief on the Sabbath constituted as much of a violation as marketing at the grocer's, then the latter becomes as inevitable as the former certainly is.

We then regard our first task to be that of doing some sifting, of setting up for ourselves criteria on the basis of which we shall discard certain restrictions as being no longer obligatory on us, and certain others on the basis of which we will hold ceremonies and customs to be binding upon us, and which we hope and pray will impel us to overcome the habit of non-observance.

Now, then. We shall regard a restriction as not binding upon us:

1. *If its going counter to the refinement of the age is palpably obvious.*
2. *If it would work great hardship on those living in our industrialized, electrified, mechanized big cities that sprawl over large areas of our land.*
3. *If the manner of its observance is unaesthetic and lends itself to ridicule.*
4. *If its observance is void of all meaning or symbolic value.*
5. *If it has been universally disregarded by those who are and strive to be an integral part of the vortex of modern life.*
6. *If it has been deduced from another restriction, in the instituting of which, none of the circumstances in which the restriction under consideration is expected to be operative, could have been conceived as ever coming into existence.*

We shall regard customs and ceremonies as binding upon us:

1. *If they are rich in historical associations.*
2. *If they accentuate our people's struggle for freedom.*
3. *If they are safeguards against superstition, idolatrous practices, and the misrepresentation of monotheism.*
4. *If they go to induce or are symbolic of lofty aspirations and high ideals.*
5. *If they are purifying and ennobling.*
6. *If they ease the torment of the mind.*
7. *If they assuage grief.*
8. *If they bring bodily relaxation.*
9. *If they are aesthetically stimulating.*
10. *If they are deeply embedded in the consciousness of large numbers of our people.*
11. *If their preservative or survival value is apparent.*
12. *If they constitute linkages to Jewish communities the world over.*

All these rules, both the positive and the negative, we fully realize, leave much to be desired. They are far too malleable and subjective. They lack the toughness and precision of the national standards by which material objects are weighed and measured. Furthermore, they cannot be stored away and sheltered against changes in weather. They must be exposed to storm and stress. Warping is unavoidable. But then no definition or equation has ever expressed the fullness of life. That is why as we go, let us say, from mathematics to psychology our disciplines and degrees of exactness vary. For as we get closer to life we tread on quicksilver, and our most carefully considered theories are little more serviceable than crutches. But they do help us limp. Even so our rules, when we come to apply them in subsequent issues of the Bulletin to the problems before us, may give us a little more balance than we now enjoy. Should that prove to be the case, we shall be satisfied that we have not labored in vain. Should others improve upon our work, we shall gladly be their beneficiaries and debtors.

Like so many other grand projects which the restless brain and fervid imagination of Solomon Goldman struck from the anvil of his ambition, this too was destined to become sidetracked in deference to more urgent demands and to the ruthless exigencies of accident and ill health. But the questions and answers which followed in the seven or eight bulletin issues give testimony to an alert congregation and a rabbi whose erudition was always laced with spice and brandy. In answering one who asks whether there are differences between the prohibitions against work on the Sabbath and on the Festivals, he answers:

> The Festival differs in naught from the Sabbath save in the preparation of food alone.

But the relaxing of any one injunction in a closely knit complex of rules and regulations is, certainly from the point of view of the proponents of the idea of the *seyag* (fence), a most precarious step to take. One can never tell what a crash will result from pulling out one peg. Give a man a finger and he will want the whole hand.[14]

In the discussion of the *agunah* (a woman who is widowed but who cannot remarry because there has been no living witness of the death of her husband) he refers to the brilliant emendation suggested by Rabbi Michael Higger who proposes that we insert in the

---

14. Goldman here refers to a leitmotif of *halakhic* interpretation that an ordinance be more demanding than necessary in order to compensate for the human tendency to do less than necessary.

Hare at[15] the words, *al da'at bet din,* and also modify the *ketubah* accordingly. "Now what is the meaning of the proposed insertion?" asks Goldman. It means "by the authority of the court." It implies that the marriage took place by the court's permission. How will that, Goldman asks, solve the problem of the *agunah*? Will it give the court authority to issue a bill of divorce? Heaven forbid! Dr. Higger takes no such "radical" step. For the law states explicitly that "he," the husband, is the owner, and that the law, in turn, is rooted in a long and honorable past when to marry and to purchase were one and the same thing. Rabbi Higger is not ready to turn the dish upside down. He is most respectful of the husband and would not allow a mere court to override the purchase. All that Dr. Higger empowers the court to do is to nullify the marriage retroactively; that is, make believe that the husband has not spoken (as is done in some of the best Catholic circles when there is enough money and prestige to hire canonical lawyers).

"If there is a lack in the law of Moses and Israel" for such a condition as Rabbi Higger proposes, then why not assume that it was comprehended in the marriage formula from the beginning and leave it as is? No. We will not chop logic. For we are not moving here on the highways of reason but seeking to effect an ignominious retreat by way of dark alleys, or as it might be put in our day, fighting a kind of guerrilla war against the *halakhah*.

Goldman approves a proposal that would recognize the indispensable dynamic quality of law, permit the infusion of new ideas, take the husband down a few pegs, and emend *at* 'thou' to *anu,* 'we' and the singular *mequdeshet,* 'art betrothed,' to *mequdashim,* 'are betrothed,' and *li* 'to me' to *zeh lazeh* 'to each other.' Once this emendation is made there should be no lack of ingenuity in emending the other words in the formula.

Your question as to whether I approve of my members coming in their cars to the synagogue, I answer unhesitatingly, yes. We Jews have our choice between making total war on civilization or learning to live in it. If we wish to live by the rigidity of the traditional law we would be wise to reject our environment altogether. You cannot live in elevator buildings, with telephones, radios, electric lights, central heating, running water and not be a

---

15. The first words of the oath repeated by the groom when he places the ring on the finger of the bride.

sinner. If you wear yourself out walking on the Sabbath from the South Side to the West Side to attend the Bar Mitzvah of your nephew you have violated the spirit of the Sabbath as if you had spent it in your automobile. Never mind what a thousand pilpulists say to the contrary. Hairsplitting will not help make the Sabbath a day of spiritual delight. We may ride on the Sabbath when it is unavoidable, turn the lights on, carry on ourselves the things we need, and yet enjoy the day. We may do none of these things and make the Sabbath a burden.

Goldman devoted a great deal of time and energy to the service of worship. He had long ceased to belabor the congregation for irregular attendance. He realized early that the blame rested at least as much with the undue lengthiness and repetitious dullness of much of the service. He thought that removing the archaic portions of the service, returning to the three-year cycle of Torah reading, and introducing singable hymns would be making a good start. When a grateful worshiper wrote to thank him for the delight these innovations had afforded him, Goldman replied:

All the same we are a long way from a satisfying and inspiring Service. To begin with there is no Jewish prayer book and only a very few hymns which speak to the heart of the American Jew. Almost all existing prayer books are repetitious, erudite, laborious, metaphysical, apologetic, and cast in a mood that is foreign to the modern man. In the second place the reading of the Torah must be completely reconstructed. We must cease to speak of reading the Torah since we pretend to be teaching it. . . . It is neither edifying nor enlightening to read before a congregation what cannot be brought within its understanding except by lengthy interpretations. But the most experienced, gifted and resourceful teacher could not explain adequately, say Jacob's Blessings in less than two or three hours. Neither could he do much or in less time with the chapters devoted to the building of the Tabernacle unless he had some knowledge of architecture, carpentry, and many other crafts, and had appropriate graphic illustrations. What sense can the manual for the Levites have for the average congregant? What does the "quickening of the dead" mean to him and can he believe it if taken literally. Since most congregants do not look forward to the restoration of the Temple, the priesthood, and sacrifices, their *musaph* (additional service) is mere rote and it makes the Service needlessly repetitious.

To a parishioner who wrote that he saw evidence of a return to mysticism, a greater interest in "theological" problems, a conversion to faith, and wondered if these phenomena augured an abandonment of science and a return to organized religion, Goldman replied:

> I doubt it. Fads and fashions are as common in the realms of thought as they are in diet and dress. Yesterday we blamed religion for all our ills, today we blame the lack of it. The fact is that both our religions and sciences, disposed as they are to promise more than they can fulfill, inevitably fall periodically into disrepute. . . .
>
> Men came to feel that religion had betrayed them, and some two centuries ago became the devotees of Enlightenment. Enlightenment or rationalism was no less confident and promissory of splendid days to come than religion had been. By the time the theory of evolution was properly expounded and Spencer had designed the New World with the same assurance and precision with which Ezekiel designed the Temple of the future, the laboratories had begun to pile up inventions and men made ready for utopia. Two world wars, the implementation of totalitarianism and the theory of racial superiority, the infection of the Orient with militarism, and the imminence of an atomic war has resulted in a loss of intellectual nerve, and a return to the heavens that have previously been discarded.
>
> As I see it, science will no more be forsaken now than religion was a century ago when naturalism, materialism, mechanism, psycho-analysis and behaviorism were the order of the day. Sober reflection will convince most thinking men that neither science nor religion nor philosophy has as yet said its last and best word.

A member who wrote asking if the Reconstructionist Movement came close to expressing his views on the nature of Judaism and the program for its revitalization received this answer:

> You are right, I am closest in spirit to Reconstructionism. My disagreements with it are minor. My approach to Halacha and my conception of a modern prayer book may be somewhat to the right or left of it as you please. . . . The Halachists have produced nothing really significant in centuries. . . . If we are to make its study fruitful and pertinent to our requirements we must bring to bear on it, as Kaplan has most ably done, the social sciences, examine the social, economic, and psychological forces that have made it what it is, diagnose the travail of the rabbis in striving to remain true to their concept of revelation, but buffetted by circumstances so frequently counter to it. As to the reconstruction of our worship, the prayer book should be much briefer, less apologetic, argumentative and sermonic than the Reconstructionists have made it. The Jews of today may perhaps still form the habit

of praying if we give them little, and direct that little to their emotions. In other words a service must become in our modern setting, what it was at its inception—drama, pageantry, song. It would make me happier if the Reconstructionists were to organize synagogues rather than fellowships; if they realized that for those of us who take a modern view of revelation the theological discussion of the selection of Israel has become superfluous and monotonous; if they were less vague about their community approach. But there is blessing in what the Reconstructionists have thus far done, and of all our present Jewish ideologies they hold out the greatest promise.[16]

To one who asked if it were wise for Jews to anticipate that America would become only another temporary home in their long trek among the nations, and that it would be smart for those who could move to Israel to do so, Goldman answered:

No friends, America is not for the Jew a boarding-house. It is home. We have dug deep roots here and have harvested fruit aplenty. There is no doubt that a small number of American Jews will settle in Israel. A somewhat larger number will forever be on their way at least by word of mouth, but for some mysterious reason will never get there. Many American Jews will dissolve into thin air and disappear from our midst. Most of us will have the pride of heritage and the love of peoplehood, sense vaguely the blessedness of both for ourselves and humanity, and possess the resolution, fortitude and wisdom to preserve our identity and our creative continuity. I cannot say for how long, except to predict that the grandchildren of your grandchildren will be known as Americans and Jews. Beyond that my line of vision does not extend. What will happen on our much-troubled globe after a lapse of a century is anybody's guess. A hundred atomic years is a far longer "end of days" than any of the ancients ever dared envision.

When asked how he apportioned his loyalties and commitments between his Americanism and his Zionism, Goldman quoted from an address he had given to the United Synagogue's Convention:

---

16. See Chapter II for further treatment of Goldman's relation to Kaplan and Reconstructionism. When Kaplan did decide to eliminate "Thou hast chosen us from among all peoples" on the ground that the chosen-people concept had been made dangerous by Hitlerism, Goldman thought it unwise to make an issue of something so archaic, while Milton Steinberg, one of Kaplan's most brilliant collaborators, refused to give up this historic concept, which was a call on our uniqueness as servants of God. We should not sacrifice an important religious value because the Nazis in their madness had distorted the concept into a rationale for vicious racism and truculent chauvinism, he argued.

Strange that despite this warmth for Israel, my sense of kinship with it, it never occurred to me to regard myself as an Israeli national, nor did the shadow of dual allegiance ever cross my path. What surprises me even more is that I should not have felt the need of meticulously defining what of me belongs to Israel and what to the United States. Indeed, I have had no inclination to, in fact, I have shied away from cross-examining my heart throbs, having let them have their way—to beat for the U. S. or Israel as they please. I have seen no reason for unlacing my emotions or wearing my heart upon my sleeve for cowards, evil men or pundits to peck at. The generality of men do not as a rule probe the respective depths of the love they bear their dear ones, nor do they experience any difficulty in determining what they owe one or another among them. When confronted by a crisis of extreme emergency they act instinctively seldom being able to explain later even to themselves as to why they acted as they did. Intelligent human beings do not go around speculating as to whom they would rescue first, mother or daughter, if the need arose to make a choice.

A large congregation requires the wisdom of Solomon, the strength of Samson. The reader must not get the impression that Rabbi Goldman had the congregation in the palm of his hand, that he merely spoke and the word became flesh. He had attracted thinking Jews, and there were many who flattered the rabbi by imitating his own fearless individualism. There were some who listened to his advanced ideas and often applauded the eloquence with which they were expressed, but still insisted on following the practices to which they were accustomed. These, in fact, developed a *kleisel* or chapel of their own. They delegated laymen with some knowledge of Hebrew and possessed of a pleasantly loud voice to read the daily morning and late afternoon service. These services were conducted in the Orthodox manner and were in no way affected by Reconstructionism or even the innovations and experiments which Goldman introduced into the Friday-night and Saturday-morning services in the main sanctuary. The traditional services attracted genuinely pious Jews who wanted sincerely to pray in the manner of their fathers and some who were inclined to use the familiar ritual as an escape or a substitute for the ethical mandates of prophetic Judaism. They found it more convenient and less costly to chant Amos and Isaiah in the proper *Haftarah nigun* than to take their admonitions to heart. Goldman was aware of their hypocrisy but preferred not to make an issue of this for fear of denying the truly pious a chance to pray in the traditional manner. He took seriously the prophets command that "My house shall be a house of prayer for all people."

Nor did all of Goldman's plans find the implementation he had hoped to give them. As meticulously as he defined his projects, as carefully as he described each staff member's job, he found stubborn resistance, sheer ignorance, petty personal peeves, vain egotistic pretensions, downright envy, conspiring to take a significant toll from the envisioned ideal. Anshe Emet became a sizable corporate entity, with a permanent staff of more than fifty and a budget close to $300,000 a year. The lay leadership was often strangely loathe to apply basic principles of institutional or corporate management to a synagogue. They often expiated a guilt feeling engendered by the hard efficiency of their own businesses by going soft when it came to making tough decisions around the temple. They were often surprised that Goldman did not consider this a virtue or a valid expression of *rachmonis* (compassion). He often failed to convince certain board members who were indulgent toward incompetence that these small personal kindnesses were obstructing the larger justice and benefits which a well-organized and disciplined synagogue might achieve. Goldman was often given to pondering the peculiar dilemma of the institutional synagogue—that the curse of bigness became apparent much more quickly than in the case of other institutions. So much depended on the warm personal rapport with the rabbi and, when the congregation exceeded 1,500 families, this became impossible. As the people became more and more troubled they found his spoken words helpful, but not as helpful as more personal pastoral counseling might be; Rabbi Goldman repeated Moses' complaint to the Lord as recorded in the eleventh chapter of Numbers:

> Why have you dealt ill with your servant, and why have I not enjoyed your favor, that You have laid the burden of all this people upon me? Did I conceive all this people, did I bear them that you should say to me, "Carry them in your bosom as a nurse carries an infant, to the land that You promised on oath to their fathers?" Where am I to get meat to give all these people when they whine before me and say, Give us meat to eat! I cannot carry all this people by myself, for it is too much for me.

Nor did he find it a ready solution to delegate responsibility to associates. The rabbinical seminaries are only just beginning to train specialists in pastoral work, youth leadership, education, ministry of music. When Anshe Emet was expanding from 90 to 1,500 families, this type of assistance was not available. Rabbi Goldman had a series of seminary graduates as assistants. When they proved competent enough to relieve him of some of his burden, they preferred to be senior rabbis in their own congregations, since there were always more congregations looking for rabbis than there were rabbis. Nor was the lack of institutional specialists the only difficulty. Congregants themselves are not trained to accept surrogate rabbis. They have accepted medical, legal, and engineering specialists, but they insist that it be the senior rabbi or no one for them. Some of this is due to ignorance or thoughtlessness, but there is perhaps a deeper motivation and a more legitimate one. The rabbi as a servant of God must be a whole man meeting the total personality of the congregant. He must be more aware than any other professional that the issues of life are from the heart, that the symptom of the present distress is but the warning signal of deeper dislocations that stem from the basic alienation of man from the center of his own being or from the bond of his faith, his peoplehood, or his God. Even as Anshe Emet was reaching out to more and more people, the possibility occurred to Goldman that the big institutional synagogue was a contradiction in terms. Before his unhappy accident in 1950, the rabbi had seriously discussed the plan of establishing an experimental synagogue in a north suburb composed of selected members from Anshe Emet and K.A.M.,[17] not only to test some of the principles of Reconstructionism but to determine the proper limits of a synagogue community, the point of marginality, the place where the numbers begin to dilute quality, where the inwardness of the religious experience becomes cheapened and synthetic as human need gives way to organizational procedures.

---

17. The initials for Kehillat Anshe Maariv—Illinois' oldest synagogue of which the author was rabbi from 1939 to 1967.

Chapter 2

Dr. Finkelstein and the Seminary

A REMARKABLE PORTION of the extensive files left by Rabbi Goldman is his correspondence with Dr. Louis Finkelstein. The letters recall their first meetings as teen-age lads in the Brownsville section of Brooklyn where their families knew each other and where Louis' father was esteemed as a learned and scholarly rabbi with a very special gift in Midrash, the literary and folklore interpretation of the Sacred Scripture. This was a friendship that was to hold fast to the very day of Goldman's death, almost fifty years from its beginning in the study house of the elder Rabbi Finkelstein's *shul*. Solomon was almost two years older than Louis and seems to have been more of an extrovert, a boy who could easily relate to all ages and conditions of the human family, while Louis was more withdrawn and more singlemindedly dedicated to the study of the Torah. Louis acknowledges that it was Solomon who first encouraged him to look beyond the pages of Gemarah to the world outside, who persuaded him to become the president of the freshman class at the Isaac Elchanan Yeshivah, and planted in him the desire to read human beings with the same avidity with which he read Talmud. The letters capture rare and beautiful incidents such as their decision to publish a magazine, the *Jewish Forum,* and present the first issue on the first night of *Selichot,* since the burden of the first issue was a call to *heshbon ha-nefesh,* an inventory of the inward parts, a call to Jews to wake from their slumber, slough off the strangling coils of the outworn past, and begin at once to build a new heaven and a new earth. The letters tell us how the two decided to enroll in the Jewish Theological Seminary where they believed the climate would be more congenial to secular studies, and where they might better fashion the intellectual weapons with which they could wage the battles of the Lord against the modern idolatries. Other adolescents might cut a covenant with a pin prick and mingle their blood with a sacred oath to stand by each other through fire and water in pursuit of their mysterious goals. Solomon and Louis seem to have made an informal convenant with each other to work together for the refinement of the Jewish tradition and for the salvation of the Jewish people from their long and dark exile.

The first intimation that the skill in talmudic studies which they had acquired at Isaac Elchanan Yeshivah was less than perfect came when they were examined by the then not too well known Professor Louis Ginzberg. Professor Ginzberg allowed the eloquent Solomon to parade his precocious knowledge of several tractates and then, with a devastatingly simple question, punctured the airy balloon of his *halakhic* logistics. Obviously the "professor" against whom Solomon's Uncle Mendel had warned him ("what do professors know about Talmud?") was *boki* (expert). His mild and gentle manner had subtly disguised a brain that could rear mountains of logic and as gracefully pit one Himalayan peak against another. The examinations, while a bit depressing to their egos, stirred in these freshmen and their friend David Aaronson, a vast respect for the faculty of the Seminary and a heady excitement for the vista of the years ahead.

They were soon to meet the chancellor of the Seminary, Dr. Solomon Schechter, who was living proof that the mastery of the English tongue and a thorough acquaintance with its literature was no betrayal of Torah but rather a strong and steady bow with which to project Torah wisdom into new pastures. They were to meet Rabbi Mordecai Kaplan and Professor Israel Davidson who would open new horizons for their covenanted quest. Rabbi Kaplan was the prime catalyst who was to plant a divine discontent into the mind and heart of the young Solomon and stir him to a never-ending search for the larger and more relevant context to embrace the tried and tested truths of Judaism. On more than one occasion, Rabbi Goldman would acknowledge that Kaplan had been a most formative influence in his own thinking and doing.

While at the Seminary, the paths of the comrades of the quest began to diverge. Goldman was anxious to find a congregation and begin at once to put his passionately acquired wisdom to the winnowing of experience. Finkelstein preferred to remain in the Seminary, partly because he enjoyed the atmosphere of study, and partly because he had developed a fondness for administration. Goldman had oversold his friend when he dragged him out of the hermit corner of the study house and made him taste the joys of socializing and the heady rewards of leadership. Cyrus Adler, who succeeded to the presidency of the Seminary upon the death of Solomon Schechter, was pleased to recommend Goldman to a larger congregation in Cleveland in 1918. The new president also recognized the potential of Louis Finkelstein and encouraged him to remain at the Seminary.

As grateful as Goldman was for the splendid instruction and inspiration he had received from the Seminary, he was soon to find that it had failed him when it came to guiding a rabbi in the practical problems of a congregation. When, for instance, the recalcitrant minority of the Cleveland Jewish Center took him to court on the charge that he was misleading a traditional congregation by his innovations, Dr. Cyrus Adler advised Goldman to go slowly and not to insist on mixed seating as long as any group in the congregation was opposed to it. The Seminary was still straddling the fence. It would not define its position as it related to Orthodoxy and Reform. It preferred to remain opportunistically passive and permit the tug of war between Orthodoxy and Reform to locate the ever-shifting position of Conservatism.

When Finkelstein succeeded to the presidency of the Seminary, Goldman was hopeful that the period of ambivalence might be ended. He believed that, with Kaplan's help, his friend Finkelstein

would now set the Seminary on a firm course, define the proper
stance of Conservatism and provide the rabbis in the Conservative
congregations with proper guidelines by which to create a balance
between authentic tradition and the practical needs of the modern
Jew. He was to discover that Dr. Finkelstein had developed a
rather different concept of the nature of Conservative Judaism and
the role of the Seminary, and it is this difference that inspired a
dialogue which continued for twenty-five years, sometimes calm and
conciliatory, more often sharp and bristling, but never corrosive
enough to sever the cord of affectionate friendship which began in
the *shul* of the elder Rabbi Finkelstein in Brooklyn.

Goldman and Finkelstein early assumed a proprietary interest in
each other's souls. When Goldman became enamored of Stephen
Wise and volunteered to raise a modest sum for the Jewish Institute
of Religion, Finkelstein regarded it as a dangerous manifestation, a
flirting with strange gods. He warned Goldman that the Reformers
would try to seduce him by flattery and by more subtle forms of
wooing and beseeched him to eschew this temptation and remain
with his own seminary and his own colleagues. Goldman reassured
Finkelstein that his assistance to Wise was purely a tribute to his
leadership of American Zionism and in no way a flirting with Reform for which, he insisted, he had a vast contempt because of its
abandonment of Zionism and its assimilatory tendencies. Goldman
was quick to caution Finklestein against his taking up with the
wealthy Reform Jews, the Schiffs, the Warburgs, the Lehmans, the
Strooks, and against his involvement in the American Jewish Committee which was a fierce opponent of the *kehilla* concept and, while
not overtly anti-Zionist, saw Zionism merely as one aspect of Jewish
philanthropy. He was particularly irritated with Finkelstein for
appointing to the Seminary board these Reform *Yahudim* and occasionally a Sephardic grandee from the Portuguese synagogue. This,
he insisted, was blatant catering to the moneybags, craven social
climbing, and an insult to the Conservative laymen within the
United Synagogue who were made to feel inferior and unworthy of
the highest positions within their own denomination. It was a trav-
esty, a demeaning mockery to read time and again that an active
member of the Seminary board, even at times, its chairman, was

buried at Temple Emanuel, the Reform "Cathedral," with a service conducted by anti-Zionist Reform rabbis. But more substantively, Goldman resented the extracurricular activities of the Seminary, its Institute on Philosophy and Social Sciences, its conferences on Judaeo-Christian togetherness, its "Eternal Light" program on the National Broadcasting Stations. President Finkelstein was manipulating an impressive series of letterheads and gaining nationwide publicity, but the Seminary program, Goldman insisted, was becoming more diluted, all things to all men, like Paul of Tarsus. It was selling its soul for a mess of pottage. Let the Anti-Defamation League, and the National Conference of Christians and Jews, and the American Jewish Committee take on these popular education projects and these public-relation gimmicks. Let the Seminary attend to its own ideological problems, build its own great library, give its own graduates the proper tools and techniques of the modern rabbinate, educate its own laymen to leadership, so that the Jewish communities might graduate from a charity collection agency to a Jewishly educated and a Torah-committed community.[1]

As Goldman moved from city to city, older colleagues such as Israel Levinthal, David Aaronson, and younger colleagues such as Milton Steinberg, Ira Eisenstein, and Judah Goldin revealed their own misgivings about the Seminary program and about Dr. Finkelstein's leadership. Goldman suggested that the group draw up a bill of particulars and that it be presented to and discussed with Dr. Finkelstein. He submitted the letter which he had written to the Seminary president on September 26, 1944 (see Appendix) as a statement of his own feelings. Rabbi Milton Steinberg, the brilliant rabbi of the Park Avenue Synagogue and author of *Basic Judaism, A Partisan Guide to the Jewish Problem,* and *As A Driven Leaf,* a fictionalized biography of Elisha ben Abujah, undertook to edit the memorandum. Steinberg indicated his own unhappiness in this response to Goldman's letter written October 27, 1944.

Too many movements for the vitalization of Conservative Judaism have died aborning amidst those conferences, round-table discussions, etc., of which Dr.

---

1. See Appendix, pp. 259, for an exchange of letters in late September of 1944 which best summarizes the issues over which this dialogue of two decades took place.

Finkelstein is so fond. . . . My discontent isn't something that is to be arbitrated. In addition to the many things you said in your letter to Dr. Finkelstein, I want him to begin to move toward the transfer of lay authority in the affairs of the Seminary to Conservative Jews and Conservative congregations. I mean real authority, not façade boards of overseers and executive councils. . . .

I want Dr. Finkelstein, further, to stop pussyfooting on Zionism, on the democratic organization of the American Jewish community, on the "Judaeo-Christian" tradition and quit lending the prestige of his office and of the Seminary to disruptive movements in American Jewish life.[2]

And last of all, I want the Seminary to take the lead in making Judaism really historical Judaism. That is to say, both traditional and evolving. I want the Seminary to do something practical about the Jewish law of divorce, about Shabbos Observance, Kashruth, about vitalizing Jewish worship. What else are the Seminary and Conservative Judaism for?

Goldman found himself in a most delicate position. Finkelstein kept him informed of all the actions and letters of the dissidents and sincerely asked his counsel. When Goldman suggested a full, no-holds-barred confrontation, Finkelstein agreed on condition that Dr. Kaplan and Professor Ginzberg and his assistant Simon Greenberg be included. The president of the Seminary was a great believer in conference and consensus. He knew from much experience that a conference inevitably narrowed the range of complaints because there were bound to be items on which the dissidents disagreed. He was also certain that each rabbi had enough experience with his own board of trustees to appreciate that certain compromises have to be made in any organizational endeavor.

Finkelstein exercised unlimited patience and, outwardly, never for a moment questioned the motives of the petitioners; he assumed, of course, that this assumption was reciprocal. Nor did he underestimate the silent testimony of the presence of Dr. Mordecai Kaplan on his left and Professor Ginzberg on his right with an occasional reference to Professor Leiberman and also to those practical and very busy members of the board of trustees. Nor was the president unaware that each of these rabbis was extremely busy and, when

---

2. Steinberg is referring to the withdrawal of the American Jewish Committee from the American Jewish Conference.

they realized that the reorganization they demanded would require many conferences, board meetings, referenda, assemblies, and conventions, some of their ardor might be cooled or channeled into more manageable reforms.

Dr. Kaplan faced some of the same difficulties as Rabbi Goldman did in this whole situation. His teaching and writing had provided the intellectual groundwork of this attempt to bring Conservative Judaism into the twentieth century. So much that was emphasized at the Seminary was incompatible with the basic theses of Judaism as a civilization. Nevertheless, the Seminary had been his home from the days of his youth. Its presidents, from Schechter on, had been proud of his standing in the wider Jewish community and among the general scholarly community. He somehow held to the faith that the leaven of his ideas would inform the teachings and the philosophy of the Seminary.

Goldman was not so sanguine and had hoped that Kaplan might find a more congenial place at the Jewish Institute of Religion. Both he and Milton Steinberg had strongly suggested to him that Reconstructionism would prosper more as an independent movement free from too close association with the Seminary. When Professor Leiberman, a devoutly Orthodox Jew, refused to get into the same elevator with Dr. Kaplan after the publication of the Reconstructionist prayer book, the limits of Dr. Finkelstein's consensus seemed to have been reached. But Dr. Kaplan remained on the faculty, which is a tribute both to his own Olympian tolerance and to the administrative permissiveness of Dr. Finkelstein.[3] It is a vivid if not altogether conclusive testimony that Finkelstein's belief that the Seminary must be an umbrella institution, a dynamic powerhouse for all of Jewry in America, was more than an ecumenical gesture.

Throughout all this agonizing debate, Finkelstein never wavered in his attempts to involve, encourage, entice Goldman into active

---

3. Goldman, who was deeply distressed by Finkelstein's chasing after the *goyim* in his many Judaeo-Christian institutes and assemblies, once suggested that he could better exercise his craving for ecumenicity by bringing about *sholem* between Professors Leiberman and Kaplan.

participation with him and the Seminary; raising funds, formulating policies, being displayed as the Seminary's most gifted alumnus. Under a dozen different letterheads, invitations came to Goldman to make major addresses, to meet influential prospective board members, to confer and accept honors. Goldman's refusals ranged from blunt to politely evasive. There was his ever-demanding congregation; his family, his health, his many community commitments. Out of sheer embarrassment he accepted some of these invitations and quite often found it necessary at the last hour to decline. Once or twice Finkelstein became aware that Goldman's refusals were deliberate, but he simply could not accept the fact that any differences between them could ever weaken the bond of their friendship. In the midst of the most acidulous exchange there would crop up remarks such as these:

Our long friendship going back to our early years, has been one of the great pleasures of my life—July 21, 1941—from L. F. to S. G.

All I can say at the moment is that in the last few weeks I have been studying your published speeches and papers, and I find nothing in them in any way inconsistent with the views we have been trying to develop here. In fact, I found as I always thought, that many of the things I have been trying to do were simply applications of principles you have set down. L. F. to S. G. —December 4, 1944.

The exchange of letters on Dr. Finkelstein's fiftieth birthday in July 1945, expresses so well the bond which held these two towering personalities together and explains in some measure at least, how that friendship survived the divergent views they held regarding Conservative Judaism and the role of the Seminary.

                                                                    July 1, 1945

Dear Louis:

You and I spent our early years in an environment in which birthdays not alone were not celebrated, but rarely remembered. I do not recall that you or I ever were aware of each other's birthdays. We lived in close intimacy and affection every day of the year and we know that we wished each other the realization of our hopes from day to day. This is perhaps the reason why your fiftieth birthday overtook me, as it were, by surprise. When I heard it spoken of I could hardly believe that it had come, for I went back to the earliest years of our association and I saw you in my mind's eye as a very young boy with a blue cap looking even much younger than the number of your years at that time.

I tried, in the past week or so, to relive some of those early days, to see you in my mind's eye as I saw you then. I even went back to the notes I began jotting down about the time we entered the junior department of the Seminary. The notes were welcome and helpful. Again and again I had occasion to record your matchless love of Torah, your complete absorption in study—so much so that you rarely if ever stepped out of the four cubits of the law. You studied it, lived it and loved it and meditated on it day and night.

Then there was your unswerving piety, a piety which was not burdensome, but joyous. But above all, what impressed me then was your determination to make your contribution to the creative continuity of Israel. I remember the weeks in which we were planning the issue of The Jewish Forum and the decision we had made to have it come out Selihot night, the night we assumed the heart of our people would be most receptive to what we had to say. What you were after was the bringing back of Israel to its pristine prophetic and Rabbinic heritage.

As I turned my notes, I found that shortly after we entered the Seminary, I anticipated that you would some day become a member of its Faculty and as I turned my notes a little further, I discovered that I also anticipated you in the belief that some day you ought to be its President. That these things should have come about as a mere youth read them in advance, evidences the consistency of your life and its having been marked out from the beginning for the position you now occupy in American Israel and for the leadership you are now giving it and which I pray you may continue to give *ad meah v'esrim*—unto one hundred and twenty.

All this is perhaps a strange way of bringing you greetings on the occasion of your fiftieth birthday, but I could not get myself to write a formal statement, no matter how much I tried.

With affectionate regards and best wishes, in which Alice and the children join me, I remain

Sol

Dear Sol:

It is Sunday; no one is in the office; and so I can think a little of the days which have gone by, and try to re-live the memories which your letter stirred so deeply. I received a number of communications on the occasion of this birthday; and heard many speeches but your letter touched me, as you can imagine, with singular poignancy. I so wished we could spend some time together these days, when you and I, are both passing this curious milestone, which transforms us into counsellors.

Your friendship across the years was and remains one of the deepest satisfactions of a life, which as you perhaps more than others are aware, has not been free from tragedy. You were the man (then the boy), who discovering me in the *bet ha-midrash* of the *Ohev shalom shul,* with its damp walls, and even damper floor, its candles instead of electric lights, etc. dragged me to the Adas Bnai Yisrael; and made me feel for the first time, that there is a job to be done in this world, besides study. Perhaps if it had been otherwise, I might have remained absorbed in Torah; whether that would have been better or not, I don't know. You not only thrust me into the world where Judaism had to be built as well as preserved; you also some time later made me president of the Seminary student body—to my immense surprise—and there I discovered the world in which our student body was then operating, the IZZ etc. I made new friends, developed new contacts, and began to look on the study of Torah as only one aspect of life. I think I can say truly that those two metamorphoses were the determining elements in my life; and for both you were responsible.

Very often, I need not tell you I hunger for the days when my whole life centered about memorizing an additional page of Hullin or Aboda Zara; when I literally counted my days by the number of *dafim* (pages) I had covered. Have we exchanged "an enduring world" for a "passing world"? About ten years ago, our old friend, Abraham Meyers, tried to persuade me that we had. I felt sure then that he was wrong; I believed that it was necessary to take hold of this, but also not let go of the other. Today I am less sure than I was then. And while I am trying to think it all out, here comes your letter, and adds its own persuasion to the many which stem from sheer memory and wistfulness. I think it is the old story of *Talmud gadol* or *ma'aseh gadol;* but there are so many *baale maaseh* and so few *baale talmud.*[4]

I wish very much that we were not so far separated as we are, by space, if not by thought. I wish we could spend days together, when we are together, in thinking through the days that have gone, and those that are to come. There is no one, I believe, (except my brothers Maurice and Hink) in whom I can more completely confide, because I feel that you and they understand fully both the measure of my gratitude to God for the joys and opportunities He has given me, and the measure of my grief and disappointment, in that my life has turned out so different from what I had hoped it might be. You

---

4. . . . it is the old story of either great Talmud-study or great deeds; but there are so many doers of deeds and so few men of learning.

are right; my sole hunger when we were young was to be a good Jew and a
talmid hakham. That is still my sole hunger. But being a good Jew turns
out to be a more complicated business on Broadway and 122 St. than it
seemed at one Belmont Avenue. And somehow I wish I were still at one
Belmont Ave. Maybe that is why I am so eager to go to Palestine as soon
as may be; but will Palestine be the old Adas Bnai Israel writ large; or will
it be 122 St. and Broadway, only more difficult and more confused?

Enough of this; you wrote me with deep feeling, and you have made me
tell you, what in all the celebrations and fun, I have yet told nobody else.

I am looking forward to the celebration in honor of Schechter. It ought
to be a great day for both of us. I think we can make it worthy of Schechter;
and I know that he would have enjoyed the idea of your speaking and
receiving a degree, on that day.
Do let us meet as soon as we can.

Affectionately, as ever,
Louis

Goldman did succeed, with Dr. Kaplan's help, in forcing a change
in the administrative structure of the Seminary which placed the
decision-making function on rabbinic training in a board of trustees
on which faculty, alumni, and Conservative laymen would have the
majority vote while a larger board of overseers had responsibility for
the policy of the extracurricular, the community-outreaching projects of the Seminary. The *machloka* (the dispute) proved to be
leshem shamayim (constructive for the sake of heaven) in other ways.
Certainly it hastened the loosening of the Seminary reins over the
Rabbinical Assembly and the United Synagogue and encouraged the
participation of a larger number of the rabbis and committed laymen in the work of the Seminary and in the building of Conservative
synagogues. The larger forces of history, Hitler and the establishment of the State of Israel, pushed the Seminary more deeply
into Zionist commitment, but there can be no doubt that the work
of Goldman and his colleagues helped to speed the change.

Goldman was never happy with the direction of the Seminary nor
with the position of Conservative Judaism on the American scene.

He felt at times that Reconstructionism might be the answer, but was at last convinced that it was too narrowly rational,[5] too theologically oriented, that it lacked mystique and weighed down the numina—the divine afflatus—with too much theorizing. He was firmly convinced that the nature of the Jew as conditioned by his personal experience, that the experience of the group, the influence of the Hebrew language and Jewish culture, would provide the raw material out of which the Jew could forge a religious philosophy adequate for his needs, and that the urge for survival would furnish any community of such Jews with a viable code of behavior and with the necessary principles of community existence. He truly wished that the Seminary and Conservative Judaism would become the central forces for the training of the rabbis and laymen who would prepare knowledgeable and dedicated Jews in the Diaspora and set in motion the two-way passage of interaction with the community in Israel as Achad Ha'am had envisioned.

It is true that these were the goals Louis Finkelstein claimed as his own. In the perspective of the years that have elapsed since the death of his friendly adversary, it is apparent that he pursued these goals in a more roundabout manner. He seemed to have accepted the American Jewish Committee analysis of the power relations in the American community, its judgment that America was not ripe for *kehillah,* that the best way to spread a doctrine or a point of view was to sublimate it in the midst of more generally accepted ideas or clothe it in prestigious symbols as has been accomplished with *Commentary* magazine. He learned, also, from the corporate structure of American business and from its heavy dependence on the image-making of the mass media that these instruments had to be mastered to make any idea or goal competitive in the crowded marketplace of America. The numerous institutes, conferences, publications, and radio programs, were designed to create a context in which the more special Jewish goals would gain momentum and acceptance. He was always confident, and remains so to this day,

---

5. See Goldman's *The Jew and the Universe* for a penetrating analysis of the defects of pure rationalism and of Normative Judaism's preference for a viable balance between reason and emotion, logic and intuition, a preference stemming in part from the wholeness and oneness of the *Shema.*

that safeguards could be provided to protect the basic values of
Judaism from the curse of bigness and the compromises of success.
Certainly the contributions of the "Eternal Light" program and of
many of the publications of the various institutes sponsored by the
Seminary have not only added to the prestige and effectiveness of
the Seminary but to the pride of all Jews in America and perhaps,
in some measure, to a better grasp of Jewish reality among non-Jews.
Whether the energies expended in these endeavors could have been
more wisely devoted to the strengthening of the Rabbinic Assembly
and the United Synagogue and the resolution of some of the thorny
problems such as the *agunah* and *kashrut,* and a more definitive
statement of the Conservative theological position, is still debatable.
It is *taku* (only Elijah the Tishbite will be able to decide this in the
heavenly academy). Meanwhile it is a tribute to the Jewish heart
and mind of the two principals in this dialogue, and to the human
situation in general, that bitter ideological and doctrinal differences,
which are generally the most resistant to the meliorating influence
of compromise, could not mute the memory of childhood trust and
affection, of youthful dreams shared together, of the common bond
of a historic faith which, like a mother, can suffer the pangs of Jacob
and Esau in her womb and with compassionate love embrace them
both. There were times when Goldman bewailed the fact that these
serious differences were putting severe strains on the friendship. He
found it most difficult to become the chief adversary of his oldest and
dearest friend, but when push came to shove, loyalty to the person
of a friend muted the passion to win an argument, and the basic
respect for the sincerity of each other's position prevented an open
break. This was much more psychologically punishing for Goldman
since he was by nature a passionate fighter, and when the future of
the synagogue or the Jewish people was at stake, he could lay about
him with a fierce disregard for hurt feelings. Finkelstein believed
to the last that it was a failure of communication, the inability of the
two to get together for long uninterrupted stretches of time that prevented them from recognizing that they were agreed on essential
goals—that they differed only on their instrumentation. It could
very well be that they needed each other's loyal opposition, to be
ezer kinegdo (helpmates one against each other); that their youthful

study of Talmud together had bred into their unconscious the need to strengthen each other's mental muscles by offering the resistance to evoke the sturdiest response. They were keepers of each other's conscience, wardens of integrity and satans in the Jobian sense—agents provocateurs of each other's intellectual potential.

If a Reform colleague can be so forward as to anticipate the judgment of Elijah the Tishbite, he would say that in the perspective of the three decades since the dialogue took place that the re forms suggested by Goldman and his colleagues—in the Seminary curriculum, in the training of the rabbis, in the intensification of Hebrew studies in the religious schools, in a more direct involvement with the building of Zion, in the encouragement of day schools, in the training of Jewish lay leadership—might have made the Jewish establishment more responsive to the needs of Jewry today and preserved for the Jewish community some part of the gifted young men and women who have given themselves so passionately to the New Left and to other political and avant-garde movements which are indifferent or hostile to Judaism and to Jewish peoplehood. Dr. Finkelstein's program undoubtedly solidified the position of Conservative Judaism, slowed down the conversion of traditional Jews to Reform and, in addition, influenced the Reform movement to hold fast to much of the tradition which the founders had heedlessly abandoned. There can be no doubt, however, that the elaborate superstructure of the institutional apparatus which he largely built has taken excessive toll of the spiritual and cultural goals he envisioned. This was a prediction which Goldman made frequently in his letters to Finkelstein.

Chapter 3

The Zionist Organization— Ordeal by Glory

On 4 July 1938 in Detroit, at the Zionist Organization of America's annual convention and after heated debates and the kind of caucusing and maneuvering which characterizes our quadrennial political conventions, Rabbi Solomon Goldman was elected president. He had been making fiery addresses up and down the land exposing the weaknesses of the Zionist organization, its administrative incompetence, bureaucratic rigor mortis, its inability to attract the young, and the intellectuals, and its pathetic subordination to the special agencies which by right and the logic of common sense should be integrated parts of the Zionist organizations. His devastating exposures were often followed by rather detailed suggestions as to what might be done to reconstruct the organization to make it worthy of implementing the high goals of establishing a Jewish National Home in Palestine. It was these specifics that caught the eye and ear of many who had long been aware of the shocking paradox that the organization that represented the most persistent hunger of the Jewish people and the fulfillment of its oldest collective dream should not have attracted as many able and dedicated men and women as the defense agencies, the fraternal societies, and the philanthropic auxiliaries. Even some of the veteran leaders, Stephen Wise, Louis Lipsky, Louis Levinthal, and Robert Szold, were convinced that a new reformist leadership was needed; they were equally convinced that Solomon Goldman, the dissenter, was the man who could attract new blood to the organization without losing sight of the practical necessities of institutional life that would inevitably impose restraints on the transformation of an organization that perforce had to be all things to all men.

Rabbi Edward Israel and Rabbi James Heller, who headed two of the oldest and most distinguished Reform congregations in the land, served as Goldman's floor managers in the heated convention fight. They were drawn to Goldman by deep personal ties of affectionate regard and by their agreement with Goldman's philosophy of Zionism. It was a philosophy that he had first stated in 1930, when he proposed to Harper and Brothers publishing company the need for a new history of the Jews which, rather than emphasizing monotheism as the most important and revolutionary contribution of the Jews to civilization, would stress the group personality based on the ethnic and cultural continuity which the Jews had miraculously and uniquely maintained through three millenia. In this conception, Zionism played a key role and one much more consistent and realizable than that of the universal acceptance of Judaism's God. The idea of One God was not unique even among ancient peoples, and it tended to become fragmented the moment one began to draw particular and relevant directives for conduct from the unity of the Godhead.[1]

The centrality of the return to Israel became more and more the leitmotif of Goldman's thinking. The unity of land, language, and faith became the essential framework in which the purpose and the character of the Jewish people and its historic experience could be understood. His mastery of the Bible and Talmud, and the Hebrew and Aramaic languages in which they were written, gave him a

---

1. Absorption with the many tasks incident to the building of Anshe Emet prevented Goldman from writing this history but Harper did later agree to publish *Crisis and Decision, The Jew and the Universe,* and the first volume of *The Book of Human Destiny.*

deeper appreciation of the quality of Judaic civilization and a profounder sense of commitment to the preservation of the people who would guard and enhance this distinctive culture. Happily this mastery of the culture, its language and its content served as an antidote to parochialism or to that inverted patriotism which lead so many other Zionists to disavow the Diaspora—to become *sholel hagalut.* Goldman saw the people Israel as a cosmic experiment in a universal humanity. Its sages and poets had hit upon ideals and values which were indispensable to Israel's survival, but equally so to mankind's survival and spiritual growth. His pride in the moral and ethical genius of Israel did not blind him to the values of other cultures. God's love was not all on Israel spent. He therefore could never understand how one could place a hyphen between his Americanism and his Judaism. He said that he could never distinguish the heartbeat that throbbed for Israel from that which warmed to America. Only immature minds and hearts narrowed by craven fear could erect barriers between these two orders of loyalty and affection. Dedicated Zionists like Stephen Wise, Edward Israel, James Heller, and Louis Levinthal saw in Goldman a man who could persuade the amorphous, universalist philosophers of Reform to find a place in its idealistic outreaching for the romance of an Israel restored and, also, a man who could enlarge the vision of the *verbrente,* the passionate parochial Zionists, urging them to embrace Zion as a universal goal and Jerusalem as a city built without walls.

The aid and comfort of these stalwart friends and the boost to the general morale provided by some 20,000 new members brought in through a campaign led by Goldman were not enough to remove the organizational dry rot. Goldman did establish a Zionist office in Washington and found in Rabbi Isidor Breslau a most dedicated administrator, but the bureacracy remained entrenched at 111 Fifth Avenue and, by subtle and crude acts of sabotage, frustrated most of Goldman's reforms. Budgetary limitations and the low prestige of the Z.O.A. made it difficult to enlist competent staff members. The permanent staff knew that most presidents held only a two-year tenure and that, generally, they were heavily committed to many other causes. Rabbis were especially vulnerable because they were still primarily responsible to their congregations. Although Anshe Emet, out of respect for their rabbi, out of devotion to Zionism and in deference to the special intervention of Louis D. Brandeis, had granted Goldman a leave of absence to devote himself to the Zionist organization, the congregation, burdened with an ambitious program of expansion, was still in need of its rabbi's direction and fund-raising assistance. The leave of absence became more and more an honorific gesture.[2] The petty bureaucrats bided their time. They waited until the emotional storms aroused by Goldman's flaming oratory settled and then went about their business of quiet sabotage. Thus, 111 Fifth Avenue became a cave of Adullam, a den of subversion, and the realization began to dawn on Goldman that the little people were not motivated by the same selfless sacrifice that drove him from city to city, from group to group, in the cause of Zion. Not all the blame can honestly be put on the staff and the office-holders. Rabbi Edward Israel loved Goldman enough to level with him when he pointed out that Goldman should have been more decisive in getting rid of the incompetent and giving firm assurance to the competent that their tenure was secure, instead of keeping the whole office in uncertainty over a long period of time. Goldman should realize, he counseled, that men in fear of their livelihood sometimes act in unidealistic ways, that it is the nature of people to make an empire of the little involvements and kudos of their office, and that one accustomed to high honors, and self-directed withal, may not be aware of the extracurricular needs of the people in the lower echelons. Nor was Goldman sufficiently aware of the unconscious way in which routine tasks became orthodox procedures and as sacrosanct to the bureaucrat as *tallis* and *tephillin* to the Orthodox Jew. In the cause of Zionism, Goldman simply did not grant that margin of permissiveness which he often accepted in persons engaged in causes less crucial to the survival of the Jewish people and the Jewish ethic.

---

2. See the exchange of letters between Justice Brandeis and Hyman Kohn on the leave of absence.

But there was one man who very much appreciated this puritan streak in Goldman, perhaps because it was a reflection of one of the dominant traits in his own makeup. That man was Louis D. Brandeis, Associate Justice of the Supreme Court of the United States. From what Brandeis read of Goldman's addresses, and from what Robert Szold reported of his actions in the inner circles of the Zionist leadership, Brandeis took a great liking to Goldman and after several conferences determined that Goldman was the white hope of the movement, that he had the knowledge, the will, and the courage to carry through a vital reorganization of this battered and bedraggled cause. This is all the more remarkable since the Justice was somewhat allergic to charismatic persons, especially those whose charisma was a by-product of their oratory.[3] Goldman's vast knowledge of the historic and psychological roots of Zionism impressed Brandeis, but even more was he taken with Goldman's resolve to wager his future in the movement on a radical reorganization even if it required a wholesale dismissal of incompetents.

Justice Brandeis, it will be remembered, had had a serious falling out with Chaim Weizmann and Louis Lipsky in 1920, a schism which resulted in his withdrawal from the movement. One of the main points of difference in this controversy was the slack administration of the American Zionist offices, their gross inefficiency and nepotism. Brandeis would not accept Weizmann's explanation that the movement had to put up with the shortcomings of those who were willing to join it, for the most part Jews who had become accustomed to the more permissive habits of *shtetl* politics and petty graft. The wealthy Jews with modern business experience, a high appreciation of rigid accountancy, and open bookkeeping openly arrived at, had not joined the movement. Brandeis insisted that even if these elements could not be enlisted, it was the duty of leadership to insist on absolute probity in the affairs of a cause whose goal it was to restore the people who were descendants of the prophets.

---

3. Mrs. Alice Goldman recalls that the first time the Goldmans visited the Justice at Chatham, he was so aloof and so brutally caustic in his criticism of the past leadership that she almost panicked and asked her husband if there was still time to reconsider and find a way out of this patch of nettles.

The correspondence files contain several dozen cryptic notes written in the Justice's slightly slanted but vigorous penmanship calling Goldman to Chatham or Washington or agreeing to conferences requested by Goldman. It appears from these notes that Brandeis had informally assigned specialized roles to his advisors. Robert Szold was his consultant on the many special projects: nurseries, youth camps, agricultural experiments, cooperative self-help industry, etc.[4] Ben Cohen and Felix Frankfurter were consultants for American-Palestine problems. To Goldman he came to look more and more for guidance on the internal problems of the Zionist organization and the interplay of the various forces in the Jewish community. What seems to be truly remarkable in view of his humanistic agnosticism, was his acceptance of Goldman's theistic position and his tolerance for the religious mystique which was for Goldman the real springboard of his Zionist aspirations. He seems to have accepted and even relished from Goldman what he could not accept from Stephen Wise. Perhaps he recognized the authority which Goldman's profound scholarship gave to his judgments on contemporary issues. Or it may be that Brandeis had never quite forgiven Wise for veering to the Weizmann position in the bitter conflict of 1920 and 1921.

The Goldman papers reveal how, in a world that was closing in on the Jews and at a time when Hitler's genocide plan was being ruthlessly and successfully carried out, Jewish leadership grasped at straws and gave majestic rationalizations to the meagerest crumbs of hope. The very exaltation of Justice Brandeis can, in perspective, be seen as one of these pathetically noble illusions which frustration breeds in the best of us. Visits to the Justice took on the air of a special audition with the Pope. Codes were constructed so that the

---

4. In the 1938–1939 negotiations with American and British officialdom and with world-Zionist leadership, Szold was the anchor man who kept an eagle eye on all the major proceedings and acted as liaison between Brandeis and Goldman, Wise, Rose Jacobs, Routenberg, Norman, Akzin, and Ben Gurion. He held fast to Brandeis's conviction that there should be no partition or any other watering down of the Mandate's obligation to establish a Jewish national home in Palestine, a home where the Jew would be in the majority and master of his destiny.

message "Get the Justice to arrange interview with President for Weizmann at White House" was coded: "Have *Shofet* arrange *siyum skipper shushan* with Nasi." The Shofet, always mindful of the dignity of the Court, would refer the request to Ben Cohen or Felix Frankfurter who would attend to the matter. The Skipper (Roosevelt) would be congenial, exercise his tireless charm, and give noncommittal answers or suggest a visit to Cordell Hull, who would exercise his utmost in Southern hospitality and even refer to his Jewish wife. Hull naively thought that the elder Rabbi Levinthal of Philadelphia was one of the ancient prophets or one of the anonymous thirty-six saints.[5] Actual results were meager, but word went out that the highest authorities had been seen; we had friends in the seats of ultimate power. Nevertheless, Evian closed out the Jews. The president refused to command the generals to bomb the railroads leading to Auschwitz, and Jewish refugees were allowed to drown in unseaworthy vessels while British sea power looked on. Goldman was too shrewd an observer not to see this. But he was too much the rabbi to let the facts drive him to despair. He kept the faith with himself and with the people. It was better to let them believe that help would come, that our great men were not helpless in crisis.

The British White Paper, the negotiations in late 1938 and early 1939 which led up to it, and the maneuvers which followed its official publication offered a forcing house in which the faith of Jewish leadership was tested in bitter adversity and not found wanting. As president of the Zionist Organization, Goldman played a vital role as liaison between Weizmann and Brandeis, as well as being one of the chief mobilizers of American resistance to the British disavowal of its solemn obligation under the Mandate to facilitate the establishment of a Jewish national home in Palestine.

Weizmann, in his letter of congratulation to Goldman written from London on July 15, 1938, sets the scene almost in the manner of a Greek choral prologue to a tragedy.

---

5. This refers to the folk legend of the *lamed-vovnicks*—the thirty-six saintly Jews for whose sake in each generation the Lord permits the sinful world to endure.

. . . It needs no words of mine to tell you that you are taking office at a most crucial time in the history of our movement and of our people. American Jewry is now the one great Jewish community which still remains intact, and Fate has thus placed upon it, and upon you as the head of the Zionist movement in the United States, a very heavy task, as well as a great opportunity. The coming months will no doubt bring with them momentous decisions which may influence the political situation in Palestine for years to come. But whatever those decisions may be—and I must make it clear that we are still without any grounds for prophecy in this connection, either one way or the other—independently of the work of the Commission or of the attitude of His Majesty's Government, we ourselves must see to it that our work continues under any circumstances, and continues even more intensively than hitherto.

If it is brought home to the British Government and to the British people that, undaunted by all that has happened, we are still prepared to make a greater effort than ever, this in itself will be a political factor of the first magnitude. . . .

Three months later, on October 3rd, Weizmann's faith is subjected to an almost unbearable strain. He writes to Goldman:

My dear Friend,

We are now slowly recovering from the extraordinary tension which has prevailed here during the past fortnight—since we parted in Antwerp. World events have been moving so swiftly that it is still very difficult to draw conclusions, or to appraise the results of the agreement which has been reached. I fear, however, that from the Jewish point of view, the attitude of the present British Government, and the way in which they have handed over Czechoslovakia, augurs ill for us; I should not be surprised if Mr. Chamberlain's method of appeasement, applied to Palestine, should turn out to mean making terms with the Mufti at our expense in the same way as terms have been made with Hitler at the expense of the Czechs. What that means I need not tell you. Naturally, we shall have to resist to the last ditch, and our power of resistance depends entirely on the support which we can get from America, which is the only great Jewish community which still remains intact, and is capable of extending a helping hand.

You have been called to the head of the Zionist Organization in America at perhaps the most critical time in Jewish history. It would be offensive if I were to make an appeal to you, because I know exactly how you feel. But I am sending out this letter as a kind of signal of distress, so as to warn you of what we *may* expect. I am carrying on a series of conversations with Mr. Malcolm MacDonald, which have so far been quite inconclusive. He is harping a great deal on the "Arab danger," the need for "going slow," and the difficulties of carrying out partition because it might upset the Arab world. But there lurks in my mind the fear that in all these conversations he may be merely "leading me up the garden path," since quite possibly all these things may be already settled, and these conversations nothing but eyewash. I may be putting the worst construction on the present position because I am still under the influence of the last few weeks here. Possibly I may be wrong; this is why I would ask you to regard this letter as very strictly private, and as intended merely as a warning.

I think it would be useful if you would see Ben Cohn who has just been in England, and with whom I had a number of talks. I think he has a clear idea of the situation here, and it would be a good thing if you would talk matters over with him and see what can be done at your end. . . .

In spite of these ominous premonitions, Weizmann and his associates, Ben Gurion, Professor Selig Brodetsky, Viscount Bearsted, and Dr. Stephen Wise, met with the representatives of the British government, Mr. Malcolm MacDonald, the colonial secretary; Lord Halifax; Undersecretary Mr. Butler, and Lord Dufferin. The Arabs were represented by Aly Maher Pasha, Taufiq Bey Suwaidi, H. H. Lloyd, Fuad Bey Hanza. This was the conference on Palestine called in the middle of February at St. James Palace. The Chamberlain government hoped by this conference to find a way to continue the Mandate or, failing that, to establish an independent state wherein the Jewish and Arab population could eventually develop self-government. The first sessions were devoted to procedural matters. When these were agreed upon, the Arab and Jewish delgations would meet separately with the British government representatives.[6]

Ben Gurion immediately asked for joint face-to-face meetings with the Arabs. On the basis of private conversations held with the more moderate Arabs, this seemed a possibility. But when the chips were down, the moderate voices were vetoed by the Arab extremists and direct negotiations never took place. The Arab militants were for freezing the Jewish population in Palestine at the level then existing

---

6. The more recent refusal (1970) of the Arab governments to engage in face-to-face negotiations has at least two precedents: once in 1938 and again in 1948. Pride and prejudice can pervert memory and lead a people to repeat the costly mistakes of its past.

(1938). They insisted that Palestine remain Arab even if, to keep it
so, it had to close its doors to the refugees from Hitler. The Jewish
delegation insisted that to accept a permanent minority status was
unacceptable and was in addition a violation of the purpose of the
Balfour Declaration and a betrayal of the conditions on which the
Mandate over Palestine was granted to Britain by the League of
Nations. The Jewish delegation was willing to consider parity with
the Arabs on a non-domination basis and, failing that, were willing
to discuss a partition of Palestine into Jewish and Arab enclaves
within some overall federated structure. The Arabs adamantly refused parity. The British offered various compromises; a period of
limited migration until the Jewish population came to 35 percent
of the total, then further immigration subject to Arab consent; land
purchase was to be prohibited in certain areas, limited in others,
and free in some. Neither Jews nor Arabs were willing to accept
this solution. The British finally declared the negotiations and the
conference at an end. The cabinet presented a plan embodying,
largely, the compromises outlined above. The plan was debated in
Parliament, where it met with much opposition. Winston Churchill
vehemently declared the plan a betrayal of England's solemn promise and, ultimately, a betrayal of England's best interest. But the
unity engendered by the approach of war muted the wide dissent
and obvious dissatisfaction with this decision, and the plan carried.
Ben Gurion did not waste energy lamenting this decision. He immediately set about to nullify the White Paper by bringing in
thousands of Jewish immigrants and refugees and by building
overnight settlements in areas which had already been purchased.
He cabled Goldman constantly to find the funds which would enable him to accomplish these ends.

Weizmann still believed that diplomatic channels were not closed,
and hoped that Jewish will, ingenuity, and sacrifice could negate
the evil decree. He wrote to Goldman from Palestine on 28 April
1939:

My dear Dr. Goldman,

Ben-Gurion has sent me a copy of your letter of April 6th, in which you
gave details of your interview with the President. I was delighted to read it

and in these times of stress it was a great comfort to feel that a man of Roosevelt's calibre is beginning to understand the importance of Palestine and the severity of the struggle through which we are passing at present.[7] I am now three weeks in the country and cannot do better than send you a copy of a letter I am sending to our friend William Bullitt in Paris, and which gives a good picture of the situation as I see it. I have really nothing more to add to it. I shall be grateful if you will circulate this letter and the enclosures to our friends and naturally show it to Judge Brandeis. I also enclose a cutting from the Egyptian Gazette which is, as you may know, the official organ of the British in Egypt and in particular the British Embassy, which clearly indicates their attitude and methods of propaganda in the neighbouring states. With such an attitude, which completely ignores all the moral and contractual obligations of the British towards the League and us, you can clearly understand that it makes it very difficult for us to get on a footing of negotiations with the Arabs although the time seems to me at present more propitious than it was in the history of the last twenty years. Perhaps the attached short statement on our program of work among the Arabs which was drawn up by our Political Department might give you an idea of the lines along which we would like to proceed.

. . . Although the London Conference has brought us a great deal of disappointment, it has, on the other hand, produced the effect of establishing some personal contacts between ourselves and some Arab leaders in Iraq and Egypt and I am trying actively to develop these relations which with care might in time lead to some positive results. Although my visit to Egypt was merely a courtesy visit, it strengthened the friendly relations between us and some of the leading Egyptians. If the British were not blinded by abject fear of phantoms they could not only help us in settling the Palestinian difficulties but would for all times make a substantial contribution to the friendly relations between us and the Arabs in spite of the Mufti and his satellites. Whatever is it that has come over the British, whether it is fear or the infection by the virus of Hitlerism or something else, . . . it is certainly a bitter disappointment and a great tragedy. Should any of our friends have the opportunity of a further talk with your President you might point out this Druse question to him as a typical example of the unsoundness of what British official quarters have been saying about Upper Galilee since the publication of the Peel Report. Their thesis was that the Peel Commission had blundered in offering the Jews a part of Palestine which is so thickly

---

7. The revelation of Roosevelt's indifference to the plight of the Jews condemned by Hitler in Morse's *While Six Million Died* reveals how even such sophisticated men as Wise, Goldman, Weizmann and Brandeis could be misled by the vague assurances of the Skipper—hope, it seems, mingles heartening illusions with its balm of sustaining faith. . . .

populated by Arabs that its colonisation would mean a constant war with them. The heart of Upper Galilee is not Arab, but Druse, and we could acquire it peacefully with the consent of the Druses. All the district along the Acre-Safed road as far as Hanitah and Nahariah could become Jewish in a perfectly peaceful manner, with the added benefit of the emigration of something like 10,000 souls. This is a typical example of the grotesque exaggeration preached by these British officials all these years. I cannot help feeling that this distortion of facts is intentional and malevolent. Unfortunately, one must not breathe a word about it publicly as it would ruin the prospects of the purchase but to our friends in America this could be pointed out as a typical example of mendacious anti-Zionist propaganda.[8]

Affectionately
Yours Ch. Weizmann

A month later on May 30th Weizmann, in his letter to Goldman, analyzes the strategy of non-cooperation in greater detail:

At the present time we are passing through a very indefinite period; our relations with His Majesty's Government are very strained, non-cooperation has already set in. It is essential that it should not assume violent forms, but can it be avoided? . . . I count to a great extent both on the ingenuity and sense of responsibility in the Yishub, except of course the Revisionists for whom these are heydays.

In the course of this letter, Weizmann expressed his profound dismay and discouragement at reports that the British undersecretary, Butler, was conveying information that he was receiving no real opposition or even criticism from the American Department of State on Britain's interpretation of the Mandate. Having no faith in Joseph Kennedy, our ambassador to Britain, he urged Goldman to discover the real attitude of our government. Weizmann still believed that if the Mandate Commission of the League of Nations rejected the White Paper as betraying the objective of the Mandate, that the British government would reconsider. That is why he resented Lady Astor's suggestion that he accept the White Paper and

8. Recent criticisms of Zionist leaders, especially Weizmann and Ben Gurion for not having done enough to win over the Arabs (see Nahum Goldman in *Foreign Affairs Quarterly* for April 1970), seem not to be aware of the many attempts by Ben Gurion, Sharret, David Ha-Cohen to enlist moderate Arab leadership, nor do they give due weight to the deliberate policy of the British to discourage these attempts.

stay away from America. He even more sharply rejected her advice that he cultivate the good will of Mr. Arthur H. Sulzberger who happened to be in London:

> I have refused to do so and have asked her to tell her friends in the government that they will meet with nothing but uncompromising hostility as far as I am concerned and that at some time I shall be going to U.S.A. As for Sulzberger—he is a cowardly Jew!
>
> Now what I would like to understand however is whether the general attitude and feeling of the Jews is very different from Sulzberger's and his paper.

This letter inspired Goldman to include this indictment of timid Jews in his address to the Forty-first Annual Convention of the Zionist Organization in June of 1939:

> But even as we resolve to confront the external events unflinchingly, we must not neglect the danger of irresolution working from within. Anti-Semitism does not overwhelm the Jewish people, but it succeeds in terrorizing numbers of Jews. In these last few years a pitiful timidity has overtaken certain Jewish leaders; . . . There is not a more devastating commentary on what Anti-Semitism can do to individual Jews than that provided by one of the world's leading newspapers, which happens to be owned by a Jew. On the day when the White Paper was published the news was proclaimed in that publication under the headline: "Palestine Freed!" Freed from whom?—we would like to ask the publisher. Freed from the lineal descendants of his own ancestors, from the people who had come there to revive and renew the spirit of Isaiah and Hillel. . . .[9]

Zionist leadership had its finest hour in this crisis. With the cards so solidly stacked against them, they, with the exception of two or three timid ones, showed none of the stigmata of defeat. They acted as if the decision might yet be reversed, and took consolation in the thought that even if this were not to happen, the enemy would realize that the Jews can put up a fight and make it very costly for the victor even when he wins. Stephen S. Wise expressed the mood

---

9. See *Undefeated* by Solomon Goldman (Zionist Organization of America, Washington, 1940), pp. 31 and 32.

of the leadership in a letter to his children written just before his
departure from the conference at St. James.

Dear Justine, Jim and Shad:

. . . It was a long session and MacDonald really laid down the law, fore-
shadowing the worst which has now come to us in the form of written
Government proposals. It is worse than the worst that we had feared, namely,
[the end of] an independent State. . . .

We shall move as hard and as quickly as we can in order to get something
done. We are telephoning to New York and to Sol Goldman, but it all seems
of very little avail. The British Government seems to be, in their own language, "fed up with the Jews," and they know we are in their hands, because
at least we are more anti-Hitler than we are anti-British, so they probably
consider this an opportunity to get rid of the Mandate. They will have all the
advantage they think of possession and domination of Palestine without having to take us into account all the time. Some of us may try to see the Prime
Minister tomorrow and let him see how Chatham [Brandeis] feels about this
threatened repudiation of Balfour and the Mandate, but the precedent of
Munich is almost certain to be followed and we are to play the role of the
Czechs. There is no Runciman visible, but we have our own rancid men
ready to surrender and to make peace when there is no peace in the hope of
getting some sort of partition. The Arabs, we learn from Rutenberg, who is
very helpful, have accepted the proposal—I mean of the Arab State, and
they expect to win the Mufti's representative within the day. The Mufti gang
are not even satisfied with the slaughter and wish to impose further concessions, demanding the right to know in advance how land sales are to be
limited and immigration to be restricted.

Tomorrow the P.M. [Prime Minister Chamberlain] will do the thing near
to his noble heart, extend hasty recognition to Franco, and a day or two
later it will be the Arabs who are recognized and the Jews who will be pushed
aside like the loyalists of Spain. It is grotesque to the point of weirdness or
would be if it were not unspeakably tragic. What it will mean to Jews the
world over is too awful to contemplate, with their hearts set upon Palestine.

We are fighting all day and will until the decree has been finally and
irrevocably pronounced, but there will be nothing irrevocable, because England will rue the day and yet alter the decision. She will get nothing from
the Arabs. She might have gotten so much and will get so much from us. . . .

Meanwhile Weizmann took advantage of all the obligatory notes
he held from the British elite in whose homes he had often been

the celebrated lion. He literally badgered Halifax and Lothian. From one of the labor leaders in the Opposition, Mr. Herbert Morrison, he received the assurance that should Labor come to power, the White Paper would be reversed—cold comfort indeed. He made one more desperate effort with the Prime Minister on 24 March 1939. He wrote:

My dear Mr. Prime Minister,

Although I hesitate to add to the pressure on your time by asking you even to read an additional letter, I cannot leave for Palestine at this juncture without making to you a personal appeal and suggestion. Never before have I quitted England with so heavy a heart. A cloud hangs over the relations between the Jewish Agency and British Ministers. Through all the ups and downs of more than twenty years, I have found support in the thought that, to quote Lord Balfour's words, we were "partners in the great enterprise" which means life or death to my people.

In a week's time I shall be in Palestine. Even in present circumstances, it will be our duty to try and keep the spirit of our people calm and collected, and their discipline unbroken. But they have been sorely tried, and the chances of my succeeding would be greatly improved if the threatened blow of the new policy was not inflicted upon them at this time. Please consider the events of the past twelve months as they more particularly affect the Jews.

Hitler's entry into Vienna; the expulsion of the Jews from Italy and from Danzig; the Nazi occupation of the Sudetenland; the November pogrom in Germany; the anti-semitic measures in Slovakia; the Nazi invasion of Bohemia and Moravia; and now Memel. It is against this background that any threat to our work and position in Palestine will be judged by Jews all over the world.

In times so deeply disturbed, could we not avoid adding to the turmoil? For such would be the result of putting forward a policy which only raises further questions and provokes further demands, and satisfies no-one. If the announcement of the decision is postponed I do not mean to leave the time unused. Every effort will be made, and every contact used, to explore the possibility of a Jewish-Arab agreement or rapprochement. While I cannot promise any success, I would suggest that lapse of time may open possibilities in this direction.

I would like to add a word of thanks for your unfailing kindness to me throughout this difficult time. This emboldens me to believe that you may

still, even at the last moment, prevent this additional sorrow from being
added to our tragic lot.[10]

> With kind regards, believe me,
> Yours very sincerely,
> Ch. Weizmann

With the pall of certain defeat in England hanging over them,
Ben Gurion, Shertok, Kaplan and their associates began the nerve-
and-muscle-straining task of subverting the aims of the White Paper
by bringing in refugees, building settlements in border areas, and
occupying as much of the already purchased lands as possible. Goldman served as the American contact or agent. Ben Gurion cabled
him frequently detailing the projects and asking for the 7,000
pounds per week they would require.[11]

In the desperate search for help, Benjamin Akzin, a colleague of
Jabotinsky who was to become one of the leading philosophers of
the Revisionist movement, appealed to Justice Brandeis to step
down from the bench and, even at eighty-four, assume the leadership of the Zionist movement and give battle to the Chamberlain
Government. Akzin was unaware that the Justice's intervention with
Chamberlain had not even merited the courtesy of a personal reply.

For on February 25th, the Justice had cabled this message:

Right Honorable,
Neville Chamberlain, M.P.,
London.

Dear Prime Minister:

London friends advise me of the proposed intentions of His Majesty's
Government with reference to Palestine. Having discussed in detail the
problem of the Jewish National Home in Palestine with the late Lord Balfour prior to the publication of the Balfour Declaration and the acceptance
of the mandate, I cannot believe that your Government has fully considered
how gravely shattered would be the faith of the people of this troubled world
in the solemn undertakings of even democratic governments if Great Britain
so drastically departed from her declared policy in reference to the Jewish
National Home. I wire you to consider the cruel plight of the Jews in the

---

10. See also the exchange between Viscount Halifax and Weizmann in December of
1939, on pp. 235.
11. See cables sent to Goldman on May 24th and 29th by Ben Gurion, pp. 241.

world today and not to crush their most cherished and sanctified hopes. In view of your own belief in direct communication I venture to address this to you personally.

Respectfully, L.D.B.

To which, the Justice received this answer from one of the Prime Minister's secretaries on March 6:

My dear Mr. Justice,

I have been instructed to acknowledge a telegram which you sent on February 26th to the Prime Minister, protesting that the proposed intentions of His Majesty's Government regarding Palestine are a drastic departure from their declared policy with reference to the Jewish National Home.

I think you may know that any opinion you may entertain on the question of Palestine, when brought to the attention of my Government, commands their respectful and earnest attention. In the present instance I am to beg that whatever reports you may have heard, you will defer forming an opinion until my Government shall have issued an authoritative statement as to their attitude. Meanwhile you can rest assured that they are very mindful of their obligations with regard to the Jewish National Home under the Balfour Declaration and the Mandate.

Believe me,
My Dear Mr. Justice,
Yours very sincerely,
R. C. Lindsay

Frank Knox, the publisher of the Chicago *Daily News,* sent Goldman this note of comfort and consolation:

. . . One of our early American Fathers warned us to always expect in dealing with foreign nations that they will act in their own selfish interests, and how emphatically and obviously the British treatment of the Jewish problem in Palestine illumines that warning.

I cannot but believe that this fresh evidence of a cynical disregard for promises made, when fulfillment of those promises seems a temporary detriment, will inure to further depletion of Britain's already depleted international prestige. In all British history, no period has seen so swift a descent in world esteem than that suffered by the British Empire since 1931 when it, callously, ran out on its pledged word to help preserve the territorial integrity of the nations bordering on the Pacific. The failure of Great Britain to support us in our demands upon Japan to preserve the terms of the Nine-Power Pact with regard to China, marked the beginning of an era in British diplomacy, the record of which future Britains will read with shame, culminating, as it does, with the undefensible violation of the British pledge to the Jews of the world with respect to Palestine.

The lesson for America, of course, is obvious: We must make as few promises as possible in dealing with other nations, and then keep those promises inviolate.

Yours sincerely,
Frank Knox

Goldman went through a fearful struggle with his conscience and a most agonizing reappraisal of the forces of history, the motives that compel human behavior, and the prospects of sinful man ever being able, with his fellow sinners, to create a good society, much less a community of the faithful. His experience with the politics of the Zionist Organization had brought him devastating testimony that for every ounce of altruism in human beings, there is a pound of self-centeredness and rampant egotism. He had seen the clay feet of even the best of our leaders. He knew that nations generally express the lowest common denominator of the ethical and moral standards of the individuals that compose them. The aggressions which animals and primitive men developed as a mode of survival are geometrically multiplied in a nation, because to the normal defensive needs of survival are added the corrosive and insatiable urge for national power and national glory. The Talmud's hard-nosed realism and the pressures of the environment on the Jewish community had long ago deprived him of the illusions to which less thoughtful and less persecuted people can often cling. His studies in Western pragmatism, especially as developed by Dewey, James, and Marx, had given him a very healthy respect for the thesis that externally determined conditions create the channels through which the individual will operate. Just the same, he had never been able to free himself from *agadah*, from the mythopoetry of the Bible, from the tenacious whisper of his subconscious that there are "powers not ourselves that make for righteousness," that the universe is open-ended and can be invaded by forces not enslaved to its past. He had discovered in a rereading of Maimonides that even this supreme rationalist had built-in loopholes to allow the cold logic of deduction to escape from its rigid premises and reach out for that reason which is above reasons and illumines a larger truth than that which can arise from the mere addition of fact to fact.[12]

And there was that inarticulate major premise of his life, the continuity of the Jewish personality, the ongoing of the collective Jewish ethic. He could not permit the stony face of the facts of realpolitik to determine his actions. He disciplined himself, as did Weizmann and Ben Gurion, to split his loyalties in a most subtle and delicate manner, to honor England as the brave David fighting the Goliath of nazism, and to despise England as the cruel Goliath blocking the Jews who were fleeing Hitler from their one certain haven in Palestine. Perhaps never before in history has a people been called upon to become deliberately schizophrenic, and never before or since has a people accomplished so ambivalent a task as effectively as did the Zionists and the pro-Palestinians of the Jewish communities. It was as the spokesman of the profounder Jewish mystique, of an out-reaching aesthetic intuition, an out-reaching of the folk genius to clothe the bitter bones of reality with the cloak of tender hope that Goldman ended his magnificent address to the Forty-first Zionist Convention with these words:

> Today, more than ever before, the words of Herzl ring in our ears with solemn meaning: "If you will it, it is not a dream." *Wenn ihr wollt, ist es kein Märchen.* Our ancestors, in the long night of the exile put off the redemption to the coming of the Messiah. We, in our day, trusted in a charter and relied on a declaration. Now we know that the redemption of the land is in the hands of the Jew.
>
> Concerned as I am with the protest against Britain, I am concerned even more with the rekindling of hope in our hearts. Let the challenge of His Majesty's Government provoke in us a storm of strength which will recoil on those who have sought to break us. Let us remember that Palestine is ours as long as its hills and valleys lie between the Mediterranean and the Jordan. Of haunted houses it is said that they yield peace of mind only to the descendants of the original owner. Even so the soil of Eretz Israel will yield its sustenance and its beauty only to the descendants of those who wrote the Tehilim [the Psalms], and who bled at Masada.[13]

---

12. See the discussion of the *Jew and the Universe*, pp. 86.
13. See *Undefeated* (Washington, D. C.: Z.O.A., 1943), pp. 47–48.

Chapter 4

The Bookman: Scholar and Author

THE CHAPEL of the Jewish Theological Seminary of America is part of the library which houses one of the great collections of Hebraica and Judaica in the world. It has a New England meeting-house austerity reminding the visitor of the scholar's proper discipline, salt and bread to eat, the floor to sleep upon. It is also a permanent testimony to the inseparability of worship and study in our tradition, a simple architectural statement that study is indeed a form of worship in Judaism. A modest plaque in this chapel links the names of Alexander Marx, Louis Ginzberg, and Solomon Goldman whose personal libraries have been housed together in this section of the Seminary library. Dr. Louis Finkelstein quite correctly said that there could be no more fitting memorial to Sol Goldman than to link his name with these two titans in Jewish scholarship, and it was with no false modesty that he added he could wish for no better reward for his own long labors in the fields of Jewish history, sociology, and theology. If ever the subway that tunnels under the library remains quiet, and the weary laughter and sick despair of neighboring Harlem is stilled, one might easily imagine a great colloquium of the spirit as the brainchildren of these three scholars slip out of the fixed pages and hold high discourse one with another. Far more satisfying than the roast leviathan or the dedicated wine would be the intellectual banquets of the interacting thoughts of *The Work of Medieval Jewish Scholars*, *The Legends of the Jews*, and *The Book of Human Destiny*.

Solomon Goldman was primarily a man of the Book. His memory, fastidious and wide-ranging as it was, could not go back to a time when his eyes were not trained on a printed page or his ears not attuned to the chanting of the wisdom of the Book. When Emmet Dedman of the Chicago *Sun-Times* once asked Goldman why he had undertaken the massive task of a thirteen-volume work on the Bible, he replied that the Book was mother's milk to him, a familiar friend, a household presence, the guide and goal of his childhood, his youth, and his mature years. Aside from the hours he spent with Alice, and later with Gayolah and Naomi and still later with the grandchildren, no hours delighted him more than those he spent reading. Reading was not a passive pleasure. It engaged him completely. He tested unfamiliar terms against dictionary definition, he made marginal notes, underlined crucial passages, took notes on subjects he was pursuing, and these were many. He loved to check quotations, especially those of the Talmud, or Midrash or the Mekhiltahs, to discover variants in different texts. In his study, both at the synagogue and in his home, he had ladders affixed to rollers so that he could scurry from one section of the library to another. He was as busy as a papa heron feeding his fledglings as he quickly fingered the pages looking for the confirming evidence. The elusive quarry found, he came down with it, lovingly placing the book on his desk while he copied the relevant reference and then as lovingly returned the book to its proper niche, unless this latest revelation of its contents led him to reappraise its category and transfer it to more congenial neighbors. Like the father of Israel's president, Zalman Shazar, Goldman was expert in grasping the inner consanguinity of books. Titles were often misleading. He preferred to place a book by the weighted balance of its moods and content, by its true character, rather than by its formal category. Why should Graetz, Dubnow, and Baron be forced to share the same shelf with Tharaud, Chamberlain, and Toynbee, or Thomas Mann with Breasted because they were concerned with the same subject? Goldman abandoned the *mechitzah*[1] in the synagogue, but found place for it in his library. When Goldman's library was presented to the Jewish Theological Seminary, the librarian was deeply impressed with the arrangement of books. The covers of the volumes were not closed doors. The interrelatedness of content and conviction made them members of one family.

Goldman's colleagues were amazed at his productivity as book followed book from Goldman's pen. Some suspected that he kept a stable of ghost writers for they simply could not believe that the rabbi of one of the largest and most active congregations in the land could marshall the time or the effort to produce works whose footnotes alone would be considered a high scholarly achievement for any congregational rabbi. In fact one correspondent put the matter quite bluntly and vividly in these lines:

> When and how do you do it all? You are the rabbi of one of the largest congregations in the country. You are president of two national organizations —the Zionist Organization of America and the Histadrut Ivrith. You tour and lecture over half the globe. Your congregation is a beehive of activities with what is generally reported as being the largest budget of any synagogue in the land. When do you find time to accumulate your material, to survey such a large portion of the literary, political, philosophical and scientific writings of the occidental world in addition to the archeological and biblical material? How much of your work is done? How many years will be required to finish it?

To this query, Goldman replied:

> . . . I have disciplined myself to few hours of sleep. For a quarter of a century and more I have been rising approximately at a quarter of six and retiring at midnight. For the past fifteen years I have denied myself what is described as social life. A lover of the drama and music and a frequent visitor in my younger days to the theater and opera, I have in the past fifteen years probably heard a concert or opera an average of one in two years, and seen a play probably once in the same period of time. I rarely go to movies. I do not stay for wedding dinners. I do not go to Bar Mitzvah receptions.

---

1. The *mechitzah* is the divider in a one-level Orthodox synagogue that separates the men from the women.

Whenever possible, I avoid going to the cemetary though I officiate at the chapel. I husband my time. I try to the best of my ability not to waste any of it. I am at my table in the library at 6:15 in the morning. My family has made the super-human effort to guard me against interruptions until approximately 11:30.

I have always read with pencil in hand, and for more than three decades I have marked in the books that I read everything and anything that appealed to me. When I finished reading the book I wrote down the passages that I marked. When I was able to afford it, I had somebody type the material for me so that it saved me time copying. Recently, when my library was moved to our new home, I had occasion to survey the material I accumulated. I found that from the year of my Bar Mitzvah to this year when I passed fifty-six, I had accumulated approximately 150,000 3x5 index cards. In these cards I came across scores of books outlined, an endless number of selections from a wide range of the world's literature. I have a filing scheme of my own and a numeral system for purposes of classification. The "Echoes and Allusions"[2] have become so numerous that I stopped long ago making any additions. Indeed, though my second volume, *In the Beginning,* is bulky I have included there no more than 55% of the material I had available referring to that book. The cost of publication is prohibitive. By the time my work is finished, I shall have used no more than half of the "Echoes and Allusions" I have available. If the Lord grants me at least the shorter Biblical span of life and my congregation retires me at the age of sixty, I shall, God willing, have completed my work on the Bible before I go into the Great Yonder to begin my education. . . .

Alas, this modest and benign hope was not to be fulfilled. *Mann dacht und Gott lacht;* Man plans but God has his own design. As Bialik wrote of another giant in Israel:

> There was a man and he is
> no more,
> Before his time, death took him
> and
> The Song of his life was interrupted.

While only three volumes of his major work on the Bible were

---

2. These are the sections in Volumes I and II of *The Book of Human Destiny* wherein are quoted excerpts from the wide world of literature that has been inspired by the Bible.

completed,[3] these, and the books he wrote before he undertook the
Bible series and during the gathering of the material for the *magnum opus,* constitute a bibliography of which a scholar of ripe years
devoted solely to the making of books could well be proud.[4] We
shall briefly consider these publications before we evaluate the three
volumes on the Bible in greater detail.

A Rabbi Takes Stock was published by Harper and Brothers in
1931. It contains eleven essays, written between 1925 and 1929.
Goldman had come to national prominence in the famous "heresy
trial" described in Chapter I. The editor of Harper and Brothers
had been sufficiently interested to ask Goldman to write a popular
history of the Jews largely for non-Jewish readers. Goldman submitted an outline in which he made nationalism, the Jew's ethnic
identity rather than monotheism, his most unique and significant
contribution. The editor was intrigued and eagerly awaited the
fleshing out of the outline. Preoccupation with the innumerable
details of reviving Anshe Emet in Chicago prevented Goldman
from following through. He offered the collection of essays as a substitute. Harper's editor was of course disappointed, but he recognized the high quality of Goldman's writing style and the sparkling
erudition from every page of these essays, most of which had first
been delivered as sermons or public addresses. The book was not
by any means a best seller. It never went into a second printing.
It had, however, a sharp impact on the American rabbinate and on
some five thousand Jewish laymen who were both willing and able
to read a rabbi who drove them to the dictionary at least a half-
dozen times for each chapter. In the first chapter, "A Rabbi Takes
Stock," which gave the book its title, Goldman threw down the
gauntlet to Orthodoxy, Reform, and Conservatism and, in the
later essays, began to formulate the theses which were to become
his hallmark in the forums of the Jewish people and in the select

---

3. These are the general introduction to *The Book of Human Destiny, In the
Beginning,* which deals with Genesis and *From Slavery to Freedom,* on Exodus. Goldman left eight large typescripts containing translations and commentaries on most of
the Prophets and the Writings which may stimulate other scholars to complete these
books.
4. See Bibliography, pp. 287–290.

company of those concerned with comparative religion and religious philosophy. Here he raised the abrasive charge that at the end of almost a century of religious conflict in Jewry, neither Orthodoxy nor Reform could claim a victory. Both were so impoverished in spiritual and intellectual resources that neither could hope to meet the new challenges of our day: ". . . the future of Judaism would be dark indeed if it rested with the might of either group."

Orthodoxy, he maintained, has been permitted by the blindness of its leaders to slip into a cul-de-sac from which there is no hope of emergence. Reform is intellectually sterile and spiritually hollow. European Jewry is impervious to it, whereas its much advertised success in America is limited to brick and mortar. The crude way in which Reform has slashed its way through traditional Judaism has contributed to Orthodoxy's unwillingness to take its head out of the sand. But those who have looked critically at Reform find that its whole structure is reared on ill-digested Kantianism. Its prophetic pretensions sit ill on the shoulders of the wealthy merchants and bankers mouthing their mission to bring universal peace and justice to the world.

Nor has Conservatism built a sensible highway down the middle, eschewing Orthodoxy's obscurantism and Reform's vapid and rootless gentile-aping universalism. Whereas Orthodoxy has expressed its stubborn persistence to live by the *Shulchan Arukh* and Reform has rung endless variations on the mission theme, Conservatism has remained coyly silent or has palmed off a few sophistic aphorisms about not being so much Conservative Judaism as Conserving Judaism. Goldman is compelled to ask the leaders of his own denomination what they mean by the values they would conserve, how much of the heritage they meant to retain and what they plan to throw overboard. He insisted on forcing Conservatism to declare in what manner it differs from Orthodoxy and from Reform and to offer a clear unequivocal platform to those who would come under its banner and not be merely a rest camp for the malcontents from Orthodoxy and the discontents from Reform.

The value of footnotes becomes readily apparent in the first book. Goldman made clear that Professor Mordecai Kaplan of the Jewish Theological Seminary had for some years already been exploring this very area and amassing full notes on just such a transvaluation of values. He also admitted that, among the Reformers, Stephen Wise, Barnett Brickner, James Heller, and Louis I. Newman had begun to heal the breach between nationalism and Reform Judaism and had called upon their congregations to restore Zionism, not merely the dream of Zion but the State of Israel, as a central doctrine and goal of Reform Judaism. Kaplan's *Judaism as a Civilization* was to be published in 1934 and the Columbus Platform was to be adopted by the Central Conference of American Rabbis in 1937. This platform marked the official return of Reform Judaism to Zionism by declaring an end to the classical dichotomy of nationalism and universalism and accepting the goal of restoring a part of the Jewish people to the Land of Israel. It is not too much to claim that Goldman's book was an important and acknowledged factor in the publication of Dr. Kaplan's major work and equally important but not heretofore acknowledged in the promulgation and acceptance of the Columbus Platform.

It was also in *A Rabbi Takes Stock* that Goldman defined some of the central theses that were to dominate his intellectual life. He asked for a definition of Judaism in terms of the whole of life. Nothing that enhances the physical, ethical, spiritual, and esthetic welfare of the individual dare be overlooked in its perspective, he insisted. Both Reform and Orthodoxy still clung to the theology of the Middle Ages. They had not advanced beyond the reasoning of the scholastics who were themselves tied too firmly to the dialectic elaborations of Aristotle. If Judaism were to become relevant, it would have to create a new philosophic foundation based on the formal truths of science and on the more intuitive and existential data of our own experiences. As the civilization of the ancients was the result of their experience and their comprehension of that experience, so must our religion and our morality be the outgrowth of our experience. It is our task to develop not only a science of religion but a new science of our history, based on a psychologic as well as an economic and political evaluation of the data of our past. With the scholarly tools now available to us a reexamination of the data of our history and literature will, he was confident, once and forever disestablish the thesis that we are only or even mainly religionists. It will reveal the ineluctable fact of our nationhood,

> . . . that it is our common ancestry, common longings, common experiences, and common memories that have spelled our characteristics, our identity and the continuous motivation of our existence as a group, that we are a nation and not a missionary society—a national, historic group and not a league organized for a propaganda purpose.[5]

Here in this essay, Goldman insisted that the first and irrevocable tie that binds a people together in the ethnic bond is language, the Hebrew language for the Jew. The historic sense of the people had understood this and preserved only that which had been written or translated into Hebrew. Alexandrian Jewry, gifted as it was, failed to influence Jewish values because it preferred Greek to Hebrew. The amoraim of the Talmud let us down because they did not continue the practice of the Mishnaic teachers of using Hebrew. Therefore, if Jewish education is to be a real aid to Jewish survival, it must make Hebrew central in its curriculum. Not to do so is to be downright dishonest. In Palestine, Goldman wrote, these problems will be solved in the broad daylight of public life. In the Diaspora it is the synagogue that must for a long time constitute the arena.

> The reconstruction of Judaism must begin with the reconstruction of the synagogue. Ventilate it, renationalize it, beautify it, make it alive to the needs of the Jewish people today. Let membership in the synagogue express a loyalty to the group, an anxiety to continue its life-process, rather than presuppose the acceptance of certain unalterable dogmas and fixed ideas of the cosmos.[6]

Goldman was a mercurial person, a man of sensitive flesh and hot blood. He was often dominated by his moods. One day agnostic humanism was seen as the rallying creed of enlightened men, the next day it was a purged and subtly rationalized theism; one day the central hope of Jewish vitality was the Zionist organization, the next day it was a lost cause that might be usefully absorbed by the syna-

---

5. *A Rabbi Takes Stock* (New York: Harper & Brothers, 1931), pp. 16 and 17.
6. Ibid., p. 20.

gogue. A reading of all his published writings as well as his massive correspondence puts these shifts of opinion and advocacy in their proper perspective. They are seen here as very occasional eddies in the mainstream of his purpose and his philosophy. From 1925 to 1953, the year of his death, the central values of his work as writer, preacher, community leader, and scholar were the values so sharply and eloquently stated in *A Rabbi Takes Stock*: the paramountcy of nationhood, the centrality of land and language in that nationhood, the crucial importance of the synagogue as the agency of renaissance and survival, the role of Judaism as the philosophic and pragmatic expression of the values which make a people proudly committed to preserving itself and its world.

In *A Rabbi Takes Stock* are also seen some of the qualities of style which were to become part of everything Goldman wrote. There was his penchant for the rare word. He once lamented that so many precious words were imprisoned in the dictionary, words that once were common and had fallen into disuse, and had become, in fact, the silent majority. He took great delight in liberating them and setting them among the living and more popular words on the printed page. In his brilliant essay on Palestine "Where the Jew Feels at Home," a preview of the powerful and eloquent Zionist addresses he was to give to countless Jewish audiences, he uses the following obscure words in the course of two pages: limbec, lubricous, imposthume. Dr. Eustace Hayden, an admiring friend who held Goldman to be the best informed and most eloquent rabbi of his generation, admonished Goldman not to use these rare and archaic words since they created unnecessary barriers for the reader. Goldman replied that these were chastisements of love for the lazy reader. The *mitzvah* of liberating a forsaken word was compounded by the *mitzvah* of going to the dictionary and visiting a few more familiar friends along the way. The rationalization was delightful, but it did not altogether hide the aspect of flamboyant showman and superb word aerialist that lurked under the luminous brow.

There also was the need in Goldman to have a personal adversary. Personalizing his opposition lent passion to his pen. It was a calculated risk, for there were times when he came close to making an argument *ad hominem,* but most often this personifying gave an added intensity and sharper focus and impact to his plea. A mercenary realtor who insists on applying American monetary standards to the work of the early pioneers in 1926 in Palestine becomes the target for this barb:

> In all these centuries it was not only sage and mystic poet and priest that longed for the land of their fathers, the whole house of Israel faced Kadimah, eastward. Where then does our realtor-tourist come from? How is this strange phenomenon to be explained? What has happened to his spiritual antennae? Why does he no longer sense either the pain or dream of Klal Yisrael, Catholic Israel?[7]

Contemplating this ethnically unconscious Jew, he hurls a thunderbolt or two at Reform Judaism, the religious haven of so many anti-Zionists or non-Zionist Jews:

> The Jew ceased to be a Jew. At any rate nothing was left of him but a few vague, inconsequential generalities paraded under the guise of prophetic Judaism. In reality there was no relationship between Reform and prophecy. The prophets were men who suffered poverty and persecution, but delivered their fiery, spontaneous messages in the midst of the tumultuous city, into the ears of poor and rich alike. The prophets were the most zealous nationalists in the history of our people.[8]

Nor did Orthodoxy get off scot free!

> In reaction to Reform others in Jewry tightly wrapped about themselves the mantle of the past. . . . Many buried their heads in the pages of a Code and their spirits in a rigid observance of its legitimate minutiae. Whereas Reform had consciously taken German Protestantism for its model, a new Judaism dubbed Orthodoxy was unconsciously but dangerously approaching Catholicism. Whereas the reward of a *mitzvah* was considered to be the performance of another *mitzvah* now it guaranteed salvation—personal salvation in the world to come. . . . Many a *maggid* emulated revivalist and evangelist and the crackling fires of hell lent force to many a sterile *derasha*.[9]

These passages are premonitory of the stinging rebuttals he was to heap upon the heads of Breasted, Delitsch, Morgenstern, Well-

---

7. Ibid., p. 187.
8. Ibid., p. 191.
9. Ibid., p. 192.

hausen, and Toynbee in his defense of Torah against the so-called
higher Biblical criticism. More cloistered colleagues shook their
heads and expressed regret at this rough jousting, some because they
were timid and could not understand the needs of an ardent and
courageous soul, others out of an honest fear that these personal
attacks tended to become counter-productive, to shift attention from
the basic issues to the difficult gray area of evaluating personal motives and defending or attacking reputations.

The distance that has elapsed between these forensic debates and
the present, enables the chronicler to draw this conclusion: Goldman
was right in his judgments. Events have fully exposed the tragic
shortsightedness of those who considered the return to Zion as a
threat to the universalism of Judaism, or as a vulgar intervention in
God's plan for redemption. More recently discovered data and
greater knowledge of ancient languages have more sharply revealed
the pretensions and even the anti-Semitic motivations of the higher
critics. Freed from the pressure of immediate controversy and the
need to take sides, the chronicler sees that there was a built-in antidote to Goldman's partisanship, his overwhelming love for Zion, his
passionate worship of the incomparable glories of the Book of Books.
When one reads his love song to Zion at the close of his essay "Where
the Jew Feels At Home" or the concluding page of "Pro Vita Sua,"
the wrath of his diatribes against the enemies of the Land, its people,
and its Book, is seen to be but the counterpart of his love, the fierce
defense of a lover for his beloved, of a father for his children, of a
poet for his song.

The reader of these essays has an advantage over the audiences to
whom they were delivered—the footnotes. There is an average of
some forty-five footnotes to each essay. They not only provide the
exact source of his quotations and the list of recognized authorities
who back his judgments but the sources of his opponents' statements
and a list of authorities who differ from the point of view of the
adversary. Aside from this, the notes provide a well-chosen reading
list for the subject at issue and trenchant excerpts from sources not
easily available to the average reader. Collections of sermons or
occasional papers of rabbis have become a popular addition to Judaica; but it is rare to find an author who has buttressed his position

so well and consulted such vast amounts of the relevant literature as Goldman did in his passionate zeal to assist the Lord in covering the earth with knowledge as the waters cover the sea.

A Rabbi Takes Stock was but a preview of a much more scholarly work published in 1936, *The Jew and the Universe.* He explains the genesis of this book in the preface:

> In 1912 my sainted and lamented teacher, Professor Israel Friedlander, recommended to me the reading of Achad Ha'am's essay on Maimonides, entitled *The Supremacy of Reason.* In those days, Achad Ha'am was a demi-god. His name was so frequently on the lips of the learned and pronounced with such reverence that one thought of him as the greatest Jewish thinker of all time. His opinions were considered incontrovertible and final. To my amazement and unhappiness I found it impossible to accept his interpretation of Maimonides. Professor Friedlander, to whom I came with my doubts and notes, suggested with more enthusiasm than my immaturity warranted, that I develop my reactions into a thesis. A busy rabbinic career has nipped in the bud many a scholarly ambition. The musings of 1912 were soon forgotten and were not resurrected until 1935, when I was invited by the University of Illinois to deliver an address at the University on the occasion of Maimonides' Octocentenary. The following pages are an expression of last year's lecture and an elaboration of the reflections of 1912.

And what an elaboration it turned out to be! The 182 pages of text of the eighteen chapters are supported by 998 references from the works of Maimonides, the Talmud, Midrash, the medieval philosophers both Jewish and Christian including the early Greek and Latin fathers of the church, and a substantial number of modern religious thinkers. Original sources in Hebrew, Aramaic, Greek, Latin and modern sources in English, German and French are ransacked to establish the thesis which Professor Friedlander so innocently suggested in 1912.

That thesis was simply this: Maimonides was not an Aristotelian, though he admired Aristotle's deductive approach. Maimonides was not a simon-pure rationalist, though he considered reason to be man's noblest gift. Goldman says:

> Maimonides, is, after all his reasoning, not far removed from Yehudah Halevi and his insistence on the God of Abraham, Isaac and Jacob. He is

only more rigidly logical, seeking to eliminate all contradictions and to tie up all loose ends. With him everything must submit to a system, to order, to a syllogism. His basic conceptions, however, he had imbibed with his mother's milk. The unity and incorporeality of God, which necessarily implies His existence, he had had as the foundations of his faith from his earliest childhood. . . . His philosophizing made neither Greek nor Aristotelian of him. Logic and reason prevailed up to a certain point; deeply rooted in his whole being was the faith of intuition.[10]

To make certain that this interpretation would not place either Maimonides or himself in the ranks of antirationalists, Goldman probes into Hebrew, Aramaic, and Arabic philosophical terminology to show that *sechel* (wisdom) and *emunah* (faith) were not adversaries. On the contrary, *sechel* was considered even by the traditionalist Rabbi Jacob Tam, grandson of Rashi, as the source of faith, because the heart accepts intellectual proofs of God more readily than scriptural proofs. Goldman finds confirmation of his thesis in an analysis of the works of Homer, Plato, Aristotle, Saint Thomas Aquinas, Chrysostum, and Jerome, who, he insists, merely gave elaborate rationalizations for the *zeitgeist,* for the prevailing climate of opinion and folklore, a wisdom of the heart which uses reason as far as it will go. These sages then supplement and substitute for reason those yearnings and apprehensions, those hopes and aspirations which are sometimes rooted in instincts below the level of pure reason, and sometimes are winged by a power not ourselves toward realities not yet glimpsed in our philosophies.

Goldman takes the reader of *The Jew and the Universe* through some intellectually rigorous bypaths, into Plato and Aristotle, the patristic literature of the Church fathers, the medieval philosophers and the Cabala, to establish his thesis which he states succinctly in the very first page of this book:

> Man has sought to comprehend or solve the riddle of the Universe in one of two ways. Eeither he examined reality logically and philosophically, and viewed it as a concatenation of cause and effect, culminating in a First Cause, or he related himself to the world organically, intuitively, and viewed it as the unfolding of God's creative will.

---

10. *The Jew and the Universe* (New York: Harper and Brothers, 1936), p. 105.

The Greeks preferred the first approach.

> Among Jews the intuitive approach prevails. In the great writings of Israel designated Bible, Apocrypha, Talmud, Midrash and Responsa, . . . it is difficult to discover a score of logical syllogisms or metaphysical hypotheses. Throughout this literature no attempts are made to state or define concepts. Indeed the whole apparatus of rationalism is absent. Reason invariably yields the palm to intuition, speculation to meditation, formulation to awareness. In many, many thousands of pages of superb religious content we search in vain for a definition of God, religion, soul, or idea. Concepts and phenomena are not analyzed. They are seen whole and in their immediate relation to man. The universe is viewed through and in terms of personality.[11]

Goldman's attempt to free Maimonides from the rationalist stereotype in which his Orthodox opponents attempted to box him in the thirteenth century and in which Achad Ha-am placed him in the twentieth century, was seen by some rabbis as an escape from reason, as a surrender to the forces of irrationality which, they believed, would eventually embrace the intuitionists and those who place faith above and beyond reason. Rabbi Bernard Heller in a long letter to Goldman expressed his fear that Goldman had done an injustice to both Maimonides and himself by exalting intuition above reason and personality above the analyzable elements of character and will. Rabbi Milton Steinberg who was closely associated with Goldman in the attempt to reform the Jewish Theological Seminary, wrote a review of *The Jew and the Universe* for the *Jewish Frontier* in which he said:

> He [Goldman] has prepared tidy Procrustean beds one for the Jew, the intuitionist bed, and one for the Hellenic tradition, the rationalist bed. Into these logically ordered beds he tries to cram the two traditions. Unfortunately for all his efforts, limbs and bedclothes alike pour over the edges.[12]

This review evoked an answer from Dr. A. H. Friedland, the eminent Hebraist and educator, in which he said:

---

11. *The Jew and the Universe*, p. 1.
12. *Jewish Frontier*, February 1937, Vol. IV, No. 2.

The review gives the impression that according to Dr. Goldman "reason
whether empirical or rationalistic has been a total failure. . . ." On the
contrary in the very preface the position of the author is stated in quite
clear and unambiguous terms:

It is my conviction that in the prolonged search success will crown only
the labors of those who will rationalize and welcome intuition as the legitimate helpmate of reason and who will weigh the offspring of both in the
scales of experimentation.[13]

Dr. Friedland went on to say that Dr. Goldman deserved high
credit for debunking Western philosophy's arrogant claim for a
monopoly of truth and its constant downgrading of Oriental, including Semitic approaches to an understanding of life. It is high
time that someone questioned the smug assumption that any view of
the universe which cannot be stated in a major and minor premise
is irrational, uncivilized, Oriental. There was never a dogma more
false or arrogant than Hegel's belief that he could solve all the problems of reality with logic alone.

While barbs of criticism came from some rabbinic intimates, balm
of Gilead came from an unlikely source. In February 1937, Bertrand
Russell, the supreme rationalist of them all, published an article in
the *Atlantic Monthly* on "Philosophy's Ulterior Motives" in which
he made many of the same criticisms of Western philosophy that
Goldman made in *The Jew and the Universe.*

It warmed Rabbi Goldman's heart to hear from Dr. Eustace Hay-
don that his comparison of Greek thought and Hebraic thought in
The Jew and the Universe was much more profound and accurate
than Matthew Arnold's analysis in his justly famous "Hebraism and
Hellenism." He rejoiced also in the review of his young colleague,
Joshua L. Leibman who said *inter alia,* in the *New Humanist*:

This book should force Jewish scholars to reevaluate Israel's greatest thinker,
Maimonides, and intelligent Christians finally will be able to understand for
the first time the central emphasis of Judaism, namely, the unique supremacy
of human personality, not reserved for one man elevated to the status of a
deity, but shared by all men who walk the earth, and who will see in the
light of Goldman's brilliant illuminations the role that the law played in

13. Ibid., April 1937, Vol. IV, No. 4.

Israel, and what it meant in ethical terms to belong to a people living in accordance with that law. . . .

This organic approach to the world is the Jewish approach. A passionate interest in life, a profound reverence for the giant personalities who have studded the oft-clouded firmament of Jewish history, a remarkably successful pattern of associative living—these have been the pragmatic fruits of the Jewish road toward reality.

Intuition signified to the rabbis not some wild leap of the imagination, but a deep awareness of what is tinsel and what is gold in the relations of man. They never set out to define or to imprison in syllogisms the multi-colored social universe. They were content to experience it and to enrich it. The Jew emphasized concreteness as opposed to abstraction.[14]

The Jew and the Universe was translated into Hebrew under the title *Ha-Yehudi ve ha-olam,* and also into Spanish largely for South American Jewry, under the title *El Pensamiento Judio y el Universo.* Fortunately the distinguished Hebrew poet Simon Halkin undertook the Hebrew translation and did it with such intuitive grasp of Goldman's ideas that many readers in Israel thought the Hebrew version to be the original. In a life filled with many honors and not wanting in occasions of high exaltation, the day when the Hebrew translation of this erudite volume arrived at his desk was a *Yom ha-Simchat Torah* for him. The book, he thought, linked him in content to the most luminous intellect in all of Israel's long history and in language to the renaissance of his people in its land, a dream whose fulfillment had made the strongest claim upon the energies of his mind and his heart.

In 1938, Harper's published *Crisis and Decision,* a series of seventeen essays of uneven length and uneven merit. Goldman had been elected to the presidency of the Zionist Organization of America in June of that year, and the immense responsibilities of this office shrank the available time and energy needed for the kind of editing and selecting which he had given to his two previous books. The brilliant multilingual notes which warmed the hearts of scholars who read *A Rabbi Takes Stock* and *The Jew and the Universe* are

---

14. *The New Humanist, Spring* 1937.

absent from this volume. The fire and passion which incarnadines
the ink of his pen, however, are not absent. The Nazi threat to the
very survival of the Jew turned Goldman into a one-man anti-
defamation league and, converting the adrenalin evoked by fear into
an extra measure of courage and insight, he sailed into the enemies
of Israel wherever they came out of the wood.

In the first essay, "The Place of the Jew in the Modern World,"
Goldman sets the context in which he is to discuss the many aspects
of modern anti-Semitism. He quotes Leroy-Beaulieu:

> "The enemies of the Jew have always been wont to attack in him the
> stranger." The Jew is a conspicuous, ubiquitous, enduring outsider, and
> therefore suspected, feared and hated. Whenever circumstances permit, the
> skillful demagogue can make him the object of fear, suspicion and hatred.[15]

The Western Jew, Goldman states, tried to meet this situation by
inventing the formula, "a Jew at home, a man abroad," by becoming
a national of the country of his adoption and defining his Jewishness
as "Mosaic persuasion." This formula failed completely. "Zionism,"
writes Goldman, "is little more than the honest recognition of the
failure of this formula. It insists that there is no halfway stopping
place between the complete Jew and his complete disappearance."[16]

Assuming the mantle of the prophet, gathering under its ample
folds the oratorical armament he was to use so effectively to stir the
numerous Jewish audiences he was to address in the crucial White
Paper years, Goldman predicted from his intensive study of the
Jewish past the day to come:

> The Near East will unquestionably resist most stubbornly the re-penetration
> of the Jew into the lands of his origin and early history. That resistance may
> have to be checked by a major operation. But once performed the patients
> will do well. There will be for a long time internecine conflicts. But the
> conflicts will be among peers. After a century or two the Jew will be more
> at home in the Near East than he is in Europe at the end of 2000 years.

---

15. *Crisis and Decision,* p. 6.
16. *Crisis and Decision,* p. 9.

The Jew, an Oriental, will be easily reorientalized. . . . A restored Jewish nation will give the Jew new dignity in the eyes of the world. His position will become more natural and less mysterious.[17]

The Jews of Russia, France, Italy, and Germany, Goldman predicted, will largely disappear. The few strong among them will emigrate to Palestine or to the Western lands. In England and America where anti-Semitic pressures are less persistent, the Jew faces the powerful temptation to assimilate, while the only effective antidotes to this temptation, Jewish education and the synagogue, have neither the ideology nor the organizational power to avert the process. The establishment of the State of Israel will undoubtedly aid the revival of Western Jewry even though there is the risk that the Jew will be accused of divided loyalties by American jingoists. Zionists, Goldman avers, prefer to be charged, in a crisis, with loyalty to a little state in Palestine rather than to be constantly regarded as pariahs, intruders, leeches, and members of an international conspiracy to dominate the world.

The Book of Deuteronomy offers the simple admonition that the only way to distinguish the true from the false prophet is to determine whether his predictions have come to pass. In the perspective of the three decades which have elapsed, our prophet is batting over .500. In the perspective of the century or two which he suggested would be the proper time sequence into which we might fit his vision, the margin of error will be considerably diminished. Prophecy is at best a risky business especially for those who, like Goldman and Amos before him, are willing to specify as freely as they prophesy. But time and its mirror, history, have a way of vindicating those prophets who look deep into the wayward heart of man and carefully scrutinize the record of collective man on the face of this good earth. The authentic Jew does not hesitate to mingle prophecy with history since the same need which led him to posit a creator leads him to expect that events in time and space will respond to his educated instinct for justice.

In his essay "Jews and Christians," Goldman is at his best, weav-

---

17. *Crisis and Decision*, pp. 10–11.

ing his knowledge of the Greek sources of the New Testament, his
profound grasp of Talmud and Midrash and his wide-ranging familiarity with contemporary literature into a most readable, inform-
ative, and inspiring narrative. Here he shows how the abrasive
defense which Tertulian made against the Roman defamation of early
Christianity was forgotten when it became profitable for Christian
princes of the Church triumphant to use these same libelous stereo-
types against the Jews. He traces the evolution of the attitude of
honor and respect for Jews and the Judaism of Jesus and the disciples as recorded in the New Testament, with but a few conspicuous exceptions, to the bitter denunciation and defamation of Jews
and Judaism by such towering theologians as Augustine and
Chrysostum, who seem to have forgotten that the New Testament
speaks lovingly of Joseph of Arimathea, and most respectfully of
Gamaliel.[18] The Augustines and Chrysostums did not take their
bitter prejudices from the New Testament, but reached back to their
pagan ancestors for the arsenal of vilification which incited the Christians' massacres of the Middle Ages and gave powerful religious
sanction to the Czar's pogromists and the Nazi barbarians. Goldman
is impressed with the splendid attempts of George Foot Moore and R.
Travers Herford to right the record, but fears that it will require
many decades for the truthful account of Pharisaism to become
known to the Christian congregations. It is a pity that he did not
live to see the brave attempt of Pope John XXIII to atone for the
sins of the Augustines and Chrysostums.

In *Galut,*[19] a five-page statement, Goldman presents his credo that
the Hebrew language is the core of the Jewish spirit and that a
knowledge of it is indispensable to the understanding of Judaism
and the Jewish people.

Of late I returned once more to the pages of the *Tanach* seeking, and not
failing to find, an element in the Jewish soul, a certain core which finds
expression only in one language—namely Hebrew. This core only Hebrew
reveals. No other language preserves that essence, that flavor. I sense it in
the first verse of Genesis, and I feel it again instantly in the first page of

---

18. *Crisis and Decision,* p. 38.
19. *Crisis and Decision,* pp. 46–51.

Bialik. There it is unchanging, eternal, the core, the essence of the Jewish people. In the magnificent works on Judaism written through the ages in a variety of languages, I miss it. It will not disrobe itself, or yield the mystery of its being outside its home. Cohen's "Religion der Vernunft," Rosenzwieg's "Stern der Erlösing," Kaplan's "Judaism as a Civilization," Buber's "Hassidic Tales" say, "It is not in me." Maimonides' "Guide to the Perplexed" and Gabirol's "Fountain of Life" both translated from the Arabic, found it not. It is in *Bereshit,* in *Ha-matmid,* in the *Megillat ha-Esh,* even as I discover it in almost every page of Ahad Ha-Am. Even the Hellenist Tchernichowsky reveals this mystery unto me. I feel him even if I do not always understand him. But so many books on Jews and Judaism in the babel of European tongues I sometimes understand but seldom feel.

Maurice Samuel said it cryptically when he wrote that "all translators are traitors." Any writer can quote titles but only a Goldman can in the course of ten lines mention ten names of authors and titles which have the stamp of authenticity and contain within their pages a balanced concentrate of the wisdom of Judaism. Now we must wait patiently for that scholar who is a master linguist, a hard thinker and a poet withal to factor out for us that essence, that core which is not in Maimonides or Gabirol, or Cohen or Kaplan but which is in Bereshit, in ha-Matmid, in Achad Ha'am and Tschernichowsky.

Goldman included in this collection an address which he delivered at the invitation of Stephen Wise to the student body of the Jewish Institute of Religion at commencement in June of 1932. Stephen Wise—bless his ecumenical soul!—was among the first of the Cedars of Lebanon to recognize the unique gifts of Goldman.[20] In this address, Goldman makes this pungent and relevant differentiation between Christianity and Judaism:

Christianity is an ethereal religion. It is a system of dogmas and ideals not rooted in the soil, blood, life-experience or memory of any particular people. Its approach is to the individual; its emphasis is worship; its institution is the Church. Its major problems have been trinitarianism, papal infallibility, the divinity of Jesus and the Apostolic creed. Its signed promise is salvation for

---

20. See the reference to his letter to Goldman re the Jewish Center trial in 1925.

man in the world to come. It is only natural that the continued emphasis by
the social thinkers of the 19th and 20th centuries upon this world as the
scene of human hope and destiny should have made Humanism a problem
with Christians. . . .

Judaism on the other hand is rooted in the soil, blood, life-experience and
memory of a particular folk—the Jewish people. It is inseparable from
people, land, language and Torah. Its emphasis is conduct; its institutions
are the family, the schul, the synagogue and primarily society; its major
problems are national continuity and perfection, social justice and world
peace. Its signal promise is a better world order.[21]

In this explanation Goldman not only made clear why rabbis did
not jump on the humanist bandwagon when John Haynes Holmes
was the humanist leader in the 20s and 30s, but anticipated the
reasons that kept rabbis (with only two exceptions) from hopping
on the "God is Dead" bandwagon in the 1960s.

It was in this address also that Goldman admonished the rabbis
in a manner that he was to repeat time and time again throughout
his rabbinate:

I declare that the rabbi who does not make the Torah in all its ramifications
the very essence of his life has no place in the synagogue. If it has become
fashionable of late for rabbis to allow newspaper headlines and Broadway
lights to teach them what they shall say, it is only because they are out of
contact with our heritage. . . . Almost every rabbi has spoken time and again
of Gandhi . . . but why has no rabbi brought home to his congregation the
life story of A. D. Gordon? . . . If rabbis are so fond of poetry, would it be
amiss to expect them to portray the agonized soul of a Yizhak Lamdan or
the spiritual Wehmut of our own Regelson?[22]

Sensing the power of the humanist catchwords over the bright
young men before him, Goldman used this occasion to talk of Hein-
rich Heine who had for many years of his creative life been a blithe
Helene enamored of the Greek's passion for beauty in thought, in
person, in architecture, and sculpture. Compared to these gifted,
pleasure-loving, beauty-worshiping people, the ancient Hebrews

21. *Crisis and Decision*, p. 81.
22. Ibid., p. 90.

were dour, crude, dogma-ridden oafs, and Moses, their leader, was a tyrant with a puritanic zeal for chilling the senses and killing joy in all its forms. Experience with the gentile inheritors of the Greek tradition and the bitter instruction of pain and sorrow led Heine to change his judgment of these two lifestyles. He came to see the fatal weakness in the Greek view of life. The Greeks, he said, lived by thought and not by resolution; they died by reason of thought from want of resolution. It was the fate of Greece that man should know too much and effect too little. The Greeks were impressionists, connoisseurs, tasters of life and dreamers, slaves of each new novelty, contemptuous of everyday things, more like undergraduates listening to sophistry in a debating hall or a lecture than statesmen pondering a nation's welfare.

As Heine delved deeper into Jewish lore, he came to realize how mature, how serious and grown-up the Jews were. In Bible, Talmud, Gaonica, there was no sophistry, but earnest men, pondering a nation's welfare.

> Die Juden . . . waren immer Maenner, gewaltege, Maenner. "The prophets, the scribes, the Pharisees fashioned Torah—the blending of thought with resolution—thought that leads to action."[23]

The Jews survived, Goldman went on to say, because we were blessed with men who never made peace with the foibles of the people or the whims of the rulers, who would simply not allow us to sink into the sweet lassitude of dissipation and degeneracy, but rather warned us constantly "to make ourselves clean, cease to do evil, learn to do well, seek judgment, relieve the oppressed, judge the fatherless, plead for the widow."

In Moses, too, Heine, his eyes now opened, saw a great artist endowed with the artistic spirit who built human pyramids, who took a poor shepherd tribe and created out of it a people to defy the centuries, an eternal Holy People who might serve as the prototype of humanity. Heine confessed his pride in having descended from

---

23. Ibid., p. 96.

those martyrs who gave the world a God and an ethic, who struggled
and suffered on the battlefields of ideas.[24]

Of the remaining essays, we can mention the one entitled "Is Einstein Religious?" Goldman often said that one of the great joys of
his ministry was the opportunity it provided him for meeting significant human beings. His correspondence with Einstein,[25] which
began when Einstein requested Goldman's assistance in bringing
Max Brod to America that he might escape the Nazi deathtrap, soon
became an exchange of ideas. Goldman had the divine *chutzpah* to
ask Einstein how he, Goldman, might be able to make the theory of
relativity intelligible to laymen and, even before Einstein could
answer that one, sent him a copy of *The Jew and the Universe* to
read and criticize. Einstein did not answer either request directly
but did make tangential remarks about philosophy, Judaism, and
Zionism which Goldman treasured and which he often used in his
many attempts to probe the areas in which science and religion im-
pinged on one another.

It was natural that Goldman would use Einstein as the personality
around whom he would lace his attempt to harmonize the two major
streams of reflection on the nature and purpose of the human enterprise. More and more the record reveals how thoroughly Goldman
was seized by the conviction that personality is the meaningful core
of reality. When he attacked wrong ideas, it was necessary to find a
human exponent of those ideas as he did in Wellhausen, Delitsch,
Breasted, or Mr. X. When he expounded creative ideas, it was just
as necessary to find a Maimonides, a Bialik, an A. D. Gordon, a
Louis Ginzberg, an Einstein.

In this essay, he attempts to show how Einstein helps to bridge
the age-old gap between religion and science. The nub of the matter
is quickly exposed through a question asked by a fundamentalist
minister who wrote Einstein asking if the great mathematician believed in God. Einstein laconically replied:

Ich glaube an Spinoza's Gott, der sich in gesetzlicher Harmonie des Seienden
offenbart, nicht an einen Gott der sich mit Schicksalen und Handlungen der

24. Ibid., p. 99.
25. See Appendix, Einstein letters, pp. 250.

Menschen abgibt—I believe in Spinoza's God, who reveals himself in the orderly harmony of what exists, not in a God who concerns himself with fates and actions of human beings.[26]

Goldman's respect for Einstein is so profound that he will not take advantage of the expression *Seienden* (being, existence) to drive the whole existentialist carriage through. He honestly states that by accepting Spinoza's God, Einstein abjures man's free will and the whole system of rewards and punishments that many theologies have based on free will. Nor does Spinoza's God permit Einstein to posit a universe beyond our universe, or a life beyond life. Einstein divests himself of all a priori belief and simply states: ". . . that to one who is pervaded with a sense of causal law in all that happens, who accepts in real earnest the assumption of causality, the idea of a Being who interferes with the sequence of events in the world is absolutely impossible."[27]

With such lucidity, Goldman cannot even be tempted to make the Lord's shew-bread out of the crumbs left by more nostalgic and permissive philosopher scientists such as Jeans and Whitehead. But there is a loophole, a warm vagrancy in the mind of the relativity theorist. He regards imagination even as more important than knowledge, ". . . for knowledge," Einstein asserts, "is limited, whereas imagination embraces the entire world, stimulating progress, giving birth to evolution. It is a real factor in scientific research." And imagination is the searcher and finder of faith as every researcher must know. Einstein wrote:

What a deep faith in the rationality of the structure of the world, and what a longing to understand even a small glimpse of the reason revealed in the world there must have been in Kepler and Newton to enable them to unravel the mechanism of the heavens in the long years of lonely work. . . . Only those who have dedicated their lives to similar ends can have a living conception of the inspiration which gave those men the power to remain loyal to their purpose in spite of countless failures. It is the cosmic religious sense which grants this power.[28]

---

26. *Crisis and Decision*, pp. 101–102.
27. Ibid., p. 103.
28. *Crisis and Decision*, pp. 107–108.

Dayenu! Scientist and religionist can come together in the golden
links of imagination and the passionate search for truth. The
psalmist speaks for Kepler and Newton and Einstein when he sings:
"O Lord how great are Thy works! And Thy thoughts are very
deep." But Einstein goes further to meet the outstretched hands of
the religionist. To ponder interminably over the reasons for one's
own existence or the meaning of life in general seems to him to be
sheer folly. Man is here, he tells us, for the sake of other men, above
all those upon whose smile and well-being our happiness depends,
and also for the countless unknown souls with whose fate we are
connected by a bond of sympathy. Now Einstein is fellow to the
prophets whose mystique is compounded of 90 percent passion for
social justice and 10 percent awe and reverence before the majesty
of God. It is Einstein's love for his fellow man that makes him the
ardent pacifist[29] and the supporter of every effort to lift the burden
of injustice and oppression from his fellow creatures.

Goldman concludes:

> Einstein is a religious man even though he does not accept traditional beliefs
> and conceptions because we discern in him the sense of reverence and
> mysteriousness of the psalmist, the passion for justice and peace of the
> prophet and the practical interest in society of the law-giver.[30]

But there is another plus and it is this plus that delights Goldman
to the point of ecstasy. Einstein has not fallen into the cosmopolitan
trap like so many emancipated intellects. He is a nationalist, an
ardent Zionist. It is no little tribute to his genius, says Goldman,
that Einstein should have comprehended in a flash the movement in
all its aspects, that he should have recognized Herzl's Zionism as the
haven of refuge for oppressed and persecuted Jews, Achad Ha'am's
Zionism as the center for the renaissance of Jewish teachings and
Hebraic civilization, A. D. Gordon's Zionism as the return of the
Jew to the soil of mother earth, Pinker's Zionism as the healing of

---

29. See Einstein's description of the military: "The vilest offspring of the herd is the
odious militia. The man who enjoys marching in line and file to the strains of music
falls below my contempt. He received his big brain by mistake—a spinal cord would
have been sufficient. This heroism at command, this senseless violence, this accursed
bombast of patriotism—how intensely I despise them"! *Crisis and Decision*, pp. 110–111.
   30. Ibid., p. 111.

the personality of the collective Jewish people distorted and warped by the hostility of the nations.[31]

It is little wonder then that Goldman could end his essay on this ecstatic note:

> In Einstein we see the Jew at his best. He is more than a brother in the flesh of Isaiah; he is spiritual kin. Twenty-six hundred years ago the ancient seer searched for a principle of unity in the delimited cosmos of his day even as his illustrious brother is searching today in the nebular universe. . . . Einstein exhausts the physical theories and mathematical equations to establish his *Feldtheorie*. Isaiah intuitively groped his way to the feeling of Oneness. . . . Both were overwhelmed by the order and mystery of the universe and each of them devoted his life to truth, justice and peace—and both insisted on the continuity of Israel with Zion as its center, that out of Zion shall go forth the Torah and the word of the Eternal from Jerusalem.[32]

Goldman lived to complete only two of the thirteen volumes he projected to bring to the understanding of the Tanakh some of the knowledge and insights he had gathered in the course of a lifetime of devotion to the Book of Books. He edited the proof sheets of Volume I, *An Introduction,* and of Volume II, *In the Beginning*—the Book of Genesis. Volume III, *From Slavery to Freedom,* the Book of Exodus, was in its final stages when he died. Thanks to the good offices of Professor Harry Orlinsky the volume was completed in a manner most faithful to the plan and outlines of the author. Since these three volumes represent the longest and most arduous literary labors of the rabbi and embody the deepest concern of his heart and the highest reaches of his active searching intelligence, we shall try

---

31. Einstein expressed this even more clearly than Pinsker: "The immediate great contribution of Palestine and Zionism will be the restoring of a sense of solidarity which the Jew lost since his emergence from the ghetto. Our ancestors of those days were rather cramped, both materially and spiritually, but as a social organism they were in an enviable state of psychological equilibrium . . . the best in man can be brought out only when he belongs entirely to a human group. Hence, there is great moral danger in the position of the Jew who has lost contact with his own national group and is regarded as an alien by the group among whom he lives. Often enough, a situation of this kind has produced a despicable and joyless egotism." Quoted by Goldman, *Crisis and Decision*, pp. 117–118.

32. Ibid., p. 119.

to probe the quality and thrust of their contents and hazard a judgment of their impact on the world of Jewish scholarship and on the
wider world of letters.

In the preface to the first volume, Goldman articulates his plan
for the series:

> The 39 books of the Hebrew Canon will be studied individually and sep-
> arately as follows: The contents of each book will be summarized chapter by
> chapter in simple language. Selections from it, . . . whole sections of single
> verses and phrases of special significance, will be given in a translation based
> on the Hebrew text, the ancient versions, King James Version, Moffatt's, the
> American Translation, the German of Buber and Rosenzweig, and the
> Yiddish of Yehoash.[33] The selections will be annotated in two ways. First,
> directly by means of a commentary drawing on rabbinic and medieval Jewish
> sources and modern works, and again indirectly in a section entitled "Echoes
> and Allusions" where the reader will find how a particular verse or phrase
> was understood by one or another person of renown.[34]

The disarming simplicity of Goldman's outline can be appreciated when one notes that in commenting on verses 16 to 38 in the
39th chapter of Genesis, Goldman ransacks the following sources
and authorities: Alten Testament, Genesis Rabba (four times), Ibn
Ezra (four times), Rashbam (six times), Onkelos, Rabbi Saadia Gaon,
Jakob, Benziger, Coleridge, Gunkel, Rashi, and Ramban (once each).

His passionate love affair with the Bible did not permit Goldman
to remain an academic neuter even in the footnotes. Commenting
on Genesis 39: 31, "So great was his love for her," (Jacob's for Rachel) Goldman quotes Coleridge, "No man could be a bad man who
loved as he loved Rachel," and then contrasts this sentiment with
that of Gunkel:

> Though he gave a lifetime to the study and exposition of the Jew's Bible,
> could not quite divest himself of the anti-Jewish prejudices that have ever

---

33. This is the first time that a Yiddish translation of the Bible has figured in
Biblical criticism. Prof. Dan Rauber of San Diego State College in an essay on Jonah—
"Schlemiel or Saint" suggests that the best way to appreciate the few instances of humor
in the Bible is to translate them into Yiddish and thus capture the true folk flavor in
which alone the Jewish values find their truest dimension.

34. *The Book of Human Destiny*, Vol. I (Jewish Publication Society of America,
1948), pp. x, xi.

afflicted his countrymen, but spoke with biting sarcasm of the deceitful Semite falling in love.[35]

He finds Gunkel not alone in this higher anti-Semitism. He continues while commenting on verse 32, "That I may go in to her":

> Some German scholars—brothers apparently in more ways than one of the men who tormented half the women of Europe with their insolence and bestiality—are wont to berate the biblical narrator about some "obscene" details in their narrative. They find the present verse particularly "repulsive to their notions of delicacy." The more ingenious of them have discovered here the evidence of a natural Jewish propensity to pornography.

Nor does Goldman permit Coleridge to atone for his English countrymen. He continues in this same footnote:

> English scholars oblivious of *The Canterbury Tales* and *The Merry Wives of Windsor,* repeat the libelous and malicious gibberish. If only these learned gentlemen were attentive to their own motes and beams and let the blemishes of Israel be scrutinized by its own teachers![36]

It is not only with Gunkel but with Delitzsch, Wellhausen, and Breasted, especially Breasted, that Goldman converts his pen into a sword and lays heavily upon these Higher Critics who, he claims, in the guise of profound scholarship are peddling vulgar Jew-hatred. There were some who claimed that Goldman jeopardized his scholarly reputation in taking up the cudgels of an anti-defamationist, and that he created barriers against his acceptance in scholarly circles in Chicago, Harvard, and Princeton because of his sharp attacks on the venerable priests of the Higher Biblical Criticism. There is some truth in this, and it may also be true that his fervid defense of his people and his tradition prevented some readers from fully appreciating the brilliance of his scholarship and the cogency of his insights. But Goldman was never one to prefer the gains of caution to the risks of passion, and he felt, from the very beginning of his ministry, that a rabbi who does not burn his heart out for his people is soldiering on the job.

---

35. *The Book of Human Destiny*, Vol. II, Jewish Publication Society, 1949, p. 806.
36. Ibid., pp. 806, 807.

Let it not be assumed that his passionate defense of Judaism and
the Jewish people was surrogate for hard reasoned judgments. Goldman was meticulous in choosing the weapons for defending his people's honor. The scholarly apparatus and the massive confirmatory
data in all three volumes are proof indeed that the verve, the élan,
the gracious style, the emotional intensity are in addition to, not in
place of, the solid logic of his vast and dazzling erudition. Goldman
felt that the Higher Biblical Criticism was distorted not merely by
overt and subtle (often unconscious) anti-Semitism, not merely by
over-zealous advocacy of the Christian ideology, but by ignorance of
the true meaning of the Jewish medieval commentators, whose lack
of conventional system was attributed to lack of reason and authentic
research. Goldman was among the first to point out that the very
rabbis who created the mechanism for fixing the authentic text of
the Tanakh were the first to recognize that there had been altera-
tions in the text.

> They repeated time and again that scripture speaks the language of man.
> They were the first to call attention to the fact that the Divine Names
> undergo changes in the story of Creation, that the Bible is wont to speak in
> hyperbole, that it follows no chronological order, that many of its sections
> do not stand in their proper place, that verses contradict each other, that the
> same incident is now and then reported twice.[37]

What the Higher Biblical Critics presented as revelations due to
their superior knowledge of the ancient languages or to archeological
discoveries of more recent times, were known to the ancient rabbis.
The Talmud speculates that the Book of Moses was not the Torah
in its entirety as we have it. The rabbis differ as to just how Moses
wrote the Torah. Some say that he put it down gradually, while
others hold that he wrote down only the general principles, which
he imparted orally at first and wrote down forty years later before
his death. The rabbis were aware that the prophetic books were not
all of a piece, that the books of Isaiah and Jeremiah contain parts
which were not composed by the prophets. So, too, do they ascribe
different dates to the psalms, considering some of them to be post-

---

37. *Book of Human Destiny*, Vol. I, p. 41.

exilic. Neither were they taken in by the ascription of authorship to Moses, David, and Solomon.

The Hebrew lexicographers and grammarians even more than the Talmudists and philosophers offer a mine of literary and textual criticism. Gentile Biblical critics seldom quote such men as Moses ibn Gikatila, Jonah ibn Jonah, Abraham ibn Ezra, Isaac Caro, B'chor Shor, the Kimchis, or Kalonymous ben Kalonymous, but these were the men who first revealed the contradictions and repetitions of the Biblical narrative, the different names for God, and the anachronisms in the text. The Gunkels, Wellhausens, and Kuehnens who proclaimed the discovery of a Deutero-Isaiah in the last twenty-seven chapters of the Book of Isaiah, were unaware that Moses ibn Gikatila had stated some four hundred years earlier that "one set of circumstances underlies the first 39 chapters of Isaiah and another the last 27."

Long before the French Catholic doctor, Jean Astruc, came upon his documentary theory based on the two names of God in 1753, Kalonymous ben Kalonymous, in the fourteenth century, confided his bewilderment to Joseph Kaspi, that the Tetragrammaton, *JHWH*, was not mentioned in Genesis from its first verse to the conclusion of its account of the Sabbath, *Elohim* being used throughout.

The reader will be inclined to ask, if the rabbis so early detected the human fallibilities of the Scriptures, why did they not pursue these insights to their logical conclusion and treat the Bible as an inspired record of a people in history subject to the changes, forward and backward, of the particular pressures of the time and place in which they lived? Goldman's answer is that the Bible became more than a human book. It became the national literature of a people, the explanation of their origins and a prescription for their survival. It became the *arcanum* in which they invested the guidelines of their conduct and their hopes for salvation. Just as this people came to the realization of One God in the midst of primitive animism and polytheism, so they held their national literature to be a unique, even a mysterious, entity, possessing normal historic characteristics but something more (something unique to the lifestyle of the people beyond the grasp of those who have not shared their historic experi-

ences). Here Goldman takes leave of rationalist premises and, like
Maimonides, adopts a holistic intuitionism more responsive to the
existential verities, those truths that are above and below the limits
of pure analytic reason. But since reason is still the central business
of the active intelligence and since it is the best mode of communication between peoples, Goldman makes a further attempt to explain why the Bible is an eternally effective Book, still the Book of
Books, the Book of Human Destiny. Here he adds to the testimony
of the Jewish people that of the thousands not of the House of Israel
who have found in the Bible a wisdom to live by.

The Bible was, to begin with:

> . . . the common solace of mankind in all its travails and cares, helping all
> who came to it . . . to live above the ill tempers and sorrows of life. The
> Bible was explored for the sake of its wisdom, for the funded experience of
> the race crystallized in its laws, prayers, prophecies, parables, and proverbs
> and for the science of realities or art of living contained in its narratives. . . .
> The Bible satisfied the natural curiosity of man about the origin of things . . .
> gave him an answer that he could grasp and feel and weave into the pattern
> of his daily experience. It supplied him with a concrete and tangible world
> view in a simple, precise, and understandable way almost wholly unencum-
> bered by philosophical abstractions and formulations. It organized their
> experience in the light of a few simple ideas, co-ordinated their subconscious
> perceptions, and transfigured and fused their unreflective awareness into
> intelligible and sublime expression.[38]

Even the critical elite, Goldman asserts, derived satisfaction from
the Biblical narrative. Philo, Maimonides, and Aquinas found it
possible to fill out its unimplicitness and sketchiness with the profoundest and most radical implications. And so too, even now:

> The Biblical account is still as malleable as it ever was and that its descrip-
> tion of the creative process, though it might be faulty in many respects, but
> being little else than a "picture of the universe passing from the more random
> to the less random state, each step showing a gradual victory of anti-chance
> over chance" was easily adaptable to an age of stellar and atomic physics.[39]

---

38. Vol. I, pp. 106–108.
39. Vol. I, p. 109.

The Biblical view of God was congenial with the order-hungry mind of science. The Biblical authors centered causality exclusively in God and, as a result, denied it to all other entities. All things were merged in the creative whole, in God. The immediate result of this close association of the world with God and the binding of it wholly and solely to Him was the elimination of the arbitrariness and capriciousness in the order of things. It would have been ludicrous to give credence to the tale that, in a world ruled by God, the waters had been thrown into a rage by one Aeolus because he was resentful of Neptune, or that a Hera embroiled the nations in war because she was jealous of Aphrodite.

Even more than the congeniality of its metaphysics to ever-changing views about God,

> it was the portrayal of man in the Bible, the place it assigned him in the general scheme of things, the endless numbers of marvelous, multicolored, giant figures it portrayed, the pattern it designed for associative living, the proportionate rights and duties it perceived in humanity, the element of consistency it introduced into history—these were the things that have drawn men to it as iron is drawn to the lodestone. . . . The Genesis account of creation is brief, giving evidence of having been intended only as a prologue to the more important human drama.[40]

While the Bible records exquisite lamentations of man's insignificance, his innate rascality, his bitter frustrations, his tragic vulnerability, the infinite sorrow of his sensitivity, it still remains an optimistic book. It never capitulates to hopelessness, but sets forth its faith in a favorable denouement of the human drama. Indeed its greatest strength, Goldman reminds us, has perhaps lain in the fact that, fastening boldly on the reality of things, it wrestled with it and would not let go until reality was brought under control. Nor did its authors equivocate by asking for an indefinite extension of time in another world, or conveniently remove the burden of evil from the shoulders of their God by erecting a Master Do-evil, a Power of Darkness or some other super-dualistic jurisdictional scheme.

---

40. Vol. I, p. 112.

The Biblical philosophy of this-wordliness, its major emphasis on
the drive toward a more abundant life is sustained, Goldman points
out, by four profound convictions.

First, man is a free agent capable of resisting evil and choosing good; despite
his imperfections and the instability of the imagination of his heart, he can,
if he tries hard enough, reach out beyond himself, erect himself, as it were,
above himself. What he requires are fixed duties and a rigid discipline, and
these he has in the word of God and His law, obedience to which can keep
him from stumbling and reward him with the blessings of health, length of
years, family, prosperity, peace, happiness, and the respect of his fellow men.

Second, all human beings, of all races and people, the Ethiopians even as
the Israelites, since they have a common origin and a common destiny and
are implicated in one another's pains and pleasures, failures and successes,
are related to one another. Consequently they are all equal, the common man
being no less the object of God's love than the great, and his life no less sacred
nor his well-being less important. Thus he who sits on the throne of the
kingdom is enjoined to possess a copy of the law, read it regularly, and
habituate himself to stand in awe of his Maker, lest he have his heart lifted
above his subjects.

Third, righteousness is a "cosmic demand," permanently embedded in the
structure of the universe. Man has, therefore every reason to look forward
hopefully to its triumph over evil, to establishing an ideal social order here
on earth.

Fourth, Israel will be compensated for its loyalty to God and the martyrdom
it involves in this world, since its covenant with God implies the salvation of
the people as a whole. And the salvation of a people can not be easily
thought of as being transferable to another realm as might be done in the
case of an individual.

These four convictions, powerful and relevant as they were in and
by themselves, were given added propulsive power by two circumstances; namely, the fact that Israel assumed the role of being the
living embodiment of these values in history and thus gave sinews
and flesh to what might otherwise have turned into an abstract
ideology, and by the happy accident that the Judeans who wrote this
record were extraordinary masters of the word. They were adept,
Goldman tells us:

. . . at inventing the forms of sensations or thoughts and creating visions,
images, or phrases that touched the chords of the heart to exactest nicety.

Endowed with a native gift of observation and taking their illustrations from what was near at hand, from things natural and congruous, perceptible and tangible, they expressed the impact of experience on consciousness, fully and concretely. But, though their work bears the imprint of their surroundings and time, it is stamped with the likeness of no particular time or place. For, whereas most pagan writers of antiquity generally were satisfied to present the object itself, the biblical writers were more eager to represent what it implied, and as preparatory and prospective. The Greek masters, Homer included, aimed at reproducing the object complete, inclusive, finished, . . . congealed into its unalterable identity. . . . The Judeans, on the other hand, fashioned illustrative fragments, carved out symbolic torsos and left them res infectae, that is, unfinished, mutable, as restless, prying question marks. This accounts for the dynamic, pervasive, and suggestive quality of their language, its sensory and emotional associations, and the ease with which it has evoked out of the minds of men infinite worlds of beauty and thought.[41]

Still puzzled and awed that the literature of so small a band of Judeans could have so thoroughly captured the imagination and admiration of mankind, Goldman probes further into this mystery. Felicity of style, evangelical fervor, supernatural authority, these cannot account for the obvious superiority of the Bible over the best of the Greek writings, or those of the Egyptians, Chaldeans, and Babylonians. The answer resides, Goldman believes, in the outreach of the themes of the Bible. They are seriously concerned with the ultimates of life, with the great problems of the human condition, with the poignant hungers of the soul, with the eternal struggle of man with his conscience and of collective man with his vision of the good society. And the group that most set the seal of seriousness, of human urgency, of spiritual maturity on the Book of Human Destiny were the prophets. Quite properly and climactically, Goldman ends his introductory first volume with a brilliant analysis of the nature and role of this unique band of men, the prophets of Israel:

They were aflame with God, blissfully ignorant of the creative urge, innocent of the orator's tricks, unaware of the writer's lapidary skill with words, they knew only that "God stirred them up," taught their lips to speak, guided their pen, and that His word, the tormenting inmate of their breast, the

---

41. Vol. I, pp. 116, 117.

burning fire shut up in their bones, could not be held in but had to be
communicated. So absorbed were they in their message and its divine
promptings that its form was incidental, unconscious—beautiful means wooing
blessed ends.[42]

They came from all walks of life, shepherds, farmers, from the pam-
pered courts and from priestly families, but they were not trained
for this vocation. They were inspired amateurs. No wonder that the
folk who heard them pondered on how they carved out of their
humble experience the distant destiny of the race, or merged and
incorporated the remotest future in their limited present.

Nor have critical historians been more successful in explaining
the mystery of the Hebrew prophets in the conventional terms of
social or political analysis. The prophetic fire "burning unquench-
able as an anthracite coal mine" defies analysis. Goldman does not
claim to have discovered the key, but he lists those features for which
the prophets are best known and to which they owe their lasting
fame.

They were not soothsayers, foretellers, nor necromancers. They
were possessed with a divine *meshugas*. Upheaved and overmastered
by Him, they looked into the heart of reality and spoke the truth hot
from their viscera to their tongue. Nature having removed her veil
from them and displayed the true expression of her face, their souls
were kept healthy by a constant reception of the truth. They knew
what they had to do and fixed their attentions on the immediate
political and social problems of the community.

They were indifferent to public opinion. Guided by their vision
of righteousness, they spoke truth to power and flung bitter indictment into the very teeth of kings and priests.

They were sustained by a fundamental optimism which in turn was derived
from the great love and tenderness for the humanity they indicted. . . . Too
full of God and big with hope to admit of rancor or despair, they, like Keats'
poet poured balm on the world at least to the extent they vexed it, their
pity having exceeded their rage and their sense of glory having been, if
anything, as clear as their sense of doom.[43]

---

42. Vol. I, p. 121.
43. Vol. I, p. 124.

They overflowed with love for their people and their native land. "It is only a great mind and a strong character," James Russell Lowell said, "that knows how to respect its own provincialism and can dare to be in fashion with itself." The prophets cherished their provincialism though they combined with it a great catholicity. They were universalists and considered their ultimate objective to be that of erecting the conduct of their people into a universal law. They employed the terms "Israel" and "Zion" as designations of universal mankind. But they no more looked forward to the dissolution of the real and living Israel and Zion than had Emerson to that of America, just because he had conceived of it "as the great charity of God to the human race."

Finally, the uniqueness of the prophets consisted in this—that the iniquities and miseries of the race had become iniquities and miseries for them and would not let them rest. Thus, they did what no other group of men had ever done, they sustained for a long period of many generations the constant propulsion of an unbending will to destroy the wellsprings of idolatry, idolatry in all its various forms, superstition, licentiousness, oppression, violence, and tyranny. "No one doubts," Goldman assures us, "that the fury with which they vented their discontent with evil, the tenacity with which they warred on it, the self-assurance with which they anticipated a better world have remained unmatched to this day."[44]

The introductory chapters to Book I end at page 126. The section "Echoes and Allusions," consisting of excerpts from the literature of the world which quote the Bible, begins on page 128 and continues to page 358, thus comprising more than half of this volume. In Volume II, "Echoes and Allusions" occupies pages 118 to 728, or 610 pages out of a total of 892. The late Mayor Fiorello La-Guardia once said that when he made a mistake, "it was a beaut." It seems possible that Rabbi Goldman would have recognized the error in judgment that gave so disproportionate a space to "Echoes and Allusions." Certainly they constitute a most valuable collection. They have indeed enabled rabbis and ministers to decorate their sermons with wise saws and modern instances and impress their

---

44. Vol. 1, p. 125.

congregations with their literary discernment and, in some instances, even confirm the point that Goldman was anxious to make, namely that the great figures of Western literature, poets, novelists, philosophers, essayists, and dramatists, were deeply influenced by the language, the imagery, the teachings and the stories of the Bible. As a separate compendium these excerpts would have been useful literary tools for preachers, teachers and writers. In *The Book of Human Destiny* series, they occupy disproportionate space and tend to eclipse the much more important sections of the books, the essays on authorship, philosophy and style, and the commentaries. This is clearly seen when one reads the third volume, completed after Rabbi Goldman's death, which does not contain "Echoes and Allusions." Here the essay on "Style and Philosophy" is seen in a better perspective, and the commentary, with its brilliant interpretations of so many of the texts, is full and rewarding. Of course, Rabbi Goldman meant to stagger the "Echoes and Allusions" over the whole thirteen volumes and to use midrashic commentaries on Genesis as they came up in the discussion of the writings and the prophetic books. Perhaps the premonition of his death, which often assailed him during his many illnesses in the late forties, influenced him to put so large a part of "Echoes and Allusions" into the second volume.

The translation which Rabbi Goldman made of his chosen selections from the Bible had a directness and force which were a reflection of his own poetic dynamism. He followed Moffet in using terms with more American than British connotations. From Yehoash he gleaned something of that warm folk feeling, a welcome change of pace from the formal dignity of the Hebrew and the solemn cadences of the King James translation. From Buber and Rosenzweig he took the sense of the mysterious which must be part of a divine saga no matter how loyal we would be to the logicians and the fact worshipers. Goldman was willing to supplant thou and ye and thee when addressing man, but he held to Thou and Thine when applied to God. In spite of his disclaimer that he was not writing a new translation, there is his unmistakable mark on this work. The ardor of the teacher, the communicator, the passionate advocate is felt throughout. Wherever there is a vav (ו) which can be stretched into something more explicit than "and," wherever a word of the text has fallen out or become corrupted, wherever the context permits a more imaginative inference, Goldman fills the gaps, repairs the chinks, straightens the frozen tangles with his vast erudition and compassionate understanding.

A comparison of Goldman's translation with that of the 1962 version of the Jewish Publication Society of which Professor Harry Orlinsky was chief editor, reveals a considerable congeniality of mood and purpose, especially in the use of insights and interpretations of such medieval commentators as Rashi, Saadia, Ibn Ezra, and the Kimchis. Goldman, for whom the Bible was as much a spoken as a written document, could not give up so readily "spirit" of God for "wind" of God, or supplant "heaven" with "sky," or "firmament" with "expanse." It is a pity that Goldman was not a consultant on the new JPS translation. He would have brought some of the cadence of the spoken and the chanted word which is so often ignored by the language specialists who make our translations. Nevertheless, it must be said that the new JPS translation comes closer to the substance and spirit of the Goldman translation than any other.

The late Milton Steinberg, after perusing the second volume of the series, urged his friend and mentor Goldman to make a complete translation of the Pentateuch and a translation of the *sidrot* and add the commentaries so that the book might replace the Herz Pentateuch and Haftorot. He felt that Goldman's translation was much more virile and accurate and that the commentaries were much more enlightening, especially since they were not inhibited by fears of offending the Orthodox. Steinberg was confident that the Goldman volume would be adopted by both the Conservative and Reform and, most especially, Reconstructionist synagogues and would be a most acceptable text for the many Bible study classes which were multiplying in the land. Goldman was much taken with the suggestion, but, like so many desirable projects, this one too was squeezed out by the intolerable pressures of many commitments and by the loss of precious work hours due to his frequent illnesses.

Rabbi Seymour Cohen, of Anshe Emet, in a column in his bulletin expressed the gratitude of the rabbis and of many other Bible students to Goldman for having brought such scholars as Bar Deroma, Barhebraeus, U. Cassuto, I. Efros, S. I. Feigen, J. Kaufman,

Jacob Mann, and A. S. Yahuda to the attention of the Biblical critics
and Biblical scholars who, because of limitations of language skills
or for less innocent reasons, had not found their way to them. Some
Orthodox rabbis and scholars, while unhappy with Goldman's refusal to accept the tradition of the divine revelation of the whole
Torah on Sinai, were grateful for his defense of the medieval commentators. They were delighted that Rashi, Ibn Ezra, Gikitila, and
Saadia could be pitted against Delitszch, Wellhausen, Gunkel, and
Breasted and not found wanting. They agreed that Goldman had
elevated the academic prestige and conferred wider acceptance on
the tanaim, the amoraim and the rabbonim.

The Christian religious press reflected the gratitude of many ministers who recognized for the first time how slanted the Higher
Critics had been and how amateurish was their knowledge of the
Aramaic language in general and of the talmudic use of that language in particular. Christian ministers expressed their delight with
"Echoes and Allusions." It provided good copy for their bulletins,
literary adornment for their sermons, and a link with the English
reading assignments of their high-school students.

Orientalists who reviewed the volumes on the Bible for the
Journal of Religion and similar publications appreciated the vast
erudition of the author but took exception to his harsh treatment
of Wellhausen and Breasted. Thus Arnold B. Rhodes stated:

> Although the reviewer differs radically at points from Prof. Breasted in the
> interpretation of history, he does not believe that anti-Semitism was a motive
> behind "The Dawn of Conscience." Enthusiasm for his field of labor plus his
> theological and philosophical presuppositions is sufficient to account for
> Breasted's exaltation of Egypt. Goldman's position both in this chapter and
> in the book as a whole would have been strengthened considerably if he had
> emphasized more the distinctiveness of Hebrew monotheism in terms of the
> Bible's own unique framework of faith which involves such themes as redemp-
> tion, historical revelation and election—themes suggested by the author but
> not developed.[45]

Rabbis and Jewish scholars generally received the volumes with

---

45. *Journal of Religion,* Chicago, Illinois, October 1949.

ready acclaim. Dr. Chaim Pearl, reviewing *From Slavery to Freedom*, expressed an oft-repeated appraisal.

> The reader may well be amazed at the author's versatility, for he is at home not only among Jewish writers, ancient medieval and modern, but he draws with equal advantage on classical Greek and Roman authors, the Church fathers, modern historians, geographers and climatologists—a unique feast of scholarship concentrated in one book.[46]

Rabbi Felix Levy, a President of the Central Conference of American Rabbis, reviewing the introductory volume in the Chicago *Sunday Tribune* said:

> He brings to his task a thorough scholarship rigidly scientific in method, a remarkable sensitivity to the Hebrew language and literature, a keen mind, an incisive style and a complete familiarity with the entire field of his topic. He writes with the Jew's love for and understanding of his own.[47]

Rabbi Goldman was himself delighted with the review of his second volume by his trusted friend, Rabbi David Graubart, head of the Chicago Bet Din. He was especially pleased with these sentences.

> Dr. Goldman's *In the Beginning* has the characteristics of a great book. As Christopher Morley puts it in his *Parnassus on Wheels,* quoted in the Echoes and Allusions, "A great book ought to have something simple about it. And like Eve, it ought to come from somewhere near the third rib: there ought to be a heart beating in it."[48]

Trude Weiss-Rosmarin, a most perceptive editor and ardent traditionalist said:

> Dr. Goldman's "Introduction" may well be considered an effort of kiddush hashem, notwithstanding certain formal unorthodoxies, for it helps the reader to see and appreciate the full grandeur and sacredness of "The Book of Books."[49]

---

46. *London Jewish Chronicle,* April 13, 1962.
47. Chicago *Sunday Tribune,* May 23, 1948.
48. *Chicago Sentinel,* February 2, 1950.
49. *Congress Weekly,* July 16, 1948.

The only dissenting opinion amidst some hundred reviews came from Rabbi Alexander J. Burnstein in the bulletin of the Rabbinical Assembly. Rabbi Burnstein believed that Goldman had set himself an impossible task:

> . . . in attempting to combine all angles in a single interpretation because there is no way of looking at a thing from all sides at one time. . . . He has tried to examine the Book of Genesis from a variety of standpoints all compressed within the compass of less than a hundred pages, with the result that the book is uneven, sketchy and, in many instances, sadly inadequate.

Burnstein acknowledges that the summation of the contents of the Book of Genesis is a model of succinctness and precision, and that the second chapter, the translation of selected passages, is both clear and elegant and shows that the author has utilized the abundant and variegated resources of contemporary as well as Jewish Biblical exegesis. The third chapter is disappointing because of the author's "frontal attack upon the extreme, 'dated' and eccentric views of a few individual critics. . . . the role of the higher critical method as a whole is minimized and distorted. It is purely conjectural and misleading to suggest, as the author does, that we can from a scientific point of view, and, on the basis of fresh but far from established or verified facts available to us, overcome and eliminate the complex textual and historical difficulties in the study of the Bible. And how much can we depend on the materials unearthed at the northern shore of the Dead Sea, to which the author seems to attach so much importance?"

He charges Goldman with basing his arguments against the documentary theory on rhetoric rather than on proof, on stylistic verve rather than on balanced appraisal and ends with a plea for a more all-embracing acceptance and recognition of "the historicity of the patriarchs."

> Something similar can be said of the fourth chapter, "Authorship," where the author tries to settle this question by ascribing the book to Moses, Dr. Goldman's point of view is Conservative but not blindly conservative. The criticism of the Wellhausen school . . . raises the major defect of the entire approach, and reflects as vividly as possible the vague, fluctuating, and un-

certain point of view of the author: "In the midst of so much disagreement, theorising and conjecturing, why not also on the other hand, venture a *guess* that the Patriarchs and Moses had a share in the composition of Genesis and, on the other hand, humbly acknowledge that the original character of the documents embodied in it and the approximate age or ages in which they were composed, lie, despite our labors and sciences, beyond our ken."[50]

Burnstein also regretted the inclusion of "Echoes and Allusions."

Might it not have been better to devote at least part of the available 600 pages to the publication of a critical study or interpretation based upon these quotations, which would have given conviction, coherence and direction to otherwise random thoughts and selections?

Burnstein did concede, however, that despite its defects, *In the Beginning* was an interesting and useful volume, and has in it, more particularly in its well-documented commentary, index, and notes, much grist for the mill of the serious student of the Bible.

It is understandable that Burnstein should have been confused and perhaps even annoyed by Goldman's sudden reversion to the theory of the Patriarchal and Mosaic authorship of the Torat Moshe. It does appear contradictory to Burnstein, even flippant, for an author who has displayed so critical an intelligence, so devastating a refutation of other men's traditional presuppositions and vested preferences to turn about and ask that we content ourselves with an educated guess that Moses could have been the author of the Pentateuch. But it will not appear so strange to one who has read *The Jew and the Universe* where Goldman prescribes the limitations of the rational process and establishes, for himself at least, the validity of the reasons of the heart that reason knows not of, a conditional intuitionism permissible to those who have undergone the discipline of reason and traveled with it as far as it can go. In matters of vital concern to him as a Jew and to the survival of the Jewish culture and spirit, Goldman preferred to say *"I believe,"* to *"I do not know."*

A rebuttal to Rabbi Burnstein's criticism is provided by Maurice Samuel in his introduction to "The Ten Commandments," the final

---

50. Rabbinic Assembly *Bulletin* (New York, N. Y.: February 1950).

section of the third volume, *From Slavery to Freedom,* which was separately published by the University of Chicago's Phoenix Press.[51]

> Goldman makes clear his attitude toward the entirety of the Old Testament. A scholar and a specialist he did not consider the Bible as primarily the domain of scholars and specialists. He saw it as the Book of the people. He brooded on the grand mystery of its effectiveness for hundreds of millions as much as on the riddles of its origins and the puzzles on its textual construction, seeing, indeed, an organic connection between the two aspects. To him what the Bible *was* and *what it had done* were ultimately a single question, and therefore any approach to biblical study which emphasized the purely technical aspects of the origins and history of the texts, in his view, was futile and barren, if not destructive. His interest in the technical problem was, indeed, penetrating and continuous but always subordinated to the larger and more fascinating problems of the powers of the whole.
>
> It was his view that the high point of effective power was probably reached in the substance and episode of the Ten Commandments; and here substance and episode were, more than anywhere else, indivisible; for if the substance is the core of the Law, the episode is nothing more or less than the only theophany ever vouchsafed to an entire people assembled for that purpose.

The dramatic form in which Goldman presents the theophany, Samuel goes on to say:

> . . . was dictated by his feeling for the significance of the Ten Commandments in the religious and civilized history of man, by his sense of their penetration into the lives of ordinary people. . . . The Ten Commandments are not "merely" the core of a moral code, designed for all mankind. They are not "merely" an enunciation of principles conveyed to the human intelligence in a phraseology the compactness and compulsion of which Goldman analyzes with great skill. They are also the crucial initial episode in the making of a people out of a rabble of slaves that is to say, they are to the phenomenon of civilized peoplehood what Genesis is to the phenomenon of world order.[52]

Goldman's commitment to the Hebrew language was one of the

---

51. This volume was published in 1956 as the first of the posthumous works of Rabbi Goldman to be given to the public. It was edited by Maurice Samuel who was regarded by Rabbi Goldman as the most knowledgeable and most insightful Jewish author and teacher of his time.

52. *The Ten Commandments,* edited by Maurice Samuel (Chicago: Phoenix Books, University of Chicago Press, 1963), pp. viii, ix, x, xi.

most intense and consistent of his life. Early in 1927 he enlisted the eminent Hebrew educator, Abraham Hyman Friedland of Cleveland, in an enterprise which would make the reading of Hebrew texts more enjoyable and more meaningful to Jewish students. He proposed to select a series of Hebrew texts and publish them with vowels (*nekudot*) with notes clarifying unusual terms or terms used in special context, a brief biography of the author, and a listing of the entire vocabulary used in the text with its translation. He selected as the first in this series the poignantly beautiful *L'on* (*Whither*) of Mordecai Zeeb Feierberg, and thus brought a little-known author to much deserved attention and introduced a Hebrew which gracefully applied the inwardness of Psalms to the poetic, if often melancholy, imaginings of a very sensitive and very tragic artist.

When he moved to Chicago, Goldman enlisted Dr. Leo Honor and Professor Simon Halkin in this enterprise and prepared model study texts for the letters of Achad Ha'am, the *Legend of Three and Four* (*Agadat Sh'loshah Ve'arbaha*) of Chayim Nachman Bialik, the stories of Yudah Leib Peretz, The letter to Yemen (*Igeret Taiman*) of Maimonides. These constituted the *Sifriah LeTalmedim* series and proved to be a most significant contribution to Hebrew pedagogy. Goldman obtained the cooperation of Dr. Samuel Feigen and Rabbi Ira Eisenstein in addition to Halkin, Honor, and Friedland, but he bore the main burden of writing the biographical and historic introduction and of the translation or its supervision.

His introductions were clear, succinct, and lively; the guide which the notes and vocabulary provided spared the reader hours of rummaging in dictionaries and permitted him the delight of tasting the substance of the text. It required true humility and dogged dedication for a man as busy as Rabbi Goldman to undertake this spadework. And to have raised the funds which made possible the publication of these volumes was a service beyond the call of duty. Something of the *d'vekut* (passionate devotion) of a Ben Yehudah (creator of modern Hebrew) or an Achad Ha'am was required to set aside the writing of *The Jew and the Universe* or *The Book of Human Destiny,* and refuse prestigious speaking invitations to read the galleys for Hebrew-school textbooks. Goldman was eager to share with others that special insight, that special world, that unique sense of being and destiny which he found in the language of the Bible and nowhere else.[53]

Santayana once said that true piety was a sense of reverence for the sources of our being. Goldman, the *enfant terrible* of so many pseudo-pietists, the deflator of the righteous pomposity of Orthodox accountants of the Lord, was in Santayana's sense a true pietist. His love and reverence for his teachers was a constant in his being. Very early in his career he resolved that one of the literary tasks to which he would give high priority would be to create pen pictures of his beloved teachers. He fulfilled this ambition in regard to Dr. Schechter, Professor Ginzberg, Professor Kaplan, and Professor Marx. While he did not pay formal tribute through an essay to Dr. Israel Friedlander and Dr. Davidson, he made many laudatory references to them in his sermons and on many public occasions when mention of them was relevant to his theme.

His feeling about his teachers was best expressed in an address he gave in New York in 1942 to honor the sixtieth birthday of Professor Mordecai Kaplan:

No joy can be said to be purer and more blessed than that of paying homage to a teacher. In the lore of our people, there is no title more august, no calling more sacred. The wisest Jews of all ages reverently spoke of Moses as *Moshe Rabenu,* and the humblest Hasid, when affection welled up in his bosom, chanted *oi rebbenu.* In the Bible, the teacher is the messenger of the Lord of Hosts, in the Talmud, the symbol of spiritual fatherhood. Those who like myself, had the privilege of coming into the Seminary atmosphere in their early adulthood, to sit at the feet of Dr. Schechter, Dr. Friedlander, Dr. Davidson, *aleihem ha-shalom* and *yibadlu le-hayim* Dr. Ginzberg, Dr. Marx and Dr. Kaplan experienced that ineffable bliss which the rabbis termed *Nehenim Mi-Ziv ha-Shechinah.* . . . We students were not much younger than they and yet we stood in awe of them, at a distance, removed by lengths of learning, wisdom and piety, and at the same time, drawn to them by filial ties of love and intimacy. I am not romanticizing vague recollections of a

53. Goldman's assistance to Hebrew writers, publishers, educators throughout the Jewish world is detailed in Chapter 5.

receding past. I vividly recall my days at the Seminary. They were for me personally days of ceaseless toil and poverty but when I was in the presence of my teachers, I felt exalted, happy, wedded to a purpose.

In the best style of the Festschrift, Goldman then develops a brilliant comparison between the Graeco-Christian view of the universe and the Jewish view, and interweaves Kaplan's immense contribution to this constant dialogue with his own profound thesis of Judaism as a civilization:

It is because Kaplan has recognized the organic and interdependent character of all human interests that he has refused to think of Judaism as something insular from and unallied to the issues of life. More persistently and more successfully than anyone we know, he has tried to disprove the notion that religions ever existed in splendid isolation, condescending only to earthy contact for a Sabbath hour. . . . Religions were ever inseparable from the particular civilizations with which they were identified, and as much determined by the general characteristics of the peoples professing them as the flora and fauna of a geographical area are determined by its soil.[54]

Two years later in 1945, he contributed a masterful portrait of a teacher to the *Louis Ginzberg Jubilee Volume* of the American Academy for Jewish Research:

There is no doubt but that both the naturalness and brilliance of his scholarship lend a peculiar grace to the canvas. Professor Ginzberg is the least bookish of the scholars I have ever known. He is the master and not the slave of learned tomes. There is not a trace of artificiality about his phenomenal memory. It is not a carefully compiled and properly arranged file of index cards. He never conveys the impression of having laboriously barrelled up a great deal of knowledge. His erudition is not external to his thought, a mass of sediment as it were, of other people's brew. . . . In the fields in which he is preeminent (and where is there a corner of Jewish lore he has not harvested?) one seldom thinks of him as an annotator or expositor but as the pioneer and co-creator, as the associate of the sages of the past, sitting, as it were with them at the same table. The words of a *Tanna-*

---

54. We have discussed other phases of the long and fruitful relationship of Dr. Kaplan and Rabbi Goldman in the earlier chapter on the Seminary. The correspondence between them would make a sizable volume and indicates that in many ways the pupil Goldman became mentor to the teacher Kaplan.

Amora come from his lips with a freshness as if they were his own, as if he
had a share in fashioning them. . . . Seldom has any one Jewish scholar
achieved equal pre-eminence in Halakah and Haggadah as he has, or produced stupendous treatises in both, such as his *Commentary on the Yerushalmi*
and his *Legends of the Jews*.[55]

In 1950, Goldman contributed his longest portrait of a teacher to
the *Alexander Marx Jubilee Volume,* published by the Seminary. It
was written in bits and pieces during periods when his recurring
illness permitted some degree of exertion. The essay proved to be
one of the finest, most creative, most scholarly of Goldman's writings.
Even Professor Marx, not given to hyperbole or any other extravagances of expression, expressed his amazement at the thoroughness
of the research and the vast comprehension which Goldman revealed
of his scholarly career. It appears that here deep uttered unto deep,
one bookman to another. The love of books was the common bond
which created a very special kind of camaraderie between Goldman
the extrovert, man of affairs, leader and founder of movements and
this librarian who found a Steinschneider or a Bodleian catalogue
as enthralling as the Song of Songs. We quote two passages from the
learned tribute "The Man of the Book" in the Jubilee volume:

> In one of his most technical and ingenious papers, Dr. Marx, by authenti-
> cating a statement of Joseph Kimhi, establishes Ibn Gabirol's claim to the
> authorship of *The Choice of Pearls*. In another he makes it highly probable
> that the enigmatic Paltial, so enthusiastically portrayed in the Chronicle of
> Ahimaaz, is after all perhaps none other than Jaubar, vizier of Al-Muizz. In
> a third we come pretty near determining the exact numbers of Jews in Spain

---

55. "The Portrait of a Teacher" in the *Louis Ginzberg Jubilee Volume,* 1945, p. 5.
Professor Ginzberg, like Dr. Schechter, took a deep personal interest in Goldman. The
friendship between them continued throughout their lives and extended to their
families. Professor Ginzberg wrote many brief notes to Goldman in Hebrew in his
very distinctive scrawl. Many were affectionate greetings on special occasions, many
were comments succinct and penetrating on one or the other's writings. Some were
urgent pleas for help for scholarly projects. Goldman was too much in awe of Ginzberg to engage in controversy with him over Reconstructionism or over the internal
reforms of the Seminary. Goldman respected the religious Conservatism of his teacher
and recognized that there was no need for Ginzberg to declare his philosophy. His
life and his work were not only a philosophy but the proper source for many philosophies. Goldman deeply treasured Ginzberg's compliment: "You are a strong swimmer
in the sea of Talmud."

generally and in Castile particularly prior to the expulsion. In the fourth we learn that the first books to have been printed in Africa and the Balkans were respectively the Abudrahom of 1521, for which type was imported from Portugal, and the 1493 Hebrew incunabulum of Constantinople. . . .[56]

But not even this erudition and skill would have sufficed to build this veritable *Qiryat Sepher* (The J. T. S. Library). What above all, provided the holy enterprise with momentum was the hope that beckoned Dr. Schechter to come to this country and his ardent desire to make America a *mekom Torah.*

Dr. Marx knew what he wanted. He wanted to collect, as it were, the past and the present of his people in one pulsation. He craved to have a library in which every conceivable branch of Judaism would have its habitation. As if anticipating the calamities that were to overwhelm the Jewish communities of Europe and their centers of learning, he warred on every interruption in the flow of books, . . . toiling to assemble the fugitives of Israel and bring about a reunion of exiles. His solicitude and resolution proved infectious. Men brought their gifts to him as much out of reverence for the Librarian as out of interest in Jewish scholarship, and the *Qiryat Sepher* became a reality.[57]

There was one other tribute which Goldman wrote that belongs in this company, though the subject of it was not a teacher in a seminary—Justice Louis Dembitz Brandeis. In the spring of 1953, just a few months before Goldman's death, Henry Schuman published *The Words of Justice Brandeis*, edited by Goldman and including a warm and colorful biographical sketch of the Justice. The book was compiled during the most difficult days in which Goldman was torn between intolerable and slightly more tolerable pain. Goldman felt that most biographers had overlooked the Jewish component in Brandeis's character. While the many meetings which he had with Brandeis during the two years 1938–1939, when he was president of the ZOA, were largely taken up with urgent problems of the Zionist organization, they also afforded him an opportunity to delve into the origins of the Justice's return to the Jewish people. He found that it was the action of a union delegate at a hearing between

---

56. "The Man of the Book," in the *Alexander Marx Jubilee Volume* (New York: Jewish Theological Seminary, 1950), p. 19.

57. Ibid., p. 23.

the Ladies' Garment Workers' Union and management which made
Brandeis aware of the living power of the prophetic tradition. This
awareness led him to a deeper study of Jewish history and to his
first entrance into Jewish affairs in Boston in 1910 when he issued
a public statement declaring his sympathy for the Zionist movement
and "his belief that Jews can be just as much of a priest people today as they were in the prophetic days." It was a great day, Goldman
exclaims, when Brandeis discovered this affinity between his own
views and the prophetic-Pharisaic tradition. It was another great
day when the Olympian solon discovered that the Talmudic emphasis on implementing the law, on building its premises into the
very warp and woof of society, was in complete conformity with his
own pragmatic bent. He saw in the miraculous resistance of the
Jewish people to the Big Powers that would engulf them a prototype of his own resistance to the curse of bigness in business and in
government. The very essence of freedom, which, to him, was a
cardinal principle, was exemplified in the emancipation of Israel
from Pharoah and in its unswerving loyalty to the dream and promise of freedom gained in that ancient confrontation. Goldman concludes his sketch of Brandeis:

> After turning the pages of the Bible, Graetz, and Herzl, Mr. Brandeis
> realized that his people's huge affliction was the result of continuous resistance
> to world trusts. Because Israel was small and weak it was not yet sufficient
> reason why it should be swallowed up by the many and the mighty. Sheer
> bigness was a curse. God had called Amos from Tekoah and Lincoln from
> Gentryville. Mr. Brandeis recognized in the shepherd of Tekoah the spiritual
> father of the rail-splitter. Lincoln unsheathed the sword to preserve justice
> and freedom. Israel suffered martyrdom to maintain its cause and conscience.
> It was a great day for Brandeis when he discovered that Americanism and
> Judaism were of one pattern.[58]

Aside from the commanding power of Brandeis's character and
personality, and his leadership in the Zionist cause, what fascinated
Goldman was the prime example Brandeis offered of a man who
could be fervently Jewish even though nonreligious or even a-

---

58. *The Words of Justice Brandeis* (New York: Henry Schuman, 1953), p. 21.

religious.[59] It offered brilliant testimony to the validity of Goldman's thesis which he had elaborated as early as 1929 in the pages of the *New Palestine Monthly*. Here he stated:

> Yet, of all fictions the most persistent is the legend that Israel remains united because of a God idea. . . . Blasphemous and perverted as it may sound to some, it is nevertheless factually true that Israel has lived for Israel's sake. . . . It neither suffered nor fought for God—for a uniform God idea. . . . In dynamic history God must give way to Israel. . . . The dynamic approach does not jettison the theory of Israel's selection, it only explains it. The unaided, continued struggle of Israel for its distinctive personality now appears to be unparalleled in the annals of man. . . .

> Thus we discover that of all nations of antiquity we were the most nationally conscious. Indeed we constituted the first nation in the modern sense of the word. The fact that we did is our uniqueness; that we persist is our glory. . . . We, the children of Abraham, Isaac and Jacob, with our land, descent, language, religion, folkways and social instincts—our national "I"— have survived to this day. There has been in this survival no lapse of memory. . . . This consciousness of 4,000 years of uninterrupted history in the memory cells of the Jew—this is Israel.[60]

---

59. Ben Halpern in *Midstream*, November 1971, calls attention to the Frankist strain in the Brandeis family background and to the anti-religious anti-synagogue prejudice of Brandeis's mother—an attitude which was counteracted in Brandeis's philosophy by the teachings and examples of Uncle Louis Dembitz. The uncle, it seems, rebelled against the agnostic-Frankist family tradition and returned to the synagogue and traditional Judaism. When Louis Brandeis changed his middle name from David to Dembitz, he may have given symbolic testimony to a similar change in himself.

60. "God and Israel," *The New Palestine Monthly* (New York: June 1929).

Chapter 5

A One-Man Cultural Foundation

IN THE BULLETIN of KAM Temple for May 27, 1953, shortly after his death, I wrote concerning Rabbi Goldman:

> The Jewish scholar was his friend—nay his brother. Who can count the number of writers in Hebrew, in Yiddish, in German, in English who came into his study and found not a stranger, but a brother. Sol Goldman was unofficial Dean of a large private university and with utmost delicacy prevailed upon innumerable scholars to do him the honor to accept a graduate fellowship in the form of a subvention or guaranty on the book they were eager to publish.

At the time I wrote this, my information was of a general nature, hearsay, rumor, and some personal experience. Now that I have read through his vast correspondence, I see that I was guilty of understatement.

Because of the typical awkwardness of Yeshivah boys with mechanics generally, and with typewriters in particular, Goldman never mastered the machine which has often become the writing man's alter ego. When Goldman received letters in Hebrew or Yiddish, he would occasionally answer them in his own hand. But when the pressures of his many duties became mountainous, it was his custom to dictate his answer in English to his secretary who would in turn relay these dictations to Hebrew or Yiddish scholars who would translate and transcribe them on the Hebrew typewriters. Two of these transcribers and translators were Dr. Samuel I. Feigen[1] of the Judaic Department of the Oriental Institute of Chicago and Mr. Nathan Kravitz, editor of *The Jewish Way*.[2]

One anxious or penurious scholar revealed his good fortune in enlisting Goldman's aid to another. The rumor soon was bandied about that Goldman had tapped a cluster of multimillionaires who readily opened their purses to him. The fact was that the sources of Goldman's generosity were the honoraria for lectures and articles and the checks sent by grateful parishioners for special services or on the occasion of some significant anniversary. When these sums, never more than $10,000 a year, proved grossly inadequate he would summon the assistance of friends who seldom failed him. There were those who clothed Goldman with supernatural powers when it came to extracting money from Jews whether in public or private appeals. The truth was that Goldman, when fired by a cause or touched by a person, was able to communicate his own ardor to others, especially since he had prepared the ground by long years of teaching and by his own consistent example. While the administrative necessities of running a large congregation made very clear to him how important it was to have access to money, he never idolized wealth or stood in awe of its possessors. This enabled him to ask for money without fear or embarrassment. He early convinced himself that he was performing a therapeutic service, a benign bloodletting,

---

1. Dr. Feigen was a profound scholar for whom Rabbi Goldman had a deep personal affection and for whom he labored for several years to obtain a full professorship at the University of Chicago. Such a chair required large sums which the rabbi was unable to raise. But he did find sufficient funds for the university to guarantee Dr. Feigen's salary for several years. Dr. Feigen's modest salary was supplemented by compensation for this secretarial work. The eulogy which Rabbi Goldman gave at a memorial service for Dr. Feigen elicited a most extravagant compliment from Professor Hans Morgenthau; he described it as the finest, most sensitive and most scholarly appreciation of one man's lifework by another he had ever heard.

2. See Appendix III, pp. 279 for some typical examples of these communications. The entire file constitutes an index of a large part of the contemporary Jewish scholars, journalists and poets.

just the right antidote for high blood pleasure, for callousness to the less fortunate and, above all, the very best of free-will offerings to the Power that brought the sons and daughters of wandering Arameans to the green pastures of affluence in blessed America.

Still, with all his successes, the appeals that came to him proved to be far more numerous than he could meet. The letters in which he had to refuse requests were written in agony of spirit. They were often apologetic, self-immolating, taking himself to task for being ill or unable to move more Jews to greater generosity. His benefactions were not limited to checks and money orders. He often undertook to find translators, editors, and publishers for poets and scholars who were quite innocent of the intricate mechanics of the publishing world. They were unaware, for instance, that many corrections in three languages on the galley proofs could double or triple the cost of printing, a dour fact that often caught Goldman between the rigid demands of the printer and the heartrending insistence of the author that his own image would be desecrated without the corrections. Not content with midwifing a reluctant book through the printing press, Goldman undertook to distribute the book. He bought copies to send to friends and libraries, he besieged bookstores and friends to accept copies on consignment. He wrote letters to his wide circle of acquaintances extolling the book. Like Mendele Mocher Seforim, the grandfather of Yiddish literature, he peddled other authors' books while feeling very guilty about neglecting his own unfinished manuscripts. He made it a practice to invite Hebrew and Yiddish writers to the Friday-evening service at Anshe Emet, where he would introduce them, generally with a brilliant summary of their work. He would hold receptions in their honor and not too subtly inform the people in the reception line that copies of the author's books were available at the table at the end of the line. He was the master *shadchan* bringing together an eager author and a more or less willing reader.

Goldman had developed an eagle eye for detecting gifted Hebrew poets and novelists, as the names listed above fully demonstrate, and it was most rewarding to him to see how so many who had sent him their first manuscripts in fear and trembling had become, in time, acknowledged as leading artists and authors in their field. But the incredible pressures upon him made it necessary to refuse even those whom he knew to be great luminaries. Thus he had to refuse Stephen Wise who asked him to help assure the publication of the collected works of Rav Tzair, Chaim Tchernowitz. So, too, he was forced to say no to Nahum Goldman who solicited him in behalf of Jacob Klatzkin, though, it must be said, that Sol Goldman had aided Klatzkin long before he came to Nahum Goldman's attention. But perhaps the most painful refusal was that which he wrote to Professor Diesendruck at the Hebrew Union College, when that eminent scholar solicited his help for Martin Buber shortly after World War II. Buber had fled Poland, where his estate had been confiscated, and come to Israel with many completed manuscripts and some unfinished ones—all in German. He was now in great need of money to support his children and their families, needs hardly met by his modest salary as a teacher at the Hebrew University. He believed that some of his works translated into English would find a reading public in America. He asked Diesendruck if a publisher, like Schocken or an institute of some kind, might undertake to subvene his needs against the future profits from his books. All that Goldman could do was to suggest to Diesendruck that he appeal to the Jewish Publication Society, that, it turned out had already turned a deaf ear to Diesendruck.[3] Goldman did not live to realize the tremendous impact and the universal reception which the Christian world, even more than the Jews, gave to some of the manuscripts which Buber had taken with him from Poland, such as *God and Man, I and Thou, Christianity and Judaism, Chassidic Tales.* One hazards the guess that Goldman would have suffered a twinge of regret that he had passed up this opportunity to have backed a winner, but he would have consoled himself that those he did help, Bialik, Achad Ha'am, Peretz, Feierberg, Regelson, Lamdan, Lisitzky, and Halkin, had strengthened the Hebrew language and evoked the Hebrew national spirit, and firmed the survival of the Jewish people as much as the universallly admired Buber.

---

3. See Appendix for this correspondence.

It often occurred to Goldman that some of America's leading
rabbis spoke for themselves and not for their congregations, that they
were so far in front of their flocks as to have lost communication
with them. Thus, even the beloved Stephen Wise, ardent Zionist
that he was, could muster little support for the Zionist Organization
from his Free Synagogue. Rabbi Abba Hillel Silver could mobilize
even less support for Zionism or for Hebrew education from the
substantial upper-middle-class membership of the temple over which
he presided. Dr. Solomon Freehof, the most learned Hebraist and
Talmudist in the Reform rabbinate, was not able to introduce Hebrew classes into the religious school of KAM Temple. Goldman
insisted from the beginning of his ministry at Anshe Emet that the
congregation reflect and embody the principles and values which he
professed from the pulpit and elaborated in his books. That is why
he became the first rabbi in Conservative or Reform ranks to establish a day school under the auspices of a synagogue. He was immediately assailed by liberal intellectuals who saw the day school as a
Jewish parochial school and therefore a divisive force that would
jeopardize the American dream of one nation out of many, the melting pot of the peoples of Europe and Asia. There were some who
saw it as a priestly plot to thwart the challenge of science to religion
by engulfing secular wisdom in Levitical wrappings. They thought
such an experiment especially dangerous in a community where the
Catholic parochial-school system was very strong and where Catholic
pressures were already weakening the republic's founders' hope that
a common education would be a molding force for all the children.
Some of the laymen and staff members feared that the day school
would spell the death of the Sunday religious school and the Hebrew
classes which met twice or three times a week and would definitely
diminish the growing interest in Bar and Bat Mitzvah observance.

Goldman patiently answered these objections and, in the last years
of World War II and immediately thereafter, was able to surround
himself with a group of enthusiastic laymen and women who worked
out the following goals and guidelines:

Under general educational goals, they proposed:

To realize the learning potential of each student by using those instructional methods and materials that contemporary education had found to be most effective in developing skills and discipline;

To take cognizance of the changing needs of a highly technical and socially dynamic society and therefore adjust its curriculum constantly to provide an elementary education which would prepare the child to meet the changing demands of high school and college. In this task experimental methods developed by disciples of John Dewey and Montessori would be tried and if found effective, adopted;

To limit the size of enrollment so that the teacher-pupil ratio would make it possible to detect and respond to the unique needs of each student;

To provide a full program of art and music activities to encourage the aesthetic and social growth of the student. The active participation of the child would be encouraged to evoke his creative imaginative capacities;

To acquaint its children during these formative years and in terms they would best comprehend, with the responsibilities, opportunities and problems of participatory citizenship in an evolving free society.

The Jewish education goals were formulated as follows:

To give the student a working knowledge of the Hebrew language and an ease in using it in conversation and reading—so that the language will become an experience in itself and a passport to the realization of the historic and present life of the Jewish people;

To develop a familiarity with the Hebrew Bible—a knowledge of its content and of the interpretive methods by which the unique wisdom of the Bible was given universal relevance. Bible instruction is intended not merely to acquire a fund of stories, law and history but to gain a sense of personal and community identity and purpose;

To acquaint the student with some portions of the Talmudic and Midrashic literature which grew out of the peoples' love for the Bible and which became the Oral Tradition keeping fresh and relevant the wisdom of the Book of Books;

To provide a broad general overview of Jewish history so that the student will understand himself as a member of the Jewish people, and accept the responsibilities as well as the dignity and pride of this fellowship;

To make manifest the place of Israel in the historic development of the Jew, so that he will recognize the centrality of Israel to Jewish identity and survival—and see in the interaction of Israel and Diaspora the creative survival and growth of the Jewish people throughout the world.

To help the student recognize the Synagogue as the central institution of
the Jewish Community in the Diaspora and to encourage him to observe the
formal Jewish religious experience of the Sabbath, the Festivals and Holy
Days, to know the meaning of the Jewish Calendar and the essential structure
of the Synagogue service, the structure of the prayer book, and through a
planned program of student services come to know the inwardness of religious
commitment to Judaism. Since the School would be open to all the children
of the community, the services would be designed to transcend the narrow
sectarian divisions of the Jewish Community.

The above-stated goals are attended, the statement insists, by
wider objectives that cannot be specified in terms of curricular detail
or pedagogic method, but are nevertheless intrinsic to the day-school
program. These are the implicit goals that serve as a sort of ideological context or climate for the whole enterprise:

To provide leaders for tomorrow's general and Jewish communities—leaders
with high values and lofty standards;

To change the lives of the students through a positive and creative Jewish
identification that will nourish all aspects of their personalities, evoke
their highest potential, and make Judaism a joyful, meaningful, day-to-day
experience;

To make Judaism a meaningful contribution to the life and progress of
world civilization by exemplifying the working of our culture and religious
tradition in our lives;

To make our young people at home in the unified complex of American
and Jewish civilization so that they can bring to bear upon their world the
best that can be derived from the totality of their experience.

Goldman was realist enough to know that institutions, being
composed of humans, realize only some of their objectives and have
a way of strangling others in the coils of administrative organization.
He lived long enough to see that the school enlisted high quality
teaching personnel, somewhat better than in the general school system. He saw and heard enough students to convince himself that
Jewish knowledge gained in the day school was far superior to
that gained in the week-end religious school and superior even to that
obtained in the Hebrew schools which students attended after their
sessions in the secular public schools. The day-school students could

read the Bible and the prayer book with greater facility and deeper understanding. They could read and translate the Sidrot and Haftarot at their Bar and Bat Mitzvot in *Sephardit* with more grace and understanding than the students from the religious and Hebrew schools. They showed an awareness of the interrelation of the American secular and the Jewish religious cultures, and the very fact that the two cultures were taught under the same roof and were part of the same educational objective, gave them a respect and appreciation for the Jewish subjects that were often lacking in their contemporaries who studied Judaism in the afternoons and during week-ends with the leftover scraps of their energy and commitment.

Of course there were problems, not so much with the secular studies as with the Jewish curriculum. There were standards and carefully evolved criteria available in the general educational field to guide the board and staff of the Anshe Emet Day School. But in the Jewish field there was little scientifically tested material. The immense work of the Israel-based educators was not yet available, and the work of Dushkin, Honor, and Gamoran was designed to meet the needs of community federation and denominational religious schools. The Orthodox day schools were coming into being, but their material was hardly suitable for a progressive day school where Dewey, Montessori, Fromm, and Spock were the household idols. Goldman found it necessary to initiate the series of annotated texts and undertook to make Maimonides, Achad Ha'am, Peretz, Bialik, and Feierberg available to students who had come to believe that Jewish education in Hebrew was limited to the Bible and the prayer book.

For all its difficulties, the day school prospered and added grades with fair regularity. Had Goldman lived, there can be little doubt that the day school would now have added a high school. Rabbi Ira Eisenstein, who succeeded Rabbi Goldman, did not stay long enough to come to grips with the many problems of the day school and his was the unenviable task of succeeding a man whose stature was bound to serve as an obstacle, as a source of invidious comparison to any successor. Rabbi Seymour Cohen, the present rabbi, is proud of the achievements of the day school, but, given the high mobility of the Jewish population in Chicago, is constrained to look to the

Board of Jewish Education and the Associated Talmud Torahs for the sponsorship and support of the kind of facilities which a day high school would require. The dedication and skill of the two directors and the tenacious interest of a group of laymen have kept the day school, splendidly housed in the new addition to Anshe Emet, and have attracted full enrollment for the classes it now holds.

If Jewish education in America is not to be a mile wide and an inch deep, the day school must become an ever larger part of the Jewish educational establishment. The organization of the Temple Rodef Shalom Day School by the late Rabbi Louis I. Newman constitutes the first of its kind by a Reform congregation and is undoubtedly a forerunner of others to come. Unhappily, it is apparent that mixed motives elicit the present wave of interest. It is hard to determine whether the eagerness to avoid the anticipated lower standards of integrated schools or a real desire to intensify Jewish learning is the most active propulsive force. It seems that the *yetzer harah,* the evil inclination, rides tandem to the *yetzer tov,* the good intention. The pioneer work of Goldman, begun more than twenty-five years ago, will serve as a helpful guide. He was so firmly anchored as a Jew and so deeply informed as an American that he was never for a moment worried about dual loyalties. His cultural pluralism derived from Dewey, Kallen, Bourne, and Achad Ha'am was far more profound than the popular myth of the melting pot. He had enough confidence in the Jews' devotion to the best in education and the Jews' desire to remain identified as Jews to believe that they would be willing to pay the heavy costs of a fully structured Jewish education within the framework of a secular education. The only area in which he seemed off target was his conviction that this could be managed by the synagogue. He wore his heart out trying to convince his colleagues that the synagogue must become central to Jewish life and return to its auspices the educational role and even some of the philanthropies that had been surrendered to secular Jewish leadership, often nonsurvival oriented. Only the synagogue locally and nationally, he believed, could create the educational structure which would hold our youth, and, as he early foresaw, this would require a school where the content of Jewish culture would have parity with the content of the secular culture. And for him, a Jewish

Solomon Goldman as a student at the Jewish Theological Seminary.

Dr. Goldman's parents, Mr. and Mrs. Abba Goldman.

Goldman with fellow students at the Jewish Theological Seminary. The earnest young man, second from the left, is Dr. Goldman.

1930: with Yehudi Menuhin.

Dr. Goldman with Chaim Weizmann.

Dr. Goldman in 1939, presiding as president at the World Zionist Congress in Switzerland. Among the others at the table are Nahum Goldman, and Menahem Mendel Ussishkin; the others are not identified.

At the World's Fair in New York, about 1940: with Albert Einstein and Stephen Wise.

This photograph was taken when Dr. Goldman received an honorary degree at the Jewish Institute of Religion. With him are, from left to right: (Dr. Goldman), Dr. Chaim Tchernowitz, James G. McDonald, Dr. Stephen Wise, Dr. Channing Tobias, Dr. Julian Morgenstern, Dr. Nelson Glueck, and Dr. Henry Slonimsky.

Dr. Goldman delivering an address at the celebration of the seventieth birthday of Stephen S. Wise (1944).

Dr. Goldman with Professor Louis Ginzberg, teacher, and friend
—when Dr. Goldman received the first Solomon Schechter Award
at the Jewish Theological Seminary.

culture that was not anchored to the synagogue was a tumbleweed, a sometime thing. The guidelines and goals of the Anshe Emet Day School forged by laymen who were his disciples can still serve those who want Judaism to be a way of life and not a mere profession.

Chapter 6

More Than the Sum of His Parts

GOLDMAN NEVER FELT that man should not be glorified for fear of displacing God. In *The Jew and the Universe*, he maintained that the key to a proper understanding of Maimonides was to recognize in "personality" that "wholeness" which intuitive reason, the mutual interplay of logic and feeling, discerned as the essence of man and the hallmark of reality. That same criterion will help us understand Goldman himself as the distinctive style and character of his life emerges from his various moods and multiple talents. When his good friend, the late Rabbi James G. Heller, solicited memorial tributes from a circle of Goldman's friends and associates shortly after his death in 1953, the responses, while as varied as the men who sent them, nevertheless almost unanimously expressed eagerness to capture the dimensions of the elliptical field of force in which his talents and characteristics opposed or harmonized with each other. Dr. Heller included his own splendid eulogy in this unpublished collection.[1] In it, he said:

---

1. See Preface for more detailed remarks on this volume.

If I were to be asked to select the man who seemed the most creative rabbi of our generation, I would choose his name. . . . All in all, in character, in learning, in a unique synthesis of spiritual and administrative talents, in broad comprehensiveness of interest and achievement, he was *primus inter pares,* "first among equals." There were doubtless greater speakers than he, though not in his style. There were men who had a record greater than his own in bringing national organization into being. But no one was like him in the qualities which I have described, qualities which seem to me most deeply those of a rabbi, less touched by being directed from our own kind of task and duty, less marred by uncertainties concerning the quality and goal of Jewish leadership.

The poet and educator, the late Ephraim Lisitzky, caught this view of him:

Solomon Goldman was a universal man. The man usually called "universal" achieves his reputation through the conjunction of a variety of talents, native or acquired; taken individually, his gifts surpass those of his fellows by a mere hair's breadth, but combined in one man, they add a full cubit to his stature, raising him head and shoulders above his fellows. . . .

Talented as he was as a speaker, it was in his writings that his true genius showed itself. The originality of his personality and richness of his culture pervaded all his writings. He never permitted his zest for learning to deteriorate into pedantry. . . . He was intent on getting at the foundations of Jewish and world culture, tapping the sealed spiritual and intellectual springs flowing deep underground. He tried to reach the original data, establish their genuine significance, and then weave them into the tapestry of world history. And always he illuminated the material with intuitive insights.

Mordecai Kaplan, who Goldman thought had been too rationalistic in his reconstruction of Judaism in his elimination of "Thou has chosen us from among all people" and too subservient to tradition in his reconstructed prayer book—seems to have had a much less critical view of Goldman's departure from pure reason. Here is what he said of *The Jew and the Universe* and of *The Book of Human Destiny*:

When in later years the opportunity presented itself to Goldman to interpret Maimonides' contribution to the development of Judaism, his long search for the secret of Maimonides' potent influence was rewarded by his discovery that not reason but intuition was the source of that influence. It was because Maimonides had a phenomenally intuitive understanding of Judaism that he was able to take on the challenge of the most advanced thought of his time. "The whole structure of Jewish civilization is reared in intuition," writes Goldman. "Reason yields the palm to intuition, speculation to meditation, formulation to avowal." Elsewhere he writes of Maimonides, "He exercised Reason and applied it within the spirit and scope of his tradition, a tradition deeply rooted in experience and intuition. True he checked the vagaries of faith and dissolved the mists of intuition by the application of disciplined thought. But he also clothed cold reason with the warm accoutrements of living Judaism." There can be no question that Goldman's appraisal in *The Jew and the Universe* of Maimonides' mind is far more objective, and his carefully documented insight far more reliable, than Ahad Ha-Am's. . . .

This discernment of the role that intuition played in Maimonides' thinking was no doubt due to Goldman's own intuitive insight into everything that had a bearing on Jews and Judaism. What such insight consists of might perhaps be spelled out by contrasting the different types of religious believers. There have been those who expressed their religious attitude by saying, "I wish to believe in order that I may understand." Others again have said, "I wish to understand in order that I may believe." But the religious attitude of those who resort to intuitive insight is expressed in the statement, "I love in order that I may understand and believe." Only a parent's love of a child, a student's of his subject, an artist's of his art and a citizen's of his nation can lead both to understanding of, and faith in, the creative possibilities of what they love. Only a love of the Jewish people can enable us to understand the Jewish spirit and to have faith in its destiny. In the final analysis, it was Maimonides' boundless love for his people that found expression in his intuitive insight into the true nature of its Torah. It is that same love of the Jewish people that accounts for the particular task which Goldman attempted to perform by means of his scholarly endeavors. Jewish scholarship that goes by the name of *Jüdische Wissenschaft* has done yeoman service in reconstructing the body of the Jewish past. What Goldman tried to do, however, was to retrieve the soul of the Jewish past. That could be achieved only by a vividly imaginative self-identification with it, which stems from love.

This brings us to the *magnum opus* or main achievement by which Goldman has established his claim to immortality. I refer to his exposition of the Bible in the series known as *The Book of Human Destiny,* of which three volumes have already appeared, and others are still in manuscript. There we can see how the motive of *ahavat Yisrael,* the love for the Jewish people, enabled Goldman to pioneer in a type of creative scholarship which comes to the aid of a civilization when it is in danger of obsolescence or having outlived its usefulness. That is the scholarship known as "Midrash." That is the interpretive art which explores the values and ideas of a tradition to discover their perennial and universal significance.

An enlightened layman, Robert Szold, strives to capture the sweep of Goldman's snythesizing intelligence in these words:

> Rabbi Goldman revered two giants, Brandeis and Ginzberg. They gave him their trust and confidence. He embodied the full Herzlian Zionism of Brandeis without ever forgetting the traditional learning of Ginzberg. Brandeis had supreme ability in practical affairs, intellectual spirituality, the highest standards of conduct, confidence and faith in the Jewish people, and a drive for achievement. Ginzberg had supreme learning, fabulous knowledge, and the remote calmness of the sage observing current events in perspective. Goldman fused, in his life and in his being, the learning of the cloister with the action of the fray.

The scholarly conservative rabbi and author, Jacob B. Agus, concludes a masterly analysis of Goldman's contribution to Judaism with this paragraph:

> The more I delve into his letters, the more saddened I feel that so vigorous a personality and so keen an intellect has been taken from us, long before his work was done. In the entire panorama of Jewish life, there is not another Solomon Goldman—so statesmanlike and perceptive in judgment, so subtle in reasoning, so rich in erudition, so deeply in love with the dynamic spirit of Judaism, so reverent of learning, so scornful of vulgarity and sham, so courageous in battle for the integrity of Judaism, so generous and self-sacrificing at every turn in life. Whenever we of this generation gather to plan for the revitalization of our sacred tradition, liberating it from the clichés of managers, the slogans of bureaucrats, and the prejudices of vulgarians, the spirit of Solomon Goldman and his blessed memory are with us.

Maurice Samuel with whom he had the intensest and longest sustained intellectual exchange and warmest personal friendship made this trenchant evaluation in the brilliant paper he submitted to Rabbi Heller:

> These last few days I reread much of what he wrote, and a single sentence keeps ringing again and again in my mind like some tremendous organ tone, the organ tone which opens his last great work, that unfinished symphony of

his, *The Book of Human Destiny.* He opens it with a gigantic utterance: "The Book of Genesis was the great clearing which the fashioners of the Jewish saga made in the jungle of primitive folklore." It is a tremendous utterance, and characteristic of the way his mind worked. He himself served a similar biblical purpose in the modern world; for his book created a great clearance in the modern jungle of Biblical criticism, and thrust aside to right and left all the rife and luxuriant growth of an excessive rationalism, to restore with rational faith the meaning of the Jewish saga. And trying to combine these two, and the memory of his tremendous meaning to us, and the pang of a personal separation, I am tempted to ask—everyone must ask— why could he not have lived another twenty or thirty years, as he seemed destined to? . . .

In his latter years he was greatly exercised by the tensions between certain Israeli views on the diaspora and the diaspora realities which those views ignored. It was bound to be so with one for whom the tremendous word *echad* applied equally to the Jewish people and to its God. He who had been a president of the Zionist Organization of America, and a zealot of the Jewish homeland all his life, found himself defending the right of the diaspora to exist. It might be better to say the Zionist duty than the right, for Israel without a powerful diaspora was to him, at best, a truncated Jewry. Moreover the two-thousand-year-old diaspora—and it was older than that—was in its way as remarkable an achievement as the recreation of the Jewish state. To belittle it, or to despise it, as some Israeli extremists did, was to acknowledge that for these two millenia the anti-Semites had been in the right; and if Israel, admittedly too small to contain more than an important, an indispensable, segment of world Jewry, turned its back on millions outside, it was negating itself. The diaspora was not only a reservoir for Israel; it was a mighty force in itself, twin-linked with Israel.

Rabbi Israel Levinthal, gifted *darshun,* offered an exquisite rabbinic homily from which we quote these passages:

Solomon Goldman was not only steeped in our classic literature of the past but also was blessed with an understanding of the time in which he lived and of the problems and the challenges of the new age and the new world which confronted the Jew. He was well versed in the wisdom of the modern world, the philosophy, the science and the literature of our day. And because he was so doubly blessed, he knew "what Israel ought to do." To make this Torah of the ancient past the dynamic force to guide and to rule our people today, was the supreme challenge of the hour, and to this task he dedicated his entire rabbinate and unreservedly devoted all his heavenly endowed gifts. It was the combination of these qualities that won for him the recognition not only of his congregants and of his immediate community but also of his colleagues in the rabbinate who sought his guidance and leadership. The rabbis translate the Biblical expression *hakohen hagadol m'echav*, "the priest that is highest among his brethren"[2]—*gadlehu mishel echav*, "his greatness shall come from the recognition of his brethren priests."[3] Rabbi Solomon Goldman won that recognition, and he was in truth *hakohen hagadol m'echav*.

Verily we speak of him as the ideal Rabbi, for as it was said of Rabbi Eliezer B. Shimon, it may be said of him, that "he was the *karava, tanaya, paitan v-darshan*"[4]—master of the Bible, profound student of Rabbinics, poet in literary style and preacher by the grace of God.

Alas, he was taken from us in the best years of his life, when he had so much yet to offer to his people and to his people's faith. When Rabbi Zeira died, his townsmen of Tiberias mourned his loss with the dirge: "Woe to her, saith Tiberias, for she lost her *k'le chemdata*, her precious jewel."[5] In mourning the death of Solomon Goldman, we too may say: "Woe to her, saith American Jewry, for she has lost her *k'le chemdata*."

Rabbi David Aaronson, distinguished conservative rabbi, who studied with Goldman at the Isaac Elchanan Yeshivah and later matriculated at the Jewish Theological Seminary with him, adds this rounded pebble to the memorial volume:

Possessed by the historic soul, Rabbi Goldman could not conceive Jewish life without a code. How he cried out against those who charged Jewish law with being soulless and unspiritual! "Where in the records of frail and mortal men," he asked, "does one find spirits and souls finer and nobler than our ancient rabbis—who reach the very zenith of saintliness and scholarship." The Jewish law, he insisted, was mainly responsible for the survival of the Jew. He had no quarrel with the law but with some of its latter-day exponents, with the "Gaonunculi," as he called them, the petty self-titled "geniuses," the self-appointed monopolists of the God of Israel and of His Torah, who would reduce God to their own image and place the Torah in a strait jacket. The new soul which possessed him told him that the Torah can and must be a living force. The old soul taught him that many of its expressions in the past were new in their day, and that the master builders of tradition were creatively alert to the spiritual needs of their day.

---

2. Leviticus 21:10.
3. Yoma 18 a.
4. Leviticus Rabbah 30:1
5. Megillah 6 a.

Can there be a synthesis between the old soul and the new? Rabbi Goldman answered in the affirmative. The fullest expression, he maintained, will be achieved in Israel. With all the labor and troubles and set-backs, there is yet a deepening of the spirit, he pointed out. There is a searching and groping for God, for new forms of religious life, of traditional life. The mood of anti-religion which some of the elders had brought with them from the lands of persecution, he believed, would dissolve in the land where Isaiah and Amos lived and taught. And he called our attention to the new editions of the Bible, the development of the Oneg Shabbat, the deepening attachment to the Book of Books and the free opportunities for the growth of Jewish justice.

The late distinguished educator, Emanuel Gamoran, contributed a tightly reasoned exposition of Goldman's immense contribution to Jewish education in preparing and publishing adequate textbooks and in the organization of the day school and the elaborate system of adult-education courses. We quote these lines from his essay:

> We look in vain for a statement formulating Dr. Goldman's philosophy of Jewish education. However, it can be found reflected in some of the essays which he wrote on different subjects. He said, "Hebrew is the index to the Jewish soul. The national spirit was preserved in the Hebrew language." He contrasted what was written in Arabic with what was written in Hebrew. The writings in Arabic were forgotten and survived only through the translations of the ibn Tibbons. What was written in Hebrew was preserved as the vehicle of Jewish life. In another passage he wrote, "Of late I returned once more to the pages of the *Tanach* seeking and not failing to find an element in the Jewish soul, a certain call which finds expression only in one language, namely, Hebrew. This call only Hebrew reveals. No other language preserved that essence, that flavor. I sense it in the first verse of Genesis and I feel it again instantly in the first page of Bialik. There is an unchanging eternal, the core, the essence of the Jewish people. In the magnificent works on Judaism written throughout the ages in a variety of languages I miss it, but it is in B'reshit, in Hamasmid, in the *Megilat haesh*. Even as I discover it in every page of Ahad-Ha-am."

Rabbi Felix Levy, rabbi of a neighboring Reform congregation and a former president of the Central Conference of American Rabbis, pays this generous tribute in the course of an extended analysis of his life and thought:

His life was the rabbinate, and in his life his congregation was always uppermost. No labor and no sacrifice were too great for it. It was a tremendous congregation, and great not only because of the number of families it held, but because of its leader and what he stood for. He wanted to make it a pattern community, that others might model themselves after, as he wanted his rabbinate to be a standard for others to emulate. Whatever else may have changed in his personality, his ideal of the rabbi was never diminished in grandeur and he never compromised in this quarter. He might fluctuate intellectually between humanism and theism, so that the congregation as well as he might at times be puzzled about his theology; he might attack Zionists and Haddassah for some failures, but he never ceased to be the noblest kind of Jew, whose Jewishness was evident in every word he wrote or spoke, or in every act he performed. Like Levi Yitschok, he loved his fellow Jews without stint and even when he criticized—as often he did—or when he got angry at some failure of high Jewish duty in the leaders—as he sometimes did—and would express his disappointment and ire—his chastisements were those of love. No one ever doubted his "Jewish" sincerity and integrity. Because of this he could take a small congregation and by sheer effort transform it into one of the great synagogues of the country, where he made Conservative Judaism, or his version of it, respected and even socially *comme il faut;* he broke across all Jewish boundaries and wanted to do what a few others before him, like Isaac Mayer Wise and Mordecai Kaplan, his contemporary, sought: to break down all barriers among American Jews, so that we would not be sectarian or denominationalist, but a united people; and unfortunately, like them, he did not succeed.

While these eulogists were all wise men, heedful of their words, one must make some allowance for that margin of generosity which survivors always extend to the deceased and for that benign permissiveness which the role of comforter imposes on those who speak of the dead. After two years of saturation in the writings and correspondence of Solomon Goldman, after many conversations with those who were associated with him, with the benefit of the ordering and sifting which the perspective of twenty years since his death affords, I would humbly offer this evaluation of the impact and influence of his life and work.

He was among the first American rabbis to see in the ethnic continuity of the Jews the unique contribution of Judaism to history and the key to the true nature of Jewish identity.

He had the courage to forsake the credit which many historians and theologians had conferred on the Jews for being the originators of monotheism. He advanced this conception in an outline of a one-volume history of the Jews which Harper's had urged him to write in 1925. Mordecai Kaplan elaborated this idea in his *Judaism as a Civilization* published in 1934. Kaplan had been gathering the material for his magnum opus for some twenty years, so it is difficult to determine who was teacher and who disciple in this instance. Both were instrumental in turning emphasis away from monotheism and the theological centeredness of Judaism to ethnicism and nationality.

Goldman was among the first to see the importance of the Hebrew language as the chief determinant of the ethnic character of the Jew. He early recognized what Maurice Samuel described as the traitor in every translator, and drew the proper inference from the fact that only that which had been written in Hebrew survived the winnowing of acculturation. It was this perception which led him to an alliance with A. H. Friedland to make the teaching of Hebrew viable to American Jews, and later convinced him that only in a day school could the Hebrew language and its rich freight of literature be successfully taught to the young.

Certainly there were many other scholars and rabbis who grasped the uniqueness and the glory of the Hebrew language, the incomparable profundity of the Hebrew Bible, the Messianic dimension of the land of Israel, but few, if any, were able to make these values the central conviction of their lives without becoming chauvinistic. Goldman could be passionate in advocacy while remaining generous and open in thought. He could appreciate the magnificence of the Biblical saga and the maturity of Jewish thought without denigrating the sensuous beauty of Homer and Praxiteles. He could recognize the centrality of Palestine in Jewish survival without disparaging or denying the Diaspora. He saw no contradiction or fuzziness of commitment in decorating the interior of the Anshe Emet synagogue with scenes from the Bible and from America's founding fathers. His refusal to write off the Diaspora made him persona non grata with some of the East European Zionist leaders, but it gave him access to other leaders—Louis D. Brandeis, Julian Mack, Robert Szold, Stephen Wise—and enabled him to persuade men like Albert

Lasker, Richard Mayer, and Samuel Goldsmith to take a more friendly attitude toward Zionist aspirations. Over a period of some ten years, Goldman was allied with Henry Montor in the difficult, often aggravating, struggle to convert the German-Jewish leaders of the Federation and Welfare Funds to a pro-Israel, if not a pro-Zionist, position. Where a Weitzmann or a Ben-Gurion could accept the cooperation of the American Jewish Committee as an atonement offering of assimilationist Jews, a last generous gesture before escaping into the mainstream, Goldman saw their pro-Palestine support as an omen of further interest in Jewish education and perhaps even in the synagogue.

As devoted as Goldman was to Jewish education, Jewish philanthropy, and Zionism, he was a synagogue-centered Jew. His impatience with abstract theology, his sometime flirtation with humanism, never shook his belief that the synagogue was historically and physically the incubating center of Jewish identity and commitment. He never permitted the community leaders or the civic and philanthropic agency professionals to use the synagogue as a spade to dig with or as a rostrum for their propaganda. Even Zionist leaders, Hadassah ladies, and Hebrew educators had to sublimate their causes to the larger purpose of the synagogue. He often urged his colleagues not to sell the precious birthright of the synagogue for a mess of kudos from the secular leaders or for a seat on a prestigious board. He bemoaned the fact that the paucity of knowledgeable Jewish laymen made it necessary for rabbis to assume leadership roles in B'nai B'rith, in Zionist organizations, in the philanthropies.

When he accepted the presidency of the Zionist Organization of America in 1938, he convinced his board that he considered this burden an extension of the pulpit, as the fulfillment of the act of return and redemption. Even though the congregation graciously granted him a leave of absence, he kept in close touch with its needs, often flying across the continent to guide the congregational leadership. The success of the secular organizations would never assure our survival as a people if the synagogue were allowed to decay, he believed. He made several desperate but abortive efforts to rally his colleagues in the Reform and Conservative rabbinate to recapture the educational and philanthropic roles which were once cen-

tered in the synagogue. He feared that the synagogue would wither
as lay leadership was drained to secular activities and that, eventually, these activities would become absorbed into the general
community without a rooted relationship to the historic institution
of purposeful Jewish survival—the synagogue.

He made no apology for giving the survival of the synagogue the
highest priority any more than he apologized for his own survival or
for the persistence of the Jewish people. In the pursuit of that
survival he refused to push Anshe Emet as an organization into the
fields of social action. He felt that until the Jew was sufficiently
grounded in his tradition, active partisanship in political and economic causes would divide the congregation and weaken it more
than it might strengthen the cause of political reform or social
justice. He was much more responsive to the objectives of Histadrut
in Israel than to the organized labor movement in America because,
he argued, the cooperative movement was building the context for
prophetic teachings in Israel with some conscious knowledge of the
relation of social reform to Jewish character—something not yet
available on the American scene. Furthermore, he was confident that
an effective Jewish education in the synagogue day school would
predispose Jews to enter into various fields of social and economic
reform, and ultimately make a more lasting contribution to the
welfare of the community.[6]

He was not dogmatic about this, however. He conceded that
direct involvement of a congregation in social action might lead to
good results. It was all a matter, he said, of gauging how fast one
can spend his spiritual capital. Goldman was prone to spend his
own emotional and physical reserves without stint—a rabbi who does
not burn himself out for his people is a poor rabbi, he admonished
the students at the Seminary. He was a bit more cautious about
spending the spiritual capital of Judaism. He turned away from
Reform and humanism on the ground that they would dissolve our
uniqueness into the universal air without assurance of making a

---

6. These sentiments are taken from notes of conversations I had with Goldman in
1952 when we discussed the feasibility of organizing a joint Anshe-Emet-KAM Synagogue in the north suburbs of Chicago to which many of the young families in both
congregations were moving.

difference in the general environment. He railed at Orthodoxy because in the interest of preservation, it had petrified the tradition and made it unavailable to the needs of living people.

It becomes apparent that Goldman gravitated from the priestly to the prophetic role and back again. The ambivalence is embraced, however, in his philosophy of intuitive rationalism, which he expounds so brilliantly in *The Jew and the Universe*. In his analysis of Maimonides, he discovered that the great rationalist became aware that the turbulence of life could not be caught in the neat categories of reason, that it was necessary to call on a faculty that was both above and below the plateau of logic, namely intuition. The harnessing of intuition to reason enabled one to capture somewhat more of the organic wholeness of life than could be embraced by either reason or intuition alone. This wholeness, this organic interrelatedness was best summed up in the human situation as personality. In personality is that fusion of instinct and logic, emotion and reason, internal and external which we recognize as that to which we respond in another human being. So, too, we find with Goldman that personality is the key to the understanding of his many-faceted talents and the complicated colorful pattern of his character. It was this that made him ask of the prophet in himself: Where does the abstract good of change, or reform, or revolution merge with the need for security and continuity in my life? It was this that made him ask of the priest in himself: Where does the rational good of security and tradition merge with the need for innovation and experimentation in my life? The aesthetic intuitionism of personality made him ask of the scholar in himself as he sat the long morning hours in his study: Where does the accumulation of knowledge, insight and philosophy merge with my need to relate to people with their personal fears and hopes? even as he asked in the daily routine of communal and organizational tasks: Where does this busyness merge with the need for contemplation and reasoned planning of priorities in my life? It was the quality of the mix, the remarkable way in which reason antidoted feeling and feeling mellowed logic that made the whole man, the man for all seasons, which gave his books the quality of human speech and his deeds the aura of animated logic.

Much as he loved his books and his study, he could not withstand the cry of human need that beat upon his door. Much as he relished the writing of a rounded, full-bodied sentence, the face-to-face encounter with men singly or in an audience was much more rewarding. Professors Schechter, Ginzberg, and Kaplan were all disappointed and saddened that he permitted pastoral and administrative duties to distract him from scholarly labors which they believed would have longer-range effects and add more substantially to his reputation. The call of personality to personality proved more compelling. Much as he savored the rich reward of seeing his name on the cover of a book, he remembered the phrase in the Book of Books—"And all that happened here, is it not written in the chronicle of the wars of the kings?" Much that happened—even of crucial significance—had been recorded in chronicles that were lost. That did not, however, cancel out the deeds. They were recorded in the bone and blood of men and women and became forever a part of the causative chain of events. For some rabbis, writing their record in the lives of people they serve is to write in water. For others, and Goldman was among them, it is part of an act of communion and sublimation, perhaps the profoundest confession of the *Shema* that can be made. So between writing and doing, he filled the hours of the days of his years—the blessed morning hours in his study slowly building up in him a need for people, while the afternoon and evening encounters with the various foibles and fevers and insoluble problems of men and women increased his hunger for the communion of books—so much more orderly and manageable. This see-saw became the most recurrent rhythm of his creative life.

The tendency of the masses to idolize the hero is one of the most corrupting forces in our society, often more lethal than the power of wealth. One who has known the heady power of public adulation often finds that he has lost, in the process, the desire and even the ability to relate on a one-to-one basis, person to person. The Goldman correspondence contains ample and eloquent testimony that the rabbi of Anshe Emet lost neither the desire nor the ability to make and maintain profound personal friendships. For him, friendship was an act of sacred obligation and of joyous opportunity. He was not satisfied merely to receive requests for assistance—"Come, speak

to my congregation"; "Persuade my board to give me a Sabbatical";
"Write a foreword to my book"; "Introduce me to your publisher";
"Review my book"; "Counsel my son"; "Comfort my wife." He
anticipated needs. A title or an excerpt of a sermon in a bulletin
moved him to encourage a colleague to do an article or a book on
the subject. A pessimistic theme or a sour editorial in another bulletin was a warning to him that his friend was sliding into a slough of
despond. As one of the founding directors of the National Hillel
Foundation of the B'nai B'rith, Goldman became the special friend
and pleader of those scholarly rabbis who were attracted to Hillel
because of the opportunity afforded to do academic work. When
they failed to do justice to the routine tasks of interesting unwilling
freshmen and cynical sophomores and were given warnings of sever-
ence, they came to Goldman to plead their cases. The files groan
with the burden of the letters between Goldman and the jeopardized
rabbis, between Goldman and the chairmen, between Goldman and
the other directors. He found himself coaching rabbis he had saved
to do a better job and finding pulpits for those he could not save.
Only a man to whom friendship was a sacred obligation could have
so frequently neglected or deferred his own work to heed these calls.

It was, however, not as patron-friend, but as congenial comrade of
the quest that he revealed the profoundest gifts for that communication and interplay, that give and take of thoughts and dreams and
hopes which bind one to another in such bonds of affection and
respect as to border on the province of that love which our patriarchal and puritan traditions reserve for the opposite sex. There was
a wholeness and a mutuality in these friendships that made them
creative and contributory. Goldman's alliance with the late Edward
Israel and with James Heller in the reformation of the Zionist
Organization led to collaboration on ways to reduce the barrier
between Reform and Conservative Judaism. His work with Mordecai Kaplan on the curriculum of the Jewish Theological Seminary
led to a long collaboration on the Reconstruction of Judaism.
Friendships, begun by virtue of some personal problem with a Judah
Goldin, a Jacob Agus, a Bernard Heller, led to fruitful exchanges
of ideas which added to the creative scholarship of American Jewry.

Friendship begun on the basis of literary collaboration with Maurice Samuel, Simon Halkin, Samuel Feigen, and A. H. Friedland, became closely personal, making him a grand patriarch gladly bearing the burden of family and even more gladly rejoicing in the glory of the works of his extended family.

Dedicated rabbis who burn themselves out for their people and their faith often take great toll from their immediate families. The pages of *Pastoral Psychology*[7] and the writings of psychiatrists generally are devoting more and more attention to the special problems of the minister's family. The burden of the pastor's wife as surrogate scapegoat of the congregation and of the pastor's children who must often share a father with all the children of the congregation is becoming a recurrent theme in the literature. It is no small tribute to Rabbi Goldman, and it may be most reassuring to young men who may be attracted to the rabbinate, that he offers the example of a busy, creative, dedicated rabbi who not only did not neglect his family but rather made them willing and cheerful collaborators in his ministry. Alice came from a traditional Jewish family. She inherited a profound respect for the position and role of the rabbi and considered it a matter of personal fortune and opportunity to assist her husband in his chosen vocation. She considered it normal, even challenging, that her home would become an adjunct to the synagogue, that she would be expected to serve as exemplar of a Jewish wife and mother and reveal by her personal conduct how important and honored were the Jewish precepts in her home and in the community.

In the early years of their marriage, Alice learned the difficult art of hearing "wiser" and older heads who insisted on bootlegging advice to the rabbi through her. "A wife and mother," they reminded her, "must keep her feet on the ground and know the price of groceries." "The rabbi has such beautiful thoughts and speaks so eloquently," they murmured, that "they simply did not have the heart to recall him to the facts of life." This task, they suggested, in a conspiratorial way, she must undertake. And there were incidents in the first years at Anshe Emet when Alice could admit to herself

---

7. A monthly magazine published in New York devoted to the problems of the pastorate in the organized church, in the hospitals and in the chaplaincy.

that the "friendly" counselors might have had a point. There was
that time when the rabbi had just made an appeal for a new sanctuary and, hearing no response, blurted out that he would himself
initiate the drive with a contribution of $5,000. This opened the
inhibited wellsprings of giving. But Alice had to remind him that
evening, when the sacerdotal *schnorer* was still basking in his glory,
that he had committed the total savings of the family. The rabbi,
Alice recalls, took sheepish recourse to an old adage that the Lord
sent the ravens to victual Elijah in the desert. She came, however,
to trust her husband's extravagances. She saw them in time as acts
of faith, as the proper style of a man who believed that acts of generosity were never so terrible as the gains of caution.

There were, of course, problems of privacy and priorities. It was
hard to establish fixed boundaries between the personal life of the
family and its congregational obligations. There were times when
pride in a great public figure and in the eloquent oracle of the
pulpit wore thin, and wife and daughters hungered for a more private, more accessible father. These moments were short-lived. They
were soon absorbed in the intellectual liveliness of the home and in
the never-failing joy of a father who shared his enthusiasms with his
family. Often he would come home from his study to read a marked
passage from the Bible or from Homer, from Josephus or Herodotus,
from Milton or Bialik. The burden of feeding distinguished guests
was often heavy but richly compensated for by the delightful conversation. The rabbi had a great gift for stimulating thinking people
to give their best, and for drawing the smaller streams of talk into
the larger waters where everyone could take part. His daughter
Gayola (now Mrs. Joseph Epstein) recalls an incident which is most
revealing. It happened in Cleveland where the rabbi's library was
shelved along a narrow hallway. Gayola learned to walk in that
hallway by grabbing hold of the shelves when she needed support.
She often found herself looking at the yellow binding of a book,
Fruits of Victory by Sir Norman Angell. By the time she was four
or five she had memorized the name of the author and the title of
the book. When Norman Angell came to speak to the Synagogue
Center Forum, he was a dinner guest at the Goldmans. When
introduced to Gayola, the five-year-old said, "O yes, you are the

author of *Fruits of Victory*." Sir Norman was convinced that he was
in a den of prodigies, nor did he permit mundane explanations to
shake him from that conviction. Naomi (now Mrs. Albert Zemel)
became involved in her father's intellectual pursuits and, often, with
her sister, chased references, checked sources, and prepared indices
for his books. The intellectual curiosity and concern for Judaism
of the father was caught not only by his daughters, but by their
children in turn.

Gayola offers this perceptive testimony to her father. It seems to
affirm the proposition that a great rabbi must first be a *mensch*:

> I think of father as protective, demanding, conscious and critical of faults
> and supportive and thoughtful all somehow rolled into one. I know that
> when he died and I was then married and the mother of two children, I
> very much felt the loss of a father. He was a very commanding presence in
> our lives at all times even when not there and very busy. From my earliest
> childhood he was intensely interested in selecting books for me. He took
> great pains in seeking out beautiful and unusual books for me and I can
> still see very vividly a beautiful book of Japanese fairy tales, a volume of
> Herodotus illustrated by Artzybasheff, a very fine set of all of Disraeli's novels
> that he sent to England to obtain, and Padraic Colum, and the Bastable
> Children by Nesbitt and many, many others. I was always aware that the
> world of the mind was most important to him and felt great guilt when I let
> him down in that area. He was also, however, interested in my appearance,
> and tried to make me aware of controlling my appetite (I was very fat) and
> he was the one who insisted that my Mother take me to a dermatologist when
> my skin broke out during adolescence. I suppose that what I always felt was
> that I was very important to him and even though he was very busy, he was
> giving a great deal of thought to me. We were always at the table or helping
> out and around the guests, no matter how important. Rowie Schwartz (S.D.'s
> wife) told me only recently when we saw her that she remembers vividly
> coming to our home when Daddy first arrived in Chicago (Naomi and I were
> 8 and 10) and how we waited on the table. Even as small children in Cleve-
> land when Bialik, Tszchernachovsky or Norman Angell were at the house
> we were always involved. I have been told that I sat on John Erskine's lap
> and that he told me stories; this I do not remember. When Chaim Weitzman
> came to Chicago and it was a very fancy affair at the Drake for a highly
> select group, as I recall, we were there. My 16th birthday is most illustrative;
> Daddy was going to Washington to see Justice Brandeis and we decided that
> that would be my birthday gift. First he was to go to St. Louis to speak at a
> Zionist meeting. We went and in St. Louis he sat me next to him at the

Speaker's table and next to a man who gave a few remarks. I wasn't aware until he told me years later that that man had been Harry Truman. (Truman was then a Senator.) We then went on to Washington. Daddy's appointment was at 9 in the morning and I remember arriving downstairs at five minutes to nine and standing there until precisely the hour before Daddy pressed the bell. I sat quietly during their whole conversation and it never occurred to me to ask if Daddy had asked permission to bring me. I may have been a complete surprise to the Justice. I never thought it a strange thing for him to do. I was always aware of his great love and pride in his children.

I remember the days that I was at the U. of Chicago and very involved with my radical friends. Some were Trotskyites and some Young Communist Leaguers. I never joined either group but was much influenced by their ideas. Daddy would discuss these with me but I was always completely outflanked because of his vastly superior knowledge of Marx, Engels, etc., but I never was made to feel that my espousal of them was wrong, just not sufficiently well-grounded. I was also, of course, anti-religious and this was never a problem between us. I never rebelled to the extent of being defiant of things like Seders, etc. which I adored, but tried to stay on campus on week-ends to miss Saturday morning services. But if I was home, I went. I would never have overtly hurt him, but he, on the other hand, never made us feel that as Rabbi's children it was our "duty."

He was quite strict with us and in our early years bedtime was strictly observed. We weren't allowed to go to the movies when we were very young (it was a waste of time) and were amongst the last to own a radio. Somehow I never resented these things and in a way repeated some of them with my own children. We were very tardy purchasers of a TV. People were always telling him what a shame it was that he had no sons but he would always answer that his daughters were interested in his work and that he considered himself lucky. I never realized that this might not be the whole truth until my son Jeremy was born and saw the ecstasy with which he greeted him. He absolutely adored him. Jeremy was 3 when my parents moved to the country and we spent much time out there in the summer. Although Jeremy was not quite 7 when Daddy died, he remembers him well, probably because they spent so much time together when we were out there. Jeremy would sit on a little chair in the library and draw or color while Daddy worked at his desk and would teach him Hebrew words for common objects. He told us when he was very little that Jeremy had a very good ear for language which has turned out to be quite true. They would lunch together and take naps on the two couches in the library. In the afternoon Daddy would take him out to the swings or sandbox which he had put on the grounds for him.

Death came too early to enable Goldman to write an ethical will in the manner of some of the medieval rabbis. He wrote it more subtly in the very air of his home and synagogue. Something radiated out from him that evoked in others a love of ideas and a respect for the pursuit of wisdom. He was a prophet with honor in his own home and in his own synagogue; an *ish tam*—a whole man. His personality was not a series of masks, but rather the radiant center of a happily wedded mind and heart. The public man and the private man were one man.

Chapter 7

The Legacy

THE EXTENSIVE WRITTEN RECORD and the memories of those who knew him conspire to create the image of a whole man—a man who sharpened immensely the gifts of Providence and acquired others congenial to his nature and responsive to the needs of the people he served.

In his warning against false prophets, Moses declared a rather simple test by which to distinguish the true from the false. If the thing prophesied comes to pass, he said, then the prophet was a true prophet. Goldman early recognized that the remarkable ethnic continuity of the Jewish people was a much more significant claim to uniqueness than its early acceptance of monotheism. He early foresaw the doom of Jewish collective existence in Eastern Europe and pleaded with the Federation leadership as early as 1925 that they concentrate on the settlement of Jews in Palestine. With Achad Ha'am, he was among the first to recognize that the Diaspora was here to stay and that, in order to create a mutually supportive two-way passage between *Eretz* and *Galut*, it was essential that Zionists recognize the ancient basis for the permanence of the dispersion, and that Diaspora Jews become seriously knowledgeable about Judaism.

He was a pioneer in the recognition of the crucial importance of

151

the mastery of the Hebrew language not only as a medium of communication between Jews but as an indispensable key to the understanding of those semi-historical, semi-mystical qualities of the collective Jewish experience and character.

He was the first of the Conservative and Reform rabbis to recognize the fact that neither the Sunday school nor the week-day Hebrew school would be able to convey adequately the essential facts or guiding purpose of the Jewish story to American Jewish youth.

What distinguished Goldman from others who accepted and advocated these judgments was that he embodied them in action. He gave them high priority in the programmed schedule of his daily work. He actually refused to campaign for remedial charity in the Pale of Settlement when Palestine was available as a more hopeful alternative. While Mordecai Kaplan spelled out with exquisite detail and clarity the Israel-centeredness of a viable Judaism, Goldman was meeting with the decision makers in many large communities to establish the ratio of allocation between local civic and charitable needs and Palestine-centered overseas needs. He accepted the onerous burden of the presidency of the American Zionist Organization to convert an almost moribund bureaucracy into a more effective instrument of the Zionist ideal. He was not satisfied to bemoan the inadequacy of the Sunday religious school or the three-afternoons-a-week Hebrew school. He set about organizing a day school which would place Jewish learning on a par with secular learning and provide a much better opportunity to integrate the value-forming and character-forming potential of both traditions—the Jewish and the American. Just as he refused to reject the Diaspora in frenetic abandonment to Israel, so he would not reject the adults in overcompensating guilt-ridden enthusiasm for the messiahship of the young. He set about to shore up and redeem the neglected, shallow Jewish education of those who were nominal Jews and still willing to bear the label of Jew. Therefore, he organized one of the most complete and far-reaching systems of adult education to be sponsored by any congregation in the land. He participated in the active teaching of classes—especially Hebrew classes, to satisfy himself that the adult Jew could successfully be brought back to the tradition of Talmud Torah.

But it is for the rabbis of America that the Goldman legacy may prove the most helpful. That is why we have subtitled this biography—*A Rabbi's Rabbi*. Goldman was intensely aware of the ambivalence, the undefined quality, the all-things-to-all-men nature of the non-Orthodox rabbi's role in America. The vast correspondence with President Louis Finkelstein, with Mordecai Kaplan, Milton Steinberg, and several hundred other rabbis, testify to his constant concern that the seminary training of American rabbis be adequate to their demanding many-faceted tasks. He was not satisfied that the curriculum merely provide the prescribed courses in Bible, Talmud, Midrash and the Codes, plus a few modern courses in pedagogy, philosophy, public speaking and pastoral psychology. He insisted that the seminary should be responsible for adequate guidelines to assist the rabbi in grasping the mood and the tempo of the evolution from traditional to modern forms of belief and practice. He would not permit the seminary to hide behind its ivory tower and let the push and pull of circumstances, especially the obduracy of Orthodoxy and the shallow radicalism of Reform, prescribe the areas of relevancy for Conservative Judaism. Even as he experimented with a new Code of Practice for his own synagogue, he was constantly in conference with colleagues, both Reform and Conservative, to establish some basic consensus of practice for Jews who were ready for a more meaningful commitment to Judaism. It was a matter of great disappointment to him that the creative genius of Mordecai Kaplan and his well-reasoned program of Reconstruction was not accepted by the Jewish Theological Seminary as the basis, at least, of a program for bringing Judaism into the twentieth century.

He did not permit this disappointment to discourage his own efforts to make Anshe Emet a model of what a synagogue could become in spite of the alienation of the majority of American Jews from the sources of authentic Jewishness, the critical intellectual revolt against all forms of organized religion, and the rampaging secularization of life in success-oriented, status-conscious, materialistic America.

Goldman firmly believed that the synagogue, which had survived two thousand years of transitional adjustment in a variety of national and cultural settings, must remain the central institution of the Jewish community. He considered it, at best, an evil necessity when the care of the poor, the sick, the orphaned, the education of the young, and the civic defense of the Jewish community were channeled into secular specialized agencies led by social work professionals and laymen from the business world who were seldom rooted in Jewish learning or Jewish commitment. He recognized that it was no longer possible to return these roles to the synagogue, but that it was possible for committed Jews to take over the leadership of these agencies so as to make them instruments of Jewish survival and identifiable examples of Jewish culture. He called upon his colleagues to guard against these agencies using the synagogue as a recruiting station for volunteers for their purposes and as campaigners for their funds—as a kind of glorified public relations and cheering squad for the civic, charity and defense organizations. He insisted that these causes be seen in their total relation to Jewish teachings and Jewish character. He demanded that even his Zionist colleagues restore Zionism to its profound religious roots before making the synagogue a Zionist membership promoter. While he spent many hours in personal conversation with community leaders to convince them that a strong synagogue was inherently the best guarantee of continued support for Jewish secular agencies, he spent equally long hours with colleagues and seminary heads working out the general principles for the kind of cooperation between synagogue and community agencies which would be mutually supportive and most conducive to the ultimate establishment of a survival-centered over-all community organization. His success with his own business and professional laymen encouraged him to counsel his colleagues to demand standards of Jewish knowledge and Jewish commitment from those who would undertake the honor and privilege of Jewish lay leadership. The character of his own leadership provided excellent testimony that the rabbi could do some of his most effective teaching in the councils of board meetings and committee meetings of Zionist, Federation, and defense agencies.

One cannot help but speculate on how Goldman might have faced the present challenge to the Jewish synagogue and to the

entire cluster of Jewish values in our tradition. The resident rebel
in him would have found much in common with many of our youthful dissenters. He could have given them rich Biblical precedents
from "Echoes and Allusions" and from many of his other writings
for their contempt of our joyless pursuit of wealth as the badge of
success, for our craven obedience to the status symbols of our market-
oriented society, for the conventional lies and outrageous falsifica-
tions of our commercial advertising and the mean subservience of
the communications media to the hustler's con artists. He would
have said a hearty "right on" to the young who accuse their elders
of giving a life for a living, of having lost the will and the art for
meaningful intimate rapport with their own families in their ambition to get to the top of the ladder in their business or profession.
He would applaud and aid their efforts to free themselves from the
phony ceremonialism and fake ritualism which corporate salesman-
ship and the etiquette high priests of the society columns have
imposed on our culture. In all their attacks on the idolatries of our
profit-seeking commercial Baalism, they would have found in Goldman an eager ally.

By the same token, they would have found him a tough adversary
in their rationalization of sexual freedom, in their abandonment of
family ties, in their simplistic devil theory of the Establishment, in
their acceptance of the strident ideologies of the New Left. (One
shudders to think of his reaction to the oft-repeated charges of
Imperialist Zionist Chauvinist Militarism); and most especially in
their cop-out through drugs or through deliberate isolation from the
still viable liberal, socialistic reformist elements in our society.

His deep understanding of the historic process of change, of the
styles of generation gaps, would have alerted him to the significance
of our young dissidents groping for religious roots, for beautiful
ceremonials to celebrate the gifts of nature and the ecstatic moments
of personal friendship and the old, old rite of love.

The humanist and intuitionist in him would have quickly tele-
graphed to him the relevance of Biblical poetry, of the Essenes, of
the Zohar and Hasidism to much of what the dissident young
are searching for. Builder of institutions though he was, he would
not hesitate to challenge the institutions to shape up, to find the

means and the methods to bridge the generation gap, whatever this may have required in decentralizing synagogues and centers or in the training of a new personnel for youth leadership. In his analysis of the commandment to keep the Sabbath, Goldman found in the concept of the Sabbath a turning away from the secular pressures of the daily grind, a restoration of the image of man as co-partner with God in the work of Creation, the presence of an opportunity once each week to regain the simple order of priorities by which a man becomes a mensch, the obligation to tune in on the rhythms of nature and breathe in the beauty, the harmony, the generous opulence, the built-in good sense of God's universe.

Our young people are in the wilderness of their discontent. They charge the Establishment people as the Israelites accused Moses, of luring them to a false promised land that they might die in the desert. They will not listen to any explanations because they have lost confidence in those who speak with authority and are most suspicious of the ability of anyone in authority to speak anything that could make sense to them. Sooner or later, as time blunts the sharp edge of their disillusion and their anger, as they continue to search for more positive binding principles than are now provided by hostility to the Establishment, as they begin to face the subtle task of harnessing a generalized love into the courtesies, the obligations and the disciplines of family and community, as they grope for an authentic folklore and folk-ceremonies to simplify and democratize those aesthetic raptures which great artists have generally provided for the privileged, they will reexamine the record of the past. They will look especially for those interpretations of literature and history which are instinct with a feeling for the glory and the tragedy of man who bears the poignant burden of mortality and the more corrosive yoke of boredom. They will look for those authors who not only have read the written record and evaluated it with all the tools of their science, but who have had inside themselves a wisdom of the heart, an intuitive reason to give just weight to the intangibles and to give to the truth of fact the resilient dimension of living reality. For those among them who will revisit the three-millenial Jewish story, the writings of Solomon Goldman will have much to tell. Those writings will break through their defenses for they speak with the passion of the lover and the seeker, the lover of man as God's creature and the seeker for that environmental order which might evoke man's Godlike qualities.

Many dissident Jewish youth discovered during the Six Day War, in 1967, that the ethnic tie with the people Israel was much stronger than religious or Marxist dogma and found it possible to apply for service in the Israeli army and failing that, to serve on the farms or in the factories. The threat to the Jewish State reached beyond and below the shallow canons of cosmopolitanism or the more structured internationalism of Marxism, or even the firm directives of absolute pacifism. The phenomenon adds another proof, if more were needed, to Goldman's thesis that ethnic continuity more than mono- theism is the true badge of all our tribe. The keen interest of many of our rebellious youth in Hasidism, an interest which has led some of them to the study of the Zohar, confirms the validity of Goldman's thesis that intuition, the sense of wholeness as implicit in personality, the uneasy synthesis of reason and feeling, of logic and irrationality as exemplified in folklore, is more honored in our tradition than is pure rationalism. Goldman's analysis of Maimonides' thought in his *The Jew and the Universe* entitled Maimonides to a place, together with Kierkegaard, Bonhoefer, and Buber on the reading list of the serious thoughtful young who are seeking a philosophical orienta- tion, an umbrella context for those guiding truths and principles with which they might forge some viable priorities for their lives.

There would be one area, however, where Goldman and the mod- ern rebellious generation might come to a parting of the ways. This modern generation holds to an apocalyptic view of revolution. Their refusal to cooperate, they say, will break the line of apprenticeship and our highly automated civilization will collapse from the mere absence of those who have the brains to prepare the input—or some trigger-happy president or commissar will push the button that will release the world-destroying missile. It will only remain for the sur- vivors, if some there be, to rebuild a better society on the scraps of earth that might remain viable.

Against this reasoning, Goldman would place what were for him the prototypes of successful revolutionaries, the prophets of Israel. They may have let the hair grow on their faces, they may have worn old tenting and abandoned sheepskins, they undoubtedly fed on wild berries and sunflower seeds; Goldman wrote:

> But there is no indication that any of them were at any time unhinged by millenial visions of wingy mysteries. They were, to be sure, possessed with what amounted to Mania, but their madness stemmed from God. Upheaved and over-mastered by Him, and not by idols or fetishes, they not only remained singularly free of irrelevances, delirium, and other worldliness but abhorred artificiality, theatrical enthusiasm, diseased sentimentalism, and hocus-pocus. Mystic in mind and ecstatic in mood they were, and most probably not strangers to auto-suggestion, but they never were caught away from the sober knowledge of the world and the normal experiences of mankind. Nature having removed her veil from them and displayed the true expression of her face, their soul was kept healthy by a constant reception of the truth. Thus they knew with distinctive clearness what they wanted to say and do and fixed their attention on the immediate political and social problems they wished to present to the people.[1]

The mysticism of today's rebel youth, like their drugs, is a cop-out, drop-out mysticism. Their soul food, their mind-expanding, their love-in outreach, tend to blur the edges, distort horizons, confuse goals, emasculate purpose and anaesthetize will. Not so with the prophets of Israel! This is the way Goldman saw them:[2]

> The uniqueness of the prophets consisted in that the iniquities and miseries of the race had become inequities and miseries for them and would not let them rest. Thus they did what no other group of men had ever done, certainly not in antiquity, they sustained for a long period of many generations the constant propulsion of an unbending will, an unflinching resolve, a single idea to desiccate the feculent well-springs of Baalism—the Baalism that polluted everything it touched, that debased religion to falsehood, perverted ritual into fashion, degraded prophecy to mere frenzy and hocus-pocus, and made associative living synonymous with oppression, violence and tyranny. The prophets acted . . . as if they had been summoned for no other purpose than to engage idolatry, in whatever shape or form it appeared, . . . blot out its beliefs and practices, and, in so doing, open up a clearance for a renovated society, or to put it in their own language, to give man a new heart and create a new heaven and a new earth. The fury with which they vented their discontent with evil, the tenacity with which they warred on it, and the self-

---

1. *The Book of Human Destiny*, Vol. I, p. 123.

assurance with which they anticipated a better world order remains unmatched to this day.[2]

Thus we complete another step toward the building of the immortality of Solomon Goldman—a task to which Maurice Samuel summoned us at the funeral services in May of 1953. We have striven to be loyal to the written record and to the comments and interpretations of many of those who were part of that record. They reveal an intellectually robust man, a passionate and dedicated man who made a difference in the temper and tenor of his time. He was one of a diminishing band who had his fingers on the pulse of the entire history and literature of Israel. He made the agonizingly difficult choice of limiting his scholarly research in order to put into practice some part of the values and insights of the civilization of Judaism. As the expansion of our knowledge further diminishes the possibility of the universal mind and ineluctably leaves the field to the specialist, the life and work of Solomon Goldman will offer a worthy model of wholeness—an example of how one man made himself master of a sizable portion of Jewish learning and fashioned an effective synthesis of thought and action, of mind and heart, of past and present, of East and West, Israel and America. To avoid the sin of pride, we speak too glibly of the expendability of any person. The legend of the *lamed vovnick*—the sacred thirty-six—is the folk attempt to restore our confidence in the far-reaching importance of the individual. The life of Solomon Goldman offers convincing testimony that one man in his time can make a gift without which his generation and those that come after would be much poorer indeed.

---

2. Ibid., p. 125.

PART II:
EXCERPTS

Appendix I

Excerpts from

The Book of Human Destiny

A. VOLUME I—THE BOOK OF BOOKS: AN INTRODUCTION

  1. *Out of Apostasies, wrestlings, and aspirations came the Bible*

The Bible is the outgrowth of the divine wrestlings, endless frustrations, and deep optimism of the Jewish people. It had its beginnings in the tales of a bold skeptic of whom it was recounted that, having rejected the beliefs universally adhered to in his day, he set out to transform the face of the earth. How he came by his skepticism or new faith is a question easier asked than answered. The past buries its secrets deep down beyond the reach of the archaeologist's spade or historian's acumen. Of this much we are certain: once, in the ancient world, there lived a Jew, or one whom the Jews came to regard and claim as their own who, repelled by idolatrous creeds and pagan practices, groped his way to a glimpse of the One God, perfect in all perfections.

His descendants, or at any rate some of them, brooded on this God with such constancy and concentration that it became the passion of their being to mold humanity in His likeness. Never again would they recognize progress or see any purpose in the dazzling civilizations upreared by the

163

empire builders and hoarders of wealth on the misery and poverty, sweat and blood of the slave, soldier and drudge. For they had discovered in the holiness of their father's God man's sanctity, his common origin and destiny; in His eternity the principle of the consistency of history; and in His goodness the coherence of humanity or the brotherhood of men. They desired nothing more out of life than to make of their people the agent that would bring the whole world to live by these insights.

The people responded readily and agreed to do and obey. It resolved never again to be like unto the nations—but could not abandon their ways. It accepted the Eternal as God—but upon every hill and under every green tree it erected altars to wood and stone. It urged that man was God's image—but it would not abolish slavery. It apprehended the vanity of life—but was tempted by the gold of Ophir. It longed for justice—righteousness had made Jerusalem its lodging-place—but, fond of bribes, it neither judged the orphan nor did it plead the cause of the widow. It looked forward to peace but periodically became enmeshed in the web of imperialistic ambitions of Egypt, Assyria, or Babylonia as the case might be. In a word, it dreamed and prophesied of the ideal society and even legislated for it, but never got down to build it.

—page ix

Yet, this disparity between faith and conduct, these habitual backslidings and innumerable frustrations, much as they tormented the people, never hardened into cynicism or pessimism. Israel wrestled with its conscience and no less with an inscrutable Providence that paid it double for all its sins. If it laid bare in its national literature its own evil doing with an openness and candor that no people was ever to emulate, it also demanded of the Judge of all the earth an accounting for chastising the innocent and making the guilty to prosper. It would neither desert its God, nor cease to vex Him; nor would it despair either of its own ultimate regeneration or of the salvation of mankind. And it was out of these apostasies and wrestlings and aspirations that the Bible came into being.

—page x

2. *The amazing vitality of Hebrew—its energy not exhausted by the flame*

The only other virile surviving Semitic language is Arabic, a member of the South branch. But we shall not find in it the clue to the riddle of Hebrew. Certain important contributions Arabic did indeed make to Hebrew. Arabic is a language of immeasurable richness, and the Arabs are prepared to proclaim its superiority above all the other tongues of the earth. Its verbs and nouns show high flexibility, and can be quickly adapted to any scientific or philosophical concept. Its syntax is equally elastic, and the Arab stylist interlaces primary and secondary clauses with the ingenuity and play of fancy that we find—not unnaturally—in the plastic creations of the Arab artist, and to which the proper name of arabesques has been given. It may well be that in the Bible itself there is the echo of more than one guttural, the reflection of more than one fantastic metaphor, originating in the desert spaces below Canaan. The imprints of Arabic on civilization at large are numerous, their distribution almost world wide. A single Arab book, *The Arabian Nights,* has become a universal source of amusement—if not always of edification. For centuries it served to inflame the wasted passions of princes and stir the dormant desires of paupers. The more visible influences of Arabic on Hebrew relate to the Middle Ages, when Hebrew philosophers and poets leaned heavily on the language. But that came late in the history of Hebrew; and what is more important to the pursuit of our theme, a language cannot impart that which it lacks itself. Despite its abounding wealth and its high refinement, Arabic is deficient in energy. All its fire is contained in its flame, and even the flame flickers at times, as in the pages of the Koran. But the energy of Hebrew is not exhausted by the flame; a deeper source of heat and power lies in the foundations of the language, like the latent fires heaped in the bowels of the volcano.

—page 2

3. *Five hundred root words—three primary sounds, two tenses*

The mystery of Hebrew deepens when we approach the technical side of its structure. "It is impossible to conceive anything more simple and unadorned" than the Hebrew language. Its grammatical resources are meager in the extreme. Etymologically it is no better off. It cannot boast of more than five hundred root words. Its vowel system is confined to three primary sounds, its verb to two tense forms. The formation of compounds, verbs or nouns, and the construction of rolling periods in such a medium is virtually impossible. The direct conquests of the Hebrew language, as distinguished from the indirect influence it has exerted through the translation of its supreme utterance, are nil. It never became the language of more than one people, and throughout the major part of its history, that people made Hebrew a sanctity walled off from the invigorating effects of secular usage. We are not even sure that the original pronunciation has been preserved correctly. The very name by which the language is now known, Ivrit, or Hebrew, is absent from the Bible, and remained unmentioned for fifteen hundred years after the records began. Of the cousins of Hebrew we have made mention; the grandmother of the language, the proto-Semitic type, disappeared so early that its existence must be assumed. . . .

By far the greater part of the Hebrew vocabulary consists of nouns and verbs. Of the other parts of speech we obtain only an occasional glimpse. Even the personal pronouns, which belong to the oldest component elements of the language, usually appear as appendages to nouns and verbs.

—pages 2–3

4. *A language of action—the thought is in the thing*

Most Hebrew nouns can themselves be traced back to

verbs. One can see them at a glance on any page of Hebrew he wishes to examine. For the general reader, the following illustrations may not be altogether without interest. The noun *azil*, nobleman, is derived from *azal*, set aside, separate; *be'ushim*, wild, bad grapes, from *ba'osh*, to spoil; *het*, a sin, from *hahate*, to miss (one's aim); *qeren*, a ray, from *qaron*, to shine; *mizbe'ah*, an altar, from *zavo'ah*, to sacrifice, slaughter; *ma'arav*, an ambush, from *arov*, to lurk; *ahuzah*, a possession, from *ahoz*, to take hold of; *zahav*, gold, from *zahov*, to be yellow; *ochel*, food, *ma'acholet*, a knife, from *achol*, to eat; *davar*, a word, from *dabber*, to speak; *sa'ir*, a he-goat, from *sa'or*, to be shaggy; *alumah*, a sheaf, from *allem*, to bind; *michtav*, a letter, from *katov*, to write; and finally, *melech*, a king, and *malkah*, a queen, from *maloch*, to rule. All the nouns, then, are verbal, and even as substantives they suggest movement and activity. The act lingers in the object, the effort of creation in the thing created, the inspiration in the achievement, the idea in the petrifact, the thought in the thing.   —pages 3–4

This is the source of the buoyancy and vividness of Hebrew, its natural animation and vividness, which in turn were bound to have a profound effect on the thought habits of the people. We shall yet come to the cause behind the source; meanwhile let us observe that they did their thinking in pictures rather than ideas simply because the ideas were implicit in the pictures. The words are so heavily freighted with emotional (or motional) overtones that even when they are used to convey philosophic concepts they are alive with the sensuous and the graphic. The Torah, said the Rabbis, speaks the language of the common man. They did not mean thereby that the Bible is devoid of psychological or philosophical reflections; they meant rather that it conveys these reflections by imagistic association rather than by syllogisms. Ideas are made to emerge as the accompaniment of the primary stuff of experience, of incidents and objects apprehended by the five senses; . . .   —page 4

5. *Not the form but the substance makes the Bible great*

The beauty of a land, however, and the virility of a language do not yet, by themselves, give birth to a great literature. The splendid rays of Palestine's sun gilded the tall cedars and towering mountains in the land aeons before Father Abraham began to trace his footprints on its hot sands; the Hebrew language, too, was fluent on the lips of Canaanites centuries before Moses carved its characters on the tables of the law, but the literary monuments of those ages, though constructed in Canaan and in Canaanitish, are devoid of beauty and dignity. No, the ineffable sublimity of the Hebrew Bible—sublimity, Coleridge said, was Hebrew by birth —and the divine pulses of its power are not the product of these outward causes but of a people's history and its religion. Hebrew literature is incomparably great because Hebrew writers employed the energy of their language and the dignity of their style on great themes. How true that is, even a hasty and casual comparison of the Bible with any part of Greek literature, the only other truly great literature of antiquity, will show.

pages 7–8

Only the utmost nobility of theme could have created so powerful a sequence of universal metaphors. It is to the theme that the Bible owes its unique place in the world's literature. Its authors were not poets of dalliance, weaving, out of the scenic beauty of their country and the strong language of their people, charming and gracious patterns. They were not concerned with tropes and rhetoric. They spoke under compulsion and poured themselves out with the unevenness and impetuosity of a torrent. They had a cause and they pursued it, or were driven by it relentlessly, breathlessly. If the intensity of mood made for disregard of the rules and refinements of composition, if it resulted in abrupt and precipitate turns of speech, violent changes of tenses, the Bible gained in exotic power what it may have forfeited in polish.

For it was unstudied, a by-product of the ultimate purpose and of the theme it rehearses; and it is thanks to the theme that the Hebrew Bible, even in translation, fans the imagination into a flame and remolds to its spirit languages unborn at the time of its writing.

—page 12

6. *Light on the prohibition of graven images*

This brief sketch, we hope, shows the presence of an art sense among the Jews no less keen or refined than that of any cultivated people. Perhaps no more need have been said than that the Pharisees, who despised idolatory vehemently and remembered with equal loathing both the cruelty and the degeneracy of Antiochus Epiphanes, the self-styled apostle of Hellenism, nevertheless admired Hellenic culture primarily for its beauty and the Greek people for their language. How, then, shall we explain the Second Commandment and the horror that the foremost representatives of the Jewish people, throughout many centuries, experienced in the presence of the plastic arts. The reasons for both lie deeper than is generally assumed, and we shall invite the reader to follow closely our exposition of the matter. For it is germane to a proper understanding not only of the Jewish religion but of the Bible as literature as well. The Jewish genius rebelled against art, as it was generally conceived and practiced, because of its identification with religion and the deleterious effect on morals that ensured from the apposition, and because of its limitation as a statement of reality.

—page 17

In the opinion of the Jew, this intimate relationship between the two was responsible for the worst evils of paganism. In the apotheosis of the image, he saw the beginning of the debasement of man and the degradation of life. He refused to believe that the generality of pagans were able to find in the physical representation of the forces of nature as celestial beings, and in the bold emphasis given to their sexual organs, any particular stimulus for the love of pure beauty, let alone for the worship of divine essence. One of the fathers of neo-paganism writes that "It is impossible for a human being to prostrate himself before a misshapen block of wood or piece of stone without losing all sense of the good together with that of the beautiful." Jewish experience was that the exquisiteness of the contours hardly made any difference. Idolatry was an abomination no matter what form it took. The author of the Wisdom of Solomon, who anticipated the modern view that art is born in leisure and who was certainly no enemy of beauty, testified that "the devising of idols was the beginning of fornication and the invention of them the corruption of life." That which moved the artist to fashion images or the skill with which he executed them was, the Jew suspected, of little concern to the people. Everywhere female divinities predominated, and "the taste of the multitude awoke to the lowest pleasures."

—pages 18–19

7. *The limitation of art as statement of truth*

But beyond the question of moral effect, the Jew further rejected form because of the ultimate inadequacy of the medium as a statement of truth. As long as the ancients confused it with religion, he resisted its witchery. It was not without a deep sense of loss perhaps that he sacrificed part of the enjoyment of the plastic arts, but he could not accept idols as a substitute for God, or allow imagery to veil reality. "Our intellectual love or understanding of the universe," Spinoza wrote, "is not possible if our view is limited to a single moment. Such a limitation may help us to form definite images but no adequate ideas. Ideas must not be viewed as lifeless pictures on a panel." The essence of matter, the nature of reason, the foundations of the earth, the heights of heaven, the surge of appetite, the tug of conscience are unfathomable and tormenting riddles. When men reach out for their solution, their horizon may widen—but it widens into infinite mystery. If, however, wisdom is Ptah, the vault of heaven Zeus, the earth Geb, and love Aphrodite, and these in turn are handmade, then the idea itself is vulgarized and superseded. And it is this narrowing of an idea or concept that is almost unavoidable in art. Confining its imitative effort to one single moment, art splits up reality, segregates an incident, episode, or phenomenon, and treats it as if it were self-sufficient. Self-inclusiveness or completeness is of great advantage to a work of art. To achieve it, the artist subjects inner essence to form, the form of accidental existence, disregarding all distinction between appearance and substance, existence and essence, the real and unreal. For art is not merely the reproduction of the actual or physical; it is interpretation or mood. Contradiction is therefore inherent in its very nature, since it must work with elements that it seeks to deny, transcend, or transform. The ordinary pagan and, not infrequently, the pagan artist were unaware of this contradiction, and became idolaters. They accepted form as a finality and worshiped it rather than the idea it symbolized. For the Jew, however, it was no more possible to see God in an immobile and finite symbol than he could have conceived of Him as nonexistent.

—page 21

8. *Monotheism as the source of metaphor*

And since he was incapable of or unwilling to express absolute Being in tangible, material, and lifeless form, the Jew learned, as compensation, to think and speak of it plastically in vivid, living images; to engrave it, as it were, in words. Mental and verbal plasticity had this advantage over physical form—it could not become an object of worship. It was too mutable, fluid, and interdependent with everything that exists to be regarded for more than a fleeting moment as a separate and fixed entity. Mental images, as instantly as they come into being, merge into the totality of existence; therefore, the Jew felt at liberty to exploit them, and Hebrew metaphors grew apace.

Another factor that contributed to the development of the Hebrew metaphor was the early evanescence of the myth among Jews. A polytheistic system of thought, by isolating and personifying phenomena and endowing each with an independent will, stimulates the growth of myths. When the sun and moon, wind and sea, wisdom and folly, love and hate are envisaged as separate persons, they are quite naturally imagined as being in perpetual conflict with one another. The heathen mythologies are little more than an account of the struggles that are said to have prevailed among both natural phenomena and human passions. Upon such a level of faith, myth and metaphor are as little distinguishable from each other as art is from religion on the same level. At this stage, the relationship between a concept and an image, which is expressed metaphorically, is one not of analogy but of identity. A "singing tree" is a metaphor only when the descriptive term "singing" is not "literally applicable" to a tree. But if the tree is a sprite capable of song, then the metaphor either ceases to be or else is one and the same with the myth. Such terms as "Mazda," "Lilith," "Limbo," "Dwarf," "Valhalla," "Lethe," and "Ambrosia" are, properly speaking, metaphorical only for those who have ceased to believe the myths underlying them. For the believer, they are not figures of speech but actualities. It is only when a monotheistic view of the universe purges the myth that it makes available a wealth of primitive, sensuous imagery as metaphor.

This is exactly what the Biblical writers did. They converted myths into metaphors. Instead of utilizing the plastic arts, they illumined and vitalized the nonhuman world through analogical comparison with the world of man. By restricting themselves to mental and verbal plasticity, the greatest seers and sages among the people were able to describe deity with amazing vividness and sensuousness, as father, friend, husband, guardian, and judge, and, at the same time retain the concept in its intellectual purity, transcendent and awful. And finally, without the myths to embarrass them, they felt free to speak of man as being the image of God, and of nature as His garment, and of God as all.

—pages 25–26

9. *Contra-Wellhausen—the Achilles' heel of Higher Criticism*

Nevertheless, the Achilles' heel (of the Higher Criticism) became visible when Wellhausen started it off on new adventures in the writing or, more precisely speaking, the rewriting of Jewish history. In the first place, students of comparative religion showed that his extreme view of a rectilinear evolution in religion was untenable. Ethnologists and folklorists revealed that they had discovered on the one hand, monotheistic trends among the most primitive of peoples and, on the other, periods of religious and cultural retrogression among those who had attained some degree of civilization. In the second place, as soon as archaeologists had pieced together some information about the ancient Near East it cut the ground from under his conception of Israel as an isolated Arab tribe. The structure, Kittel commented, lacked the foundation and the builder the gauge. Left only with its critico-literal methods to support it, Wellhausen's inferential reading of the Jewish past, carried to ridiculous extremes by some of his followers, was so much at variance with the as yet meager but factual evidence that it emboldened many a scholar to attack the whole critical problem anew. The methods these scholars applied and the results they achieved will be considered more or less in detail in the volumes on the Pentateuch and elsewhere in the present work. Here we can only record briefly in what manner they approached their task. Some of them merely replaced the "dominant hypothesis" by one of their own, others were satisfied only to expose its errors, and still others rejected it altogether with the triumphant cry of *Los von Wellhausen* (Away from Wellhausen)!

—pages 51–52

10. *The corrective work of B. Jakob and U. Cassuto*

Most recently B. Jakob and U. Cassuto undertook in their

impressive commentaries on Genesis to cut up the Graf-
Wellhausen hypothesis root and branch. Both of them have
examined to the minutest detail the difficulties it was invoked
to remove, and attempted to explain them without its aid.
Jakob, the more conservative and less methodical of the two,
accepts practically no theory of documents whatsoever. The
most he will concede to the critics, it seems, is that the author
of the Pentateuch made use of such earlier sources as the
Sepher ha-Yashar, Milhamot ha-Shem, and others to which
reference is made in the Torah itself. Respecting the Book of
Genesis he is convinced that it emanated from one source and
author who, favored by Divine Revelation, conceived and
executed it alone as a uniform coherent whole. Cassuto, on
the other hand, though he rejects practically all of the critical
criteria of the Wellhausen school, comes dangerously close to
formulating a Fragmenten-hypothese of his own. Discovering, as he believes to have done, traces of oral and written
traditions that go back to the earliest beginnings of the Jewish people, even in such post-Biblical works as the Book of
Jubilees and the *Midrash Rabba* on Genesis, he maintains
that they were woven together in the closing years of King
David's reign, in the Book of Genesis, by a religious and literary genius of the first rank. He would make no allowances
for any interpolations of a later date.

Starting out with the assumption that the Tetragrammaton
and Elohim were never used interchangeably, he asks, is
it conceivable that the Torah, whose chief purpose it was
to lead men to know and love God, would have varied
His Names arbitrarily without characterizing scrupulously
and accurately the subtle nuances of His Being and Essence?
Shall we assume that the writer of the Torah was some indo-
lent scribbler who listlessly allowed his pen to dash off the
Names of Deity at will? Such supposition, Cassuto asserts, is
inadmissible, and he proceeds to differentiate between the
respective connotations of Elohim and the Tetragrammaton.
The former, he propounds, is essentially a collective or appel-
lative name, common, to the One God and to the numerous

heathen deities. The term "city" in Hebrew literature, he offers by way of illustration, at one time designated any city and more particularly the city of Jerusalem. The Tetragrammaton, on the other hand, was a proper name and was reserved for the One God in His perculiar relation to Israel.

—page 54

11. *How archaeology refutes the fragment-hypothesis*

The archaeological material that illustrates and substantiates the Biblical narratives will be best cited as parallels to them in their place. Here it is sufficient to point out in a general way that it is "enough to disprove any radical reconstruction" of the early Jewish past. Nothing, to be sure, has as yet been excavated to confirm definitely the existence of Abraham, but, on the other hand, everything that the spade has thrust up makes its negation somewhat of a strain on the most plausible of critical hypotheses. The tradition of "his birth at Ur may be fearlessly accepted . . . his sojourn there may have been under the reign of Rim-Sin or Hammurabi . . . his traditional journeying from Ur to Haran does in fact broadly correspond with a general northward transfer of the Habiru or Hebrew peoples from Southern Babylonia where they are first mentioned in secular literature." We may speak, as we shall see in the volume on Genesis, with no less assurance of the existence of the other Patriarchs. . . .

A word should also be said in this place about Moses, whom the Wellhausen school has either converted into a myth or made out to have been a superstitious devotee of a volcanic deity. To confute them, we need do no more than quote the authoritative opinion of Professor Albright, arrived at after careful weighing of the latest archaeological discoveries. "The Mosaic tradition," he writes, "is so consistent, so well attested by different pentateuchal documents and so congruent with our independent knowledge of the Near East in the late second millennium B.C., that only hypercritical pseudo-rationalism can reject its essential historicity."

—page 67

12. *From the* Dawn of Conscience *to* Mein Kampf

The Germans had their triumph. The acceptance of a
regnant hypothesis or the devising of a new one had become
the only criterion for Biblical scholarship. Unfortunately,
not all the critics have as yet rid themselves of this baneful
superstition and its ruinous consequences.

That they have not as yet done so has been due in not a
few instances to their receptivity to anti-Semitism. Someone
has well said that Hegel begat Vatke, Vatke begat Wellhausen, and Wellhausen begat Delitzsch. It may now be added
that Delitzsch begat *Die Grosse Tauschung, Die Grosse Tauschung* begat *Fort mit dem Alten Testament,* and that all of
them together had no little share in the composition of *Mein
Kampf.* So many of the critics have been led and misled by
their prejudices. In the foreground or background of their
labors there seems to have been present, consciously or otherwise, the motive to "dissipate the nimbus of the chosen people." And they have, interestingly enough, often followed a
pattern that left little room for doubt as to their intention.
It must be more than a coincidence that Wellhausen, Delitzsch, and Breasted, for example, should have each begun by
selecting a people upon whose head they placed the halo that
history had for centuries bestowed upon the Jews, then exposing the latter's lack of originality and inherent baseness and,
finally, bringing the thesis to an end with a paean to Jesus.
"Hail to thee, thou hill of Babel," Delitzsch began his apos-
trophe to the Babylonians, "and to all thy fellows on the
palm-bordered banks of the Euphrates." Then he showed that
the Jews were nothing more than hucksters, imitators, and
plagiarists. They did have a few prophets and psalmists, but
they were completely overshadowed by a Galilean who was
most likely not of Semitic, that is, of Jewish, origin. It was
he who "put aside the barriers which a particularistic national religion had erected between God and the world. . . .
He made an end of all external legality and hypocrisy." And
in a triumphant closing paragraph, Delitzsch subtly hinted
whence Jesus derived his inspiration. "When we search," he

concludes his *Babel und Bibel,* "the ancient Babylonian world and see the leading spirits of Babylon endeavoring with earnest zeal, even with fear and trembling to seek God and the Truth, we can joyously welcome the fact that the Evangelist granted to the Babylonian Wise Men to be the first to offer their homage at the cradle of the Christian faith."

In the *Dawn of Conscience,* Professor Breasted did little more than substitute the Egyptians for the Babylonians. And he too was able, so amenable are the laws of Biblical Criticism, to cite Scripture as proof. "It is not merely accidental coincidence," he wrote toward the end of his book, "that Hebrew history should have traced Hebrew national origins back to Egypt, a tradition of which there is an echo in the Christian belief, 'Out of Egypt have I called my son.'" It undoubtedly took much more than critical acumen on the part of Professor Breasted to find, in this simple verse from the Gospels, support for his Egyptian hypothesis.

Blessed are the dead, for they shall inherit the good will of the professors. As the ancient world was dug out from under the debris of millennia, the critics were ready to allow originality to any and all the peoples of the past, but not to the one surviving Israel. Any scrap or potsherd that the archaeologist's spade brought to light loomed large in their eyes as irrefutable evidence against Jewish creativity. It is when we consider what scholars have done with the discoveries in other than Biblical fields that we realize fully to what extent we have to do here with prejudice rather than science. The work of Schliemann and Evans, in Crete, to take only one example, has been used to glorify Greece and not to deny it originality and deride and besmirch it. And yet the contribution of the Aegean Mycenaean civilization was great and its imprint on Hellenism indelible.

—pages 72–73

13. *Psalm 104 vs. Ikhnaton's Hymn*

Were we to have only Professor Breasted's version, couched as it is intentionally in the Biblical idiom, we might actually believe that it goes back to an original of which the Psalm is a copy. When we turn to Professor Erman's rendition, free as it is from Biblical coloring, the gap between the Hymn and the Psalm yawns wide. It is true that they have in common a number of figures of speech, but that in no way means that one is dependent on the other. Poets of the remotest countries and times are wont to employ like metaphors and similes. The sun, beasts, men, sleeping, rising, labor, pain, food, and childbirth are the same everywhere. And as for Egypt and Palestine, their general climate and physical conditions were not so divergent as to have precluded the possibility of accidental resemblance in the "nature" poetry.

But the resemblance between the Psalm and Hymn under discussion is as nothing when compared with the essential difference between them. In the former the sun is no more than one of many bodies and substances which pay homage to the Eternal God, and which despite its mass and magnificence is a toy in His mighty Hand. Underlying the Psalm there is a concept of Personality which is separate and distinct from the whole world and the fullness thereof. On the other hand, in the Hymn the sun is and remains a god. It is supreme and creative, but the sun nevertheless. He is said to be "in the horizon of heaven"; he "glistens"; "his rays encompass the land; when he goes down, the earth is in darkness"; the people praise his "arising." All these physical properties are inherent in him because he is the sun, and the blessings that emanate from him do so for the same reason. He has neither will nor purpose, nor is he endowed with personality. Whatever he achieves for man or the world is involuntary and undesigned. The Hymn might well have been written by a sun worshiper.

So much, then, for the influence of the Egyptian Hymn on the Hebrew psalm. As far as Ikhnaton's "monotheism" is concerned, three things should be remembered. First, that the worship of the sun as the supreme deity was well-nigh universal and, in the opinion of several distinguished Egyptologists, Professor Breasted to the contrary notwithstanding, Ikhnaton's religion was little else than a refined solar religion; second, that the application by Egyptians of cosmic and ethical superlatives to the gods has no particular significance, for they applied them also to a variety and multiplicity of persons and things; finally, that Ikhnaton's reformation was more political in character than religious.

—pages 83–84

14. *The Hebrews were not born too late to be original*

"The religion of Israel revolted against virtually every external aspect of Egyptian religion, including the complex and grotesque iconography, the domination of daily life in the Nineteenth Dynasty by magic, the materialistic absorption in preparing for a selfish existence in the hereafter." It was the distinctive glory of the Hebrew faith, that it had power to throw off all kinds of superstition. . . . The Hebrews were brilliant iconoclasts." In that alone the Jews' originality was already apparent. For as he apprehended the inadequacy and folly of a polytheistic world order and refused to compromise with it, a new light entered his eyes and he beheld more clearly than anyone else the one God in all His Glory. And thanks to this Vision, his prophets and psalmists, his poets and sages were endowed and possessed of a loftiness of purpose and intensity of passion uniquely their own. To say the least—and those free from prejudice always have and always will recognize it—there is as much relationship between the literatures of the Babylonians, Egyptians, Hittites, Amorites, and Phoenicians and the Bible which the Jews have given to the world as there is between the Cretan myths and the majesty of Homer's *Iliad*, between the Italian novellae and the ineffable beauty of Shakespeare's dramas, between the love stories of the Florentines and Dante's *Divine Comedy*.

—page 103

15. *What do people carry away from the Bible?*

The Bible was, to begin with, the common solace of mankind in all its travails and cares, helping all who came to it, to an extent such as nothing else apparently ever did, to live above the ill-tempers and sorrows of life. To the weak as to the strong, to the simple as to the wise, and to the humble as to the proud, to each after the manner he required it to be, it was a very present haven against the tempest outside and the best of comforters through every change of fortune. An Abraham Lincoln, for example, recommended it amidst the unquiet thoughts and tumults of civil war, as "the best cure for the blues." A Robinson Crusoe, not an overly religious man, found it, in the utter solitude that compassed him about, an understanding and animating companion. In times of adversity, it has been well said, Christians again become Hebrew, that is, they fix upon the Bible in preference to their various national literatures or the Greek and Roman legacies. For by inculcating the steadfast assurance that God was near to all those who called upon Him, and pitied them as a father pitied his children, His anger lasting only for a moment and His kindness forever, and by further holding out, with un-flagging and unswerving persistency, the hope that God would crush evil and reward good, the inspired writing could be counted upon to replenish faith, make resolution firm and inflexible, and brace and nerve men to smile confidently at misfortune, tyranny, death—at all the horrors of Hades. What support have not even martyrs at the stake found in words such as these:

> Yet I am always with Thee;
> Thou holdest my right hand.
> By Thy counsel Thou leadest me;
> Thou wilt bring me near Thee in honor.
> Whom have I in heaven but Thee?
> And there is none upon earth that I desire beside Thee.
> My flesh and my heart fail;
> But my heart's rock and my portion is
>   God forever.

—page 106

16. *The Bible as the common man's philosopher*

It is a truism that the ordinary man—indeed, it was true even of early man though he never progressed in his thinking beyond the mythopoeic—no less than the profound philosopher is curious about the origin of things, that he, too, desires to know where the world came from, what the beginnings of the human race were, and where it is headed. Indeed, he can less easily banish an unanswered question than he can silence an unfulfilled desire. True, his curiosity is more easily satisfied by fantasy than by reason. Since either for indolence he will not or because of ignorance he cannot pursue an inquiry patiently and enduringly. But some kind of an answer he must have, and it must be one that he can grasp and feel and weave into the pattern of his daily experience. And this was exactly what Biblical wisdom offered him. It supplied him with a concrete and tangible world view in a simple, precise, and understandable way almost wholly unencumbered by philosophical abstractions and abstruse formulations. . . .

What the Bible actually did was to make explicit that which was already implicit within their mind. It organized their experience in the light of a few simple ideas, coordinated their subconscious perception, and transfigured and fused their unreflective awareness into intelligible and sublime expression. If they believed in it it was only because it spoke their mind.

—pages 107–109

17. *The genius for making universality concrete*

For by identifying [Israel's] views of the universe with and embodying them in the career of a people, it put sinews upon and covered with flesh what might otherwise have turned to be an abstract ideology. As it is, it converted philosophy and religion into a living story, into great literature.

—page 116

They were masters of the word these Judeans, adepts at

inventing the forms of sensations or thoughts and creating visions, images, or phrases that touched the chords of the heart to exactest nicety. Endowed with a native gift of observation and taking their illustrations from what was near at hand, from things natural and congruous, perceptible and tangible, they expressed the impact of experience on consciousness fully and concretely. But, though their work bears the imprint and superscription of their surroundings and time, it is stamped with the likeness of no particular place or time. For, whereas most pagan writers of antiquity generally were satisfied to present the object itself, the Biblical writers were more eager to represent what it implied, and as preparatory and prospective. Even the Greek masters, Homer not excluded, seem to have aimed at reproducing the object complete, inclusive, finished, abounding in everything that might conceivably be said of it, congealed into its unalterable identity, and imprisoned in a continuous present, fearful lest the reproduction be lacking in a single shade of color or nuance of sound or thread of texture. The Judeans, on the other hand, fashioned illustrative fragments, carved out symbolic torsos, and left them *res infectae*, that is, unfinished, mutable, a kind of restless, prying question marks. This undoubtedly accounts for the dynamic, pervasive, and suggestive quality of their language, its sensory and emotional associations, and the ease with which it has evoked out of the minds of men infinite worlds of beauty and thought.

—pages 116–117

18. *The Prophets—God's word the torment in their breast.*

Blissfully ignorant of what we have come to designate as the creative urge, conscious of words only as existents and not as a choice vocabulary painfully acquired, they knew only that God stirred them up, taught their lips to speak, guided their pen, and that His word, the tormenting inmate of their breast, the burning fire shut up in their bones, could not be held in but had to be communicated. So absolute was their identification with Him, so complete their self-effacement, that no idea flitted across their imagination or word left their mouth but they attributed it to His grace. Whether, then, or not we study the Bible as literature, it must be borne in mind that those who created it were exclusively absorbed in their message and its divine promptings, its form coming about incidentally, the accessory conforming to the essential, beautiful means wooing blessed ends.

That such fervid intensity of mood and rapture of mind would in themselves arouse interest and challenge attention goes without saying. Certainly no one doubts that the serious and passionate urgency with which the prophets had spoken have drawn thousands to the Bible, their inward and desperate drunkenness of conviction and frenzied courage having awed, baffled and intrigued the ordinary and enlightened alike. The common man gaped in wonderment at these men who stood out like mountain peaks from a range, who, out of sheer sympathy for him, had defied kings and lashed the rich. The contemplative marveled at the drive for a better social order, the hunger and thirst after righteousness, and the freeing and expansion of consciousness of a poor shepherd boy born on the edge of a desert, of a court-pampered youth, and of another raised in the narrow confines of a priestly family. From where, he sought to understand, had emanated their supreme concern with questions that go down to the ground of our existence? How, he reflected, had they carved out of their humble experiences the distant destiny of the race, or merged and incorporated the remotest future in their limited present?

—pages 121–122

19. *The quintessential truth of prophecy*

To begin with, it may be stated emphatically that their distinctiveness lay elsewhere than in necromancy or the predictive element. They were not foretellers, they were *neviim*, men who spoke out or burst forth. When they delved into the future it was not for the purpose of exploring its secrets but for that of pondering over its admonitions. There is not the slightest indication that any of them were at any time unhinged by millennial visions or wingy mysteries. They were, to be sure, possessed with what amounted to mania, but their madness, as we have seen to be the case with their eloquence, stemmed from God. Upheaved and over-mastered by Him, and not by idols or fetishes, they not only remained singularly free of irrelevancies, delirium, and other-worldliness but abhorred artificiality, theatrical enthusiasm, diseased sentimentalism, and hocus-pocus. Mystic of mind and ecstatic in mood they unquestionably were and most probably not altogether strangers to autosuggestion, but they never were caught away from the sober knowledge of the world and the normal experience of mankind. Nature having removed her veil for them and displayed the true expression of her face, their soul was kept healthy by a constant recep-tion of the truth. Thus they knew with distinctive clearness what they wanted to say and do and concentrated and fixed their attention on the immediate political and social prob-lems they wished to present to the people. If ever of anyone, it certainly might have been said of them that "God when He makes the prophet does not unmake the man." . . .

—page 123

Finally, the uniqueness of the prophets consisted in that the iniquities and miseries of the race had become iniquities and miseries for them and would not let them rest. Thus they did what no other group of men had ever done, certainly not in antiquity; they sustained for a long period of many generations the constant propulsion of an unbending will, an unflinching resolve, a single idea to desiccate the feculent wellsprings of Baalism—the Baalism that polluted everything it touched like a desolating pestilence, that debased religion to falsehood, delusion, and a congeries of superstitions, per-verted ritual into fashion, licentiousness, and a vortex of pleasure, degraded prophecy to mere frenzy and hocus-pocus, and made associative living synonymous with oppression, vio-lence, and tyranny. The prophets acted throughout their

days as if this was the beginning and end of their mission, as
if they had been summoned for no other purpose than to
engage idolatry, under whatever shape or form it appeared,
in a struggle to the death, to strip it of its imposing air,
vanquish its vain pride, blot out its belief and practices, and,
in so doing, open up a clearance for a renovated society, or,
to put it in their own language, to give man a new heart and
create a new heaven and a new earth. No one doubts but that
the fury with which they vented their discontent with evil,
the tenacity with which they warred on it, and the self-
assurance with which they anticipated a better world order
have remained unmatched to this day.

—page 125

B. Volume II—In the Beginning

1. *The clearing in the jungle of primitive folklore*

The Book of Genesis is the great clearing which the fashioners of the Jewish saga made in the jungle of primitive
folklore. In man's earliest account of beginnings nature
emerges as a vast and tangled expanse of dark forces; and the
first myths which tried to separate things out as autonomous
entities only peopled the world with a multiplicity of fantastic creatures, each with an appellation and symbol of its
own. For all these beings, including gods which were set
forth as having created the world by word of mouth, had no
identity apart from the powers they manifested or personi-
fied. The myths did not probe deep, neither did they reach
out beyond the tangible and visible. In Genesis, for the first
time, the physical universe ceases to be identical with the
universe of reality. The Deity stands forth transcendent; nature, whether perceived as animate, or an automaton, is contained within God, the only ultimate spiritual or personal
reality.

In the myths, the gods were portrayed as vulgar, spiteful,
cantankerous, perverse, and cruel—all as men made them
after the likeness of their own weak and erring flesh. And
since the worshiper is rarely better than the object of his

worship, such distorted notions of deity were bound to have a deleterious effect on behavior. In Genesis, God is perfection, as perfect as the noblest tendencies of the human heart could make Him. And since, again in Genesis, man is created in God's image, it may be supposed to have been assumed that his highest aspirations were to emulate his Creator.

In the myths, creation was represented either as a bloody triumph on the field of battle or as conceiving and begetting. For the gods, that is, the physical phenomena or human instincts they symbolized, were taken to be belligerent and amorous, forever fighting and making love. In Genesis, the absolute Oneness of God put an end to celestial strife and romance and refined and purified the creative process. God spoke and the world was.

In the myths, the orderliness of the universe was at the mercy of wayward and whimsical gods and goddesses, and the destiny of man, in so far as it was given any attention, was enmeshed in a web of fetishism and sorcery. In Genesis, nature and man are subject only to the immutable will of God and as for thaumaturgy, necromancy, and all the hocus-pocus of magic or witchcraft there is hardly a trace of them.

—page xi

2. *Abraham and Captain John Smith—two immigrants*

Such great dissimilarity of one account of beginnings with all the rest cannot be the result of accident. Nor can it any longer be attributed to ignorance on the part of the forefathers of the Jewish people of the folklore of their surroundings. The Hebrews, or whatever we call them, did not enter the stage of history as barbarians, no more than did the Puritan Fathers. The former like the latter had their childhood in the bosom of another people. The one and the other were full-grown when they disengaged themselves from their kin, and in possession of their share in the heritage of the race. Abraham (if such a man ever existed in Haran or Ur of the Chaldees—and the evidence against his historicity is far from

convincing) had in his native land every opportunity to
acquire knowledge that, let us say, Captain John Smith had
in England. He would have heard the myths recounted
orally or seen them in iconic representations in all of his
sojournings. Genesis leaves little doubt but that that was true
of its authors. For its very language is impressed with the
contemporary idiom. Even to designate the Deity, it employed a word of common usage.

No! Neither ignorance of the myths nor accident will explain why the Biblical narrator substituted for the primeval
sea monster Tiamat and all her adventures with Apsu and
her combats with Marduk the docile, unobtrusive Hebrew
monosyllable *t'hom* meaning "abyss." We are in a new world
when we go from the *Enûma elish* to this account. It is Jewish genius brooding on God. It is the progenitors of the
Jewish people examining and discarding the views of Creator
and creation universally held in their day. It was an upheaval
in the mind and conscience of man that occasioned the differences between the Biblical and the pagan narratives.

—pages xii–xiii

3. *Archaeology retrieves the historicity of Genesis*

But whatever the reasons, this much is certain—our general ignorance of the ancient Near East had given conjecture
and guesswork an air of plausibility. For at the time when
the critical exposition of the Bible began, little more was
known of that part of the world than was contained in the
sporadic and obscure Biblical references to it, in the contradictory quotations from Manetho, the Egyptian priest who
wrote a history of his native land about the middle of the
third century before the Common Era; in the uncritical works
of the Greeks and the Romans; and in the weird tales of
mediaeval travelers. The critics, no less than the generality
of men in those days, looked upon the Bible as having come
into being in a historical and literary vacuum and on the
Bible lands as having been occupied by illiterate, semino-
madic hordes. The testimony that the heaven-high pyramids

were offering to the grandeur of ancient Egypt was not enough to dissolve the darkness that otherwise enveloped it as well as the whole Mesopotamian Valley, and which, as far as the critics were concerned, also dimmed the light of Palestine. They were certainly not disposed to make an exception of the Jews, and proceeded to the study of the Bible with the conviction that the children of Israel had been as illiterate, idolatrous, and primitive as all their neighbors were assumed to have been, and that no Jew, practically up to the time of Amos let alone the generations from Abraham to Moses, ever would have thought of putting pen to paper. How, then, were they to explain the narratives of the Patriarchs except as constituting the happenings of a much later age that were projected backwards into an unrecorded past of which there had remained only the flimsiest tribal recollections, and which the prophets and priests employed to provide Israel with a unique ancestry and history.

—pages 63–64

4. *The restoration of the Bible to its original setting*

If, in more recent years, scholars have begun to modify their extreme views, our thanks are largely due to the patient toil and uncommon ingenuity of a galaxy of archaeologists who, by rediscovering the ancient Near East, have lifted the Bible out of its isolation and thrown it into a fresh perspective. We are now in a position to know that the long eras and vast areas once assumed to have been barren of civilization had in reality been far advanced in the arts of life, and that that was true not alone of Egypt, Babylonia and Phoenicia, whose might or fame or both we might have conjectured from the pages of the Bible or the classic writers but also of peoples who are never mentioned or are only names there, such as the Hittites, Canaanites, Amorites, Hurrians, or Mitannians. What is of special interest to us is that some of these latter peoples who were either indigenous to Palestine or had settled there in pre-historic times, or were its close neighbors, and whose mother tongues were akin to Hebrew, or almost indistinguishable from it, were far advanced in the arts and literature already in the third and second millennia B.C.E., and that already then they employed an alphabetic script. Little wonder that their unearthed remains should have made possible the restoration of the Bible to its original setting in general history and to have compelled the revision of extremist critical theories.

Turning more directly to the first several, or "prehistoric," chapters in Genesis, we find ourselves immediately under obligation to archaeological research for having put us in the fortunate possession of ample material corresponding to the Creation and Flood narratives, and, in a lesser degree, to the story of the Garden of Eden and the genealogical list in Chapter 5.

—page 64

5. *Putting the shoe on the other foot*

However, it must be admitted that with respect to the main issue—namely, as to whether Joseph actually lived or not—all these details from Egyptian history are inconclusive. And that may be said to characterize all the archaeological discoveries bearing on Genesis. Their evidence is limited and indirect. They have not yet favored us with anything like incontestable attestation to the historicity of a single character in the book, with a birth certificate, so to speak, or marriage contract, or tomb. In the absence of such proof there is room to argue, and some scholars have not been slow to do so, that as far as its authenticity is concerned, it has not been reinforced by archaeological research. Granted, they have reasoned, that civilization in the Near East attained a high level millennia before the Common Era and that the narratives in Genesis reflect a world that actually had being and pulsated with life and action even as the world in which we live, by what logic does it follow that they constitute history and not fiction? Is it not commonplace, the critics assert, for the latter to be as faithful to local color, and as free from anachronism as the former is wont to be? Is it not more logical to assume that the narrators, just because they knew so well the milieu which they selected as the setting for their tales, qualified so much the more to disguise fiction as history?

That is undeniably sound reasoning, only, in the face of what archaeology has taught us, the situation is somewhat altered. The burden of proof now rests upon those who deny the authenticity of Genesis. As long as the Biblical age was esteemed an age of primitiveness and illiteracy, there was some basis for the conclusion that the Patriarchs and the stories told of them stemmed from myths and were fictitious. Those, therefore, who proposed to maintain that the Jewish people constituted an exception—namely, that they had a history when there was as yet no stage for its enactment and when no other people had any—were naturally expected to attest it. But now that the situation is completely reversed, it being generally acknowledged that that distant age was culturally far advanced, and that not only the Babylonians and Egyptians but also the Phoenicians, Amorites, Hittites, Hurrians, and the very Canaanites whose home was Palestine, were in possession of a history and literature, they in turn must do the explaining who are making an exception of the Jews and denying these things to their ancestors. This much archaeology has accomplished. It has authenticated, without any reference to tradition, the credibility of Genesis as a historical source, in so far as we distinguish its natural from its miraculous accounts, no part of which ought to be discarded as fabricated without sufficient reason.

—pages 74–75

6. *Tradition expands and embellishes, but does not invent*

Tradition undoubtedly expands, embellishes, and augments by the accretion of legend what actually took place or existed, but that it invents ancestors and creates everything concerning them out of nothing is open to serious question. Furthermore, no such hypothesis has ever succeeded in removing the difficulties with which we have observed Genesis bristles. Indeed the extremists have hatched many more than they have been able to disentangle. If, for example, in consonance with their views, Lot, Ishmael, and Esau never existed and were only figurative designations for the successive separation of the Ishmaelites, Ammonites, Moabites, and Edomites from the children of Israel whence have come the marvelously human and graphic descriptions of them as real persons? If it was the intention of the Jewish narrators to stress the inferiority of the tribes that had disbranched from their people and otherwise to defame them, what prompted them to suggest that Esau was remorse-bitten when he learned that his Canaanitish wives found no favor in his father's eyes, or to suggest that he participated in his [father's] burial, or that Ishmael did in that of Abraham? If Leah were only a name for a group of tribes, what was it that started the gossip about the unattractiveness of her eyes among the Rachel or Joseph tribes? Was this the only way those inventive fashioners of the saga could hit upon in which to articulate their chauvinism? If Laban was a figment that took rise in the recollection of the Aramean origin of the Jewish people, why was he pictured as such a rascal?

These are not isolated instances. They are to be found in Genesis by the score, almost all of them stamped with the likeness of life, defying every stratagem that has been contrived wherewith to reduce them to the shadow of a shade. There they stand big with actual existence, and, thanks to the results achieved by the archaeologists, against a concrete historical background. Add to this the compelling reality of Jewish history, the conviction deeply rooted in the consciousness of the people that it was descended of Abraham, Isaac, and Jacob, and the cogent promptings of common sense to the effect that the Mosaic epoch presupposes the patriarchal as does the age of Washington in American history that of its colonial period, and the recognition of the historicity of the Patriarchs and together with it the presence of a substratum of historic facts in Genesis becomes an inescapable, logical necessity.

—pages 74–75

7. *The Dead Sea Scrolls may provide new answers*

In bringing this all too inadequate discussion of the authorship of Genesis to a close, it may be permissible to state that both the critics and the neo-critics have "unfortunately grasped at the moon and overreached themselves." Emboldened by the wide range of their researches and the complex of sciences they have brought to bear on the study of the Bible, and impressed with the ingenuity and plausibility of their own arguments, and being human, they persisted in questing for certainty, for the decisive fiat that should immediately and fully dissolve the darkness enveloping the beginnings of a people and a literature millennia old. The result has been, first, that they have come to regard and defend their theories which are at best no more than working hypotheses as scientifically established facts, and, second, that an endless number of problems has been manufactured directly in proportion to the exigencies of theories and distempers of critics. The authentic history of the composition of the Pentateuch, if we are ever to piece it together, is not likely to favor the pronouncements of extremists in either camp or, for that matter what has been generally accepted as constituting the traditional view. Conjecture, theory, logic, and reason alone will not unravel the skein of perplexity or map out plainly the intricacies of putative or real anachronisms, duplications, contradictions, and the differences of diction in old texts. Neither can it ever be the achievement of prejudice and stubborn belief. We presume too much if we consider the mind of early man as being an open book to us. The long centuries separating us from our forebears should check our overconfidence and presumption. We must rid ourselves of the predisposition to look among the ancients for our methods of reasoning and techniques of writing. If the authors of the Pentateuch were only as different from us as tomorrow's generation will be, then we know little about them indeed. The extremists, however, of both the Graf-Wellhausen school and those in opposition to it, threw caution to the wind and wished for the moon.

Fortunately, increasing numbers of Biblical scholars have come to be ever more mindful of the pitfalls and limitations of theorizing. Neither have they lacked the humility to assess their hunches and hypotheses in the light of archaeological discoveries. And fortune has been gracious unto them, perhaps at this moment more than in all the days of modern Biblical Criticism. For the phenomenal discovery in a cave near the northern shore of the Dead Sea of a complete Hebrew manuscript of Isaiah, part of a commentary on Habakkuk, a book of hymns similar to Psalms, several apocryphal books previously unknown in Hebrew, and one or two other manuscripts as yet unidentified, all dating as it seems from the second century B.C.E., offers them unlimited opportunity for further research, for substantiating or abandoning conclusions that up till now had as their basis only speculation. They should know as soon as the new text of Isaiah has been studied whether any part of the Biblical book of that name can be dated as late as the second century B.C.E. They may even be in a position, thanks to the availability of a new Hebrew hymnal, to resolve the moot question of Maccabean Psalms and that of the authorship of the Book of Psalms as a whole. Now that this sensational discovery has brought them so near to the age in which P is supposed to have been written or edited and the Pentateuch compiled, moderate critics will shy away from fanciful hypotheses and instead look forward more eagerly to even more important finds. Who knows but that they may be richly rewarded, that tomorrow another cave may yield up a manuscript from the age of Ezra himself.

—pages 98–99

8. *The prose of Genesis is singularly noble*

The prose of Genesis is singularly noble and profoundly tinged with emotion. The form rises to the content, and the majesty of the one inspires the sublimity of the other. The style is firm, concise, and free from the slightest shadow of rhetoric and artifice. The enduring aesthetic qualities of the

book that have seized upon the mind of untold generations
are its incisive, unforgettable expressions, its plastic and at
the same time transcendent images, its seductive, almost ach-
ing naturalness, its vivid portrayal of character, and its uncanny skill in storytelling.

Probably the most oft-quoted sayings in conversation as
well as in literature have come from Genesis. Simple, pithy,
and sparkling, unpretentious, as it were careless of effect,
their artless poignancy takes a strong and lasting hold on the
memory. Who has not heard them, and who that has, has
ever let slip any of them. They are without number, scintil-
lating in a constant steady stream; the reader is sure to recall
and miss many which are no less brilliant than the following
few examples culled from the first four chapters: "Let there
be light." "In the image of God created He him." "It is not
good that man should be alone." "Bone of my bones, flesh
of my flesh." "The woman whom Thou gavest me." "In the
sweat of thy face shalt thou eat bread." "Dust thou art, and
unto dust shalt thou return." "The voice of thy brother's
blood cries unto me." "Am I my brother's keeper?"

The images in Genesis are vivid, picturesque, forceful, authentic, and withal suggestive, detaching themselves from
their incarnation in the twinkling of an eye, and turning to
feelings or ideas. Invariably derived from cognate and
homogeneous subjects, or borrowed from the most obvious
and familiar objects, they are never forced or farfetched. At
times they reach like silent shadows over the landscape, and
at others they burst out in a violent blaze of fury. As a figure
of speech there is perhaps nothing comparable to that of the
spirit of God brooding over the fathomless abyss. It is awful
in apprehension and rivets the heart and mind in reverential
silence. The destruction of Sodom and Gomorrah is described in some two or three verses, but it staggers the stout-
est heart. In one second a deluge of brimstone and fire sets
the fading night aglow and in the next all is gone, even that
which grew upon the earth, and a smoke rising up from the
dreadful ruins darkens the brightening dawn. What an en-

chanting and suggestive word is Eden and what longing does it not stimulate. What an impressive and felicitous symbol of faith and deliverance is the dove with the plucked-off olive leaf in her mouth. Pronounce the words "Rebekah at the well" and the eye will behold in the midst of a scene of pastoral tranquility a maiden of sweet loveliness, blessed innocence, and gracious benevolence. Recall Jacob's ladder, that golden staircase where pure-white angels gently jostled each other, and the mind will ascend with them to the heights of heaven or descend to cheer the solitude of a weary and anxious wanderer. Finally, though in truth there is no end to these images, the lion's whelp goes up from the prey, stoops down, crouches as a lion, adumbrating, as it were, the glory of a dynasty and the destiny of a people.

—pages 103–104

9. *They read as if they were told by word of mouth*

The magnificent background of narration in which these characters have their being is the last of the literary excellencies of Genesis to claim our attention. Nearly every one of its stories, the shortest as well as the more elaborate, has been hailed a classic, and indeed most of them come near being perfect specimens of the story teller's art. They read, someone has well said, as if they were told by word of mouth. Everyone of them is cast into a single mold and constitutes a complete whole, with its own beginning and end, and yet is related to the events that precede and follow it. The design of each narrative is masterly, and the selection of details and the proportion and balance between them admirable. The psychological essentials are set forth coherently, uninterrupted by anything irrelevant. Neither are there any halting or tedious preliminaries. The action begins at once and the reader's attention is engaged immediately and without effort.

We need not search too far for our illustrations. The opening story, the account of Creation, more than satisfies the most discriminating and exacting taste. In brevity, simplicity, and swiftness, in the balance of thought and structure, lucidity of arrangement, and restraint, it never has been outdone. We search the world's literature in vain, according to Wilhelm Wundt, to find a suitable substitute for it. One only has to compare it with other compositions on the same subject, from the *Enûma elish* and even to Milton's *Paradise Lost,* to appreciate fully how great is its reserve and eloquent its silence. Its every word counts. The majesty of its ideas discouraged profuse speech and swelling diction. The very first verse, employing no more than one adverb, one verb, three nouns, and a particle, indicates the time of action, the dim, distant beginning, sets the stage, heaven and earth, and fixes our attention on the main protagonist and event, God and Creation. The next delineates, in a few steady and sure strokes, the appearance of the stage at the time of the rising of the curtain. From that point on the account of the action proceeds, rapid but orderly, with an unerring sense of detail, relating in oft-repeated, staccato phrases all that was happening. Thus, the things that came into being are presented in two balanced sections of three days each: In the first day, light; in the fourth the great luminaries; in the second the firmament; in the fifth, the birds that fly "in the open firmament," and the creatures that have life in the waters; in the third, the earth and the vegetation; in the sixth, the beasts of the earth, and man, who shall require green herb for food. The climax is reached on the seventh day, when Creation is at an end, and the Creator enjoys in sweet repose the glory and perfection of His work.

—page 107

10. *The oneness of God implied a moral world order*

It was not our author's purpose to make of the God idea an impenetrable mystery of lifeless hypotheses. He purged it, to be sure, of the mythical accretions of paganism, but he wanted it to be real, tangible, living.

The rejection of the myths affected the ethical and social thinking of Genesis no less and perhaps even more than it did its metaphysics. In the first place, the oneness of God implied His infinite perfection in every way. Having always been one, the sole creator and ruler of the world, He had to combine in Himself the endless variety of powers each of which the pagan mind was wont to build into a separate deity. If the world was to subsist, there could be no thought of any limitation to His essence. By the very fact of his oneness He had to be all-powerful, all-wise, all-knowing; which also meant self-sufficient and asexual. He was neither in need of a mate nor could there possibly be a mate for Him. That alone raised the God idea of Genesis to a level of which the pagans had never dreamed. Whereas their gods were amorous, quarrelsome, cruel and licentious—all in the image of man—Genesis, though making the concept of Personality the bedrock of its thought, was able to reverse the order and fashion man in the image of God. For there was nothing degrading reported of Him, no more than anything very debasing can be related of anyone living in absolute solitude. The God of Genesis was one conceived as just, loving, merciful, compassionate, and long-suffering. It was puerile in His instance to attribute creation to any spiteful caprice, or to any desire to outreach a rival divinity, or any other illicit impulse, except to His overflowing love. He created because it pleased Him to create, because He delighted in the goodness of all that He had created. In brief, the oneness of God implied a moral world order.

—pages 111–112

11. *The one God had to be a universal God*

The one God had of necessity to be the universal God, the God of all mankind, which idea, in turn, connoted the unity and common origin of the human race. There is not the slightest trace in Genesis of polygenesis; that is, of a plurality of origin and its vicious offspring, the theory of racial superiority. Its view is throughout monogenist; namely, that all peoples descend from one ancestral pair or, as the anthropologists would put it, from one mammalian type. That, according to our book, was as true of the generations that came after the Flood as of the antediluvians. Just as the latter had a common ancestor in Adam, so the former had in Noah, from whose three sons they branched off into three races— the Shemitic, Hamitic, and Japhetic. There is not the vaguest hint that Shem or Eber, the remote ancestors of Abraham or Terah, his father, were of superior stock. The genealogical trees are all uniformly traced to Noah and to Adam, and to no superman. The deduction made by some scholars that Noah's curse on Canaan is suggestive of a color line or some other form of racial prejudice is unfounded. If anything, Canaan was perhaps the fairest of the Hamitic peoples. Furthermore, were the motive here racial discrimination or superiority, it is hardly likely that Noah would have been made to bless Japheth so enthusiastically or to bless him at all. If Genesis had been infected with that virus, it were impossible to account for its failure to mention Palestine in the story of Adam's creation and the Jordan among the rivers that flowed from the Garden of Eden. If at all, the curse of Canaan may be an echo of the political rivalry between the Jews and the Canaanites, from whom the Jews had conquered Palestine and toward whom they were no more favorably disposed than were the early settlers in the New World toward the Indians. With respect to racial origins, however, the view in Genesis was that the first human ancestor, like his Maker, was one.

—pages 112–113

12. *Anthropocentric—the origin of humanism*

The folding up of the pagan pantheon shifted the center of interest from heaven to earth and from a multitude of fantastic beings to man. In the *Enûma elish* and the other polytheistic accounts of creation, the scene of action was heaven or somewhere in the azure far above the earth. In the Genesis account, heaven, we might say, is disposed of in the first verse, for already the first word of the second verse removes us to earth, where we remain practically throughout the whole book. And just as the view of Genesis was geocentric, so also was it anthropocentric. All the gods and goddesses vanished from before the one human pair, and the disappearance of the former elevated the latter to immeasurable heights. Man became God's sole preoccupation, not as an opponent, rival, or object of amusement but as the fulfillment of the divine purpose in Creation. He is made to appear as having been in his Creator's mind from the very beginning, in whose fashioning He experienced His deepest satisfaction. In him alone He caused a spark from the divine spirit to flicker, in that He provided him by a special act of creation with a unique organism. No other animal species was ever to become his rival. He and none else was the toolmaker, inventor, and namer of things. For him alone had He endowed with the gifts of speech and thought, thus making him the ruler of all Creation. While God extended His goodness to the whole world, He preserved His boundless benevolence especially for man. He stamped him with His own image to lend him dignity and furnish him with a stimulus to greatness. He put him to dress and keep the Garden to accustom him to be on his own and to impress him with the nobility and sweetness of fruitful labor. He himself rested on the seventh day of the week of Creation to set man an example, and to teach him how ineffably delightful were repose and meditation after honest toil. He enjoined him not to eat of one of the trees of the Garden, to train and discipline his will in self-restraint and in obedience to authority. He brought Eve to Adam that they might people the earth and find bliss in each other's company. When they sinned He did not put them to death as He had threatened to do; He imposed upon them severe hardships. He did not slay Cain, He made him a wanderer and held out to him the hope of forgiveness. He despised human sacrifice, and could not bear to hear a little boy cry. Though He had sufficient reason to repent Him that He had made man, He loved him too dearly to remove him from the face of the earth. Genesis was decidedly anthropocentric.   —page 113

13. *How Genesis resolved the problem of evil*

Side by side with the lofty position it ascribed to man it also pictured him as weak, faltering, and sinful. It even suggested that there had been disharmony in his nature from the very beginning, in the very grains of dust of which he was formed. Why that was so was not explicitly stated, neither was there any attempt to gloss away the puzzling and vexing contradiction. The assumption seems to have been that God did not create man perfect but only potentially so. For He desired him to master the contrariety of his impulses by his own strength and to achieve righteousness not under the compulsion of his being but as a free agent. Apparently, as in the conception of Deity, so also in that of man, Genesis considered an untrammeled will and freedom of choice paramount. That is why it clearly indicated that the succumbing of Adam and Eve to the subtlety of the serpent, or that of Cain to mad jealousy, or that of the generation of Noah to a welter of passions was in each instance of their own doing. They had acted of their own free volition, which means that they could also have acted otherwise and have defied evil as Noah had done. They were themselves responsible for their defeat as he himself was for his victory.

Thus, by pointing to the freedom of man's will Genesis disposed, within the scheme of its thinking, of the problem of his weakness and, for that matter, of the problem of evil generally. For since man was free to act as he pleased he could not possibly expect to escape the consequences of his acts. And Genesis, viewing everything under its moral aspect and desirous of making all men do likewise, set forth the inevitability of retribution with an earnestness and skill hardly ever matched elsewhere. Who indeed was to forget what had happened to Adam and Eve and the serpent, and Cain, and the contemporaries of Noah, and the very earth they had trod, or fail to remember that it was one righteous man who had saved the human race from utter annihilation? God, to be sure, was long-suffering but in the end He chastised sin even as He rewarded virtue. For He was a God of justice and the moral development of society required that the lesson be burned into the consciousness of a weak but free humanity. Thus Genesis resolved the problem of evil.

—pages 113–114

C. Volume III—From Slavery to Freedom

1. *Why it is reasonable to assume Moses wrote* Exodus

As for the contention of the critics that Moses and his desert followers lived in total ignorance of the rudiments of civilization, and, therefore, could not have given birth to those Commandments and the large sections of the *Book of the Covenant* which reflect the life of an agricultural community, we have already seen, more than once, that such an assertion was as ludicrous as it was unfounded. Not only these sources but the entire Biblical record knows of no Israel that had had its existence in desert caves or primeval forests, on the level, as it were, of a rude and savage people. If there ever was such a Jewish community, then its traces are to be sought in the earliest racial stocks from which it had disengaged itself. The beginnings of the Jewish people were in a way the same as those of the American nation. Abraham was no more some kind of aborigine when he entered Canaan than were the Pilgrim Fathers when they landed at Plymouth Rock. And he, even as they, did not come into his new home empty-handed. He brought with him as much of the culture of Haran and Ur as they did of that of England. What then might be the strains in the pattern of material civilization, mirrored in the Decalogue and the Book of the Covenant, that could have been strange to him or to Moses? And even if we could discover anything that might be said to have lain outside of the experience of the latter's slave and desert followers, it would not yet argue against the Mosaic authorship of these codes. What great lawgiver was not always at least a few steps ahead of his contemporaries? Who among the immortal framers of the law failed to project his vision beyond the limits of his age or to anticipate future conditions? With all the criticism that has been leveled against the makers of the Constitution of the United States and the ignorance with which they have been charged, it was found necessary to amend their work only on four or five occasions in the most revolutionary, progressive and dynamic century and a half in all human history. Evidently James Madison, Thomas Jefferson and their co-workers did not bury their heads altogether in the sands of their day. Neither did Moses. In leading his people out of Egypt it was not his purpose to consign them to perpetual wandering in the wilderness, where their history was to find its culmination. From the beginning of his career he dreamed of making of the Israelite tribes a *Kulturvolk* in a land of their own and to prepare it for a unique destiny. And it was towards that end that his legislation was directed. This alone would account for whatever we discover in the Decalogue or the *Book of the Covenant* that impresses us as being far in advance of its age. Both of these codes show clearly that the legislator's eyes were riveted on the future. He did not, for example, forget his people's final destination and homeland, or that it was bound to have in due time a central place of worship and a centralized form of government, and he made provision for all of it in his legal system.

To return then for a last word to the point from which we have set out. The Mosaic authorship of Exodus, whether in its narrative or legal portions, can neither be proved nor disproved. It has, however, much to recommend it. For one thing it harmonizes, to say the least, as well with the Biblical text, the results of archaeology and common sense as do the numerous ingenious proposals of the critics. The latter leave no fewer loose threads than does the former. The Mosaic authorship has in addition several advantages. It does not mangle the text beyond recognition. It does not make of the later prophets and priests forgerers and falsifiers who willfully and consciously turned Jewish history upside down. Above all it is consistent with Moses' reputation as the great Lawgiver. A people that has evinced through the ages such an interest in law and such reverence for its teachers as have the Jews, may be trusted to have known who was their first legislator, or to have preserved the names of the authors, if there had been any, of those legal torsos of which the critics have spoken. But since they have forgotten the others and remembered Moses, the presumptive evidence will allow that if he was not the sole author of the laws and books attributed to him, he certainly had a large share in them.

pages 24–25

2. *The Song of Triumph at the Red Sea—acme of Hebraic poetry*

All of Exodus is in prose. A notable exception is the fifteenth chapter, which contains the triumphant song celebrating the miraculous crossing of the Red Sea and the eventual conquest and occupation of Canaan. That lone poem easily takes its place with the finest products of the poetic muse. It is as exciting and elevated as anything of its kind to be found in the world's great literatures. It would unquestionably be difficult to discover anywhere so marvelous an adaptation of the sound and movement of the verse to its meaning as exists here. If it is as old as tradition claims and many of the critics acknowledge it to be, then the beginning of Hebrew poetry must lie in the remotest past. For we can not detect in the specimen under consideration a trace of rawness or an echo of the pains of growth and maturing. It stands before us full fledged, exhibiting to perfection the essential elements of Hebrew poetic composition. To begin with it is alive, restless as the waves that flung themselves roaring on the enemy. It is spontaneous, thrown out, as it were, all in a breath. Not a word in it stands still but is tumbling on another's neck, not a clause but is short and quick. Stich follows upon stich like a succession of waves to form the characteristic and effective Biblical parallelism. The descriptions are picturesque, the imagery vivid, the diction sonorous and studded with figures of speech, particularly with that of alliteration, the language, as far as meager knowledge of the Hebrew vocabulary and idiom permits us to judge, is at times archaic and exotic. The poem's opening

verse is unforgettable. It strikes us as if the unprecedented
event that had occurred at the sea's edge had itself opened
its mouth to speak. It breaks upon us with the startling sud-
denness with which those who actually witnessed the amazing
and swift end of the enemy must have begun to sing, when
they awakened to consciousness and realized what had happened. It would be hard to believe that it was a composition
of later years, an offspring of pale recollections, so instinct is
it with the turmoil of life and reality. The other verses are
equally fresh and nervous, containing not the stories of
actions, but the actions themselves. "Wonderfully sublime,"
Bishop Lowth designated verses 9 and 10, in which the Pharaoh's unexpected ruin is brought into powerful relief by his
arrogance and fury. But why attempt illustrations when the
whole poem is literally crammed with excellencies. For
whether they depict horse and rider, or God's powerful right
hand or His consuming wrath, or the enemy's sinking as lead
or melting away terror-stricken, everywhere the rolling waves
of sound, flowed on with the same rhythmic cadence, the
rising to joy and gratitude in the presence of victory, to the
breathless expression of awe in the presence of God's might.
—pages 25–26

3. *I Am That I Am—a mighty abstraction on a lowly bush*

The image in Exodus which, to express it in the language
of Lord Bacon, "raises the mind and hurries it into sublimity" is that of the burning bush. Here, as again in the chapter
on the Sinaitic theophany, the author had a theme that came
near approximating the majesty of Creation and he bestowed
upon it the simplicity and grandeur of his genius, which resulted in a happy coincidence of the conception and its representation, a perfect harmony of intention and execution.
Moses was attempting to picture and express that which after
many years of intense and ceaseless meditation, he had con-
cluded was unimaginable and ineffable. He had rejected all
representation of God in an individual or physical form as
misrepresenting and debasing the idea of God. There was no

likeness of God. That was all there was to it, and all verbal analogies were distant and no more than a courtesy of speech. And yet how was he to convey an inkling of it to his people that had been living for centuries in the shadow of Egypt's idols, bring them back to the vision of Abraham, and acquaint them with the stirrings in his own heart. He did what no other man before him had done. He engrafted the mightiest of abstractions, the universal and eternal I AM THAT I AM upon a humble bush, and in a thrice the small clump of shrubs assumed a character of vastness and sublimity. It was at one and the same time real and unsubstantial, inanimate and alive, local and omnipresent, a thing that had ceased to be a thing, and had become a process, an unending process, a burning and unconsumed bush, in a word, a sublime image of at once the humility and majesty of God.

—pages 31–32

4. *Not Moses but the "Children of Israel" is nexus of Exodus*

Altogether, Exodus covered, excepting for its first two chapters, a period of only two years. And what two years they were. They blazed and throbbed with the glow and excitement of what to the author and untold subsequent generations were breath-taking and world-shaking events. The mighty hand of God smote Egypt; the waters of the Red Sea divided and stood at attention as Israel crossed over; a whole people heard the voice of God, received His law, and entered thereby into an everlasting covenant with Him; in the desert a fully equipped sanctuary had sprung up. All this had happened in two years. Who then and what could vie with this celestial, ever-shifting kaleidoscope, to chip off a second of the time it required for its rotations. What is more to the point, Exodus is a history, exclusively the history of the Israelites as a whole, adhering zealously to a unity of design, limiting and holding its variety of character and incident to what ministers directly to its interest. It is this and not the want of the story-teller's skill that explains the utter absence of those personal experiences and vicissitudes, which are the life-blood of the short story, in whatever accounts it does trouble to give of any of its protagonists—even in the case of the most important ones, even, as we have seen, in the case of Moses. But as history, Exodus is, considering its age, remarkably well planned, brilliantly executed, and beautifully written. Strange as it may sound, it meets in some respect modern historiographical standards. Thus it does not turn into a mere chronicle of heroic persons and romantic occurrences, narrating the pleasing, dramatic or highly exceptional for its own sake. By eschewing the fortuitous, isolated and anomalous, it achieves what is a *sine qua non* in a good history, a smooth continuity, uninterrupted by the starts and breaks of accidental episodes and digressions. Having made the people the nexus of its narration, it pursues it with a setness of purpose, intensity of concentration, and precision of outline that are never relaxed. The be-all and end-all of its pages, from start to finish, that fires and colors everything they contain, is the career of Israel. It was perhaps no accident that practically the opening and closing word and thought of this history should have been not Moses but "the children of Israel."

—pages 34–35

5. *Exodus—Existentialist and slightly anthropomorphic*

Exodus enunciated at a very early stage in the development of human reason a metaphysical postulate beyond which reason seems to have been unable to advance. By formulating the essence of Deity in I AM THAT I AM, it postulated Existence, Personality and the Intelligibility of Nature. It is true that that was done by means of revelation, that is, by an arbitrary assumption. But so, in the final analysis, was also Aristotle's Prime Mover, the Unmoved Movements and the causal series that was supposed to account for them. The difference was only this, to paraphrase Emerson, Exodus concealed while Aristotle's *Metaphysics* revealed its logic. The modern scientist has been no less arbitrary. He describes the Universe in mathematical equations, but when he tries to explain it, he uses language which, while not as colorful as that of the Bible, nevertheless does not escape an anthropomorphic tinge.

—page 36

Exodus was composed in the common man's language for the common man and, seen in this light, the absoluteness of its God idea is remarkably unalloyed. Thus, if it failed to deny explicitly the actuality of other gods, it counterbalanced it by a studious avoidance of giving it the least recognition. And this is how it was done. First, it remained oblivious of idolatry as a credal system with an ideological foundation, and, perceiving the idols to be solely what they were to the eye, inert matter and not symbols of principles or forces, it prohibited their manufacture and ordered their destruction. And in doing so, it, in effect, aserted the non-existence of the gods. Second, wherever it mentioned them, it was done by innuendo, as is the case in the Second Commandment, where the expression "no other gods" is an unavoidable encumbrance, a habit of speech, just as we might say "ye gods" or speak of the rising and setting sun. Similarly, speaking of God as the God of Israel was also a constraint of speech, since Pharaoh and the Egyptians did not recognize a universal God and since it was intended, as we shall soon see, as an avowal of His peculiar relationship to Israel.

—page 37

6. JHWH—God as a process—a consuming flame

With respect to the Tetragrammaton, no matter what the origin of the word might be, the way in which it is used in Exodus makes it clear that it does not go back to a thing, or an entity, or anything tangible, but denotes being or action. To have made a verb the subject of a verb as in the clause "I AM hath sent me" is to have attained if not reached beyond the metaphysical heights of the *to prôton kinoûn* or Prime Mover. It is strictly in keeping with its representation of God as a process, that is, as a consuming flame, as in the

accounts of the burning bush and theophany. Neither in the
one nor in the other is there the slightest suggestion of a
visible, let alone, tactile form. In the former extreme care
was taken to emphasize that God was only heard but not
seen. "Lo," He said unto Moses, "I come unto thee in a thick
cloud, that the people may hear when I speak with thee."
Hear but not see. Likewise underlying the Second Commandment is the conviction that God is without form or
there would not have been a direct prohibition against the
making of an image of Him. Also in his several audiences
with Pharaoh, Moses never mentions a likeness of his God or
produces any by way of evidence of His existence. Neither
does Pharaoh, for whom a god was god only insofar as he was
visible, ask for it, presumably because this strange eccentric-
ity of his Israelite slaves, namely, that they were worshiping
some sort of a God which no eye had ever beheld, was not
unknown to him. Admittedly difficult of explanation is another presentation of the Deity, in which it is specified that
the leaders of the people saw God. But even this, the most
sensuous description of its kind in the whole book is tem-
pered, giving no hint of what they actually saw and depicting
rather the background of the vision than the vision itself.
—pages 37–38

7. *How Moses differs from the men of science*

Moses and the men of science and philosophy differ radically in their approach. Whereas the latter have always
claimed to have arrived at their conclusions by means of their
own labors and the labors of other human beings, after prolonged meditation and research or experimentation, Exodus,
though it set forth the apprehension of God's essence and
nature with considerable awareness, one might even say, in
a spirit of inquiry, does not attribute it to the initiative and
genius of Moses but to the benevolence and grace of God who
revealed Himself to him. This difference is of the utmost
importance. For it goes to the heart of all religions, and it
is this, the claim of revelation, and not their teachings that

have been responsible for skepticism and irreligion. "Tough-minded" men have not always been disposed to believe that the mystery of an infinite God, who meted out heaven with the span and weighed the mountains in scales, was ever made known to "favorite sons." It is therefore the more to be regretted that Exodus, which contains so basic a part of "the body of truth" which God has revealed to Moses, is so niggardly with its information regarding the process of revelation. Beyond saying that God spoke and that Moses or Moses and the people heard, it leaves us to conjecture the "mechanics." And the conjectures have been numerous and inconclusive. Some have rationalized it, identifying revelation with what is generally understood by inspiration; others have dismissed Moses as well as all others who have ever claimed to have been favored by divine revelations as visionaries or victims of illusions; still others have not hesitated to decry all of them as imposters. It is not likely that we shall have any exposition of the matter within reach of the average intelligence—the cogitations of the theologians are more abstruse than Occam's razor—before we understand better the workings of the human mind and its capacity to receive communications otherwise than through the channels of sense. We may perhaps discover that the religious genius is endowed with a sensitivity of imagination to the spiritual or divine such as the painter has for color, the musician for sound, the poet for words, and the scientist for the laws of nature. When that happens we may not altogether find it unreasonable to believe that such a genius, who chanced to live in an age that was comparatively naive and simple, and being unencumbered with the doubts and cynicism of modern man, might, in the intensity of his meditation, actually have heard a voice that was as real to him as were to Michelangelo the faces that beckoned to him from the marble banks of Carrara. "Who now will determine," wrote Herder with exemplary reverence, "when in the soul of such a man, learned in all the wisdom of the Egyptians, and excited and actuated by the God of his fathers, the human ends, and the more than human

begins? where, in the handwriting of the tables, his finger
and the finger of God touched. In the grammatical sense, we
all know what is meant by the *spirit* and *finger* of God, but
here there is a historical relation of what was executed and
done." And we may add that we will each take from that relation as much as his heart and mind permit.

—pages 39–40

8. *"Chosen People"—Jewish and non-Jewish versions*
    There is no doubt but that these people were conscious of
a mission and that the idea had gained a great ascendant over
their minds. If then it should be asked wherein it differed
from that of the selection of Israel as formulated in Exodus,
or why it was that the prophets, as we shall have more than
one occasion to observe, came to look upon their people as
the chosen people, a conviction which was apparently present
in the mind of Jesus when he told the Samaritan woman at
Jacob's well that "salvation comes from the Jews," or in that
of Dante, when he spoke of them as God's people, or in that
of Agobard and other prelates of the Middle Ages, who took
umbrage at what they were pleased to call *insolentia Judae-
orum*, or in that of friend and foe who to this day alternate
between blessing and cursing them,—if this question should
be asked, as indeed it has been with ever more persistency,
skepticism and resentment, then the answer to it is to begin
with, that the Jews had in this regard stolen a march on the
other peoples. The above statements from Italian, English,
French and American sources, which could be multiplied ad
infinitum, make that sufficiently clear. The very language
in which Gioberti, Hugo, Milton and Wilson, if not Shakespeare, chose to clothe the idea of their peoples' consecration
is deeply tinged with the Biblical idiom. These men could
not but be mindful that they were expressing a faith which
the Jews had been the first to enunciate and formulate in
words "fire-new from the mind." In the second place, the
Jews had kept the idea fresh and lasting in the remembrance
all through their checkered history, at all times and on all

occasions, in triumph and defeat, in crisis and tranquility. It had imprinted itself indelibly on their being; mockery, hostility, persecution, assimilation, and dereliction, the distractions and demands of the world strove in vain to efface it. In the third place, as a direct result of the long endurance of the idea, as well as of other factors which cannot be dealt with here, it had come to possess the soul not only of the nation as a whole and of its most distinguished representatives, but of its humblest and most inarticulate folk as well. In the fourth place the Jews did not think that they had come by the idea by themselves, through the promptings of their own moral sense and of their own volition which, if they had, might have made them feel free to abandon it when they so desired. Thanks to its hoary age—having been traced back as it was to Abraham—they rather believed that the idea had come to them from God, and that they had entered into a covenant to remain unswervingly and everlastingly faithful to it. It was, in short, a conjuncture of these circumstances that lay at the basis of the conception of "a holy nation" and not any theory of racial superiority or national vainglory.

—pages 44–45

9. *The codes of Moses and Hammurabi compared*

But all this does not yet make the Mosaic and the pagan code one of a kind. For their points of contact and similarities are only casual and incidental, whereas their differences are intrinsic and fundamental. In the first place, they diverge in mood and atmosphere, in their settings and in the personalities back of them. The Mosaic code is preceded by the story of freedom, the freedom of an enslaved people and followed by that of a covenant which linked the people to God. The person of the lawgiver is passed over in almost complete silence, except insofar as it is related that he had acted as the agent of God. The Prologue and Epilogue to the Code of Hammurabi are spinned out of other fancies. They offer us a magniloquent catalogue of conquests, of the subjection to the will of the conqueror. As for Hammurabi, his boastful-ness knows no bounds. By the time he is through blowing his own trumpet the gods shrink and disappear, and even Shamash, the King, is forgotten. What does not Hammurabi say of himself? He is the exalted prince, the perfect King, the monarch of kings, the supreme ruler of kings, the god of kings, the wise, the perfect, the mighty bull who gores the enemy, the stormer of the four quarters of the world, who caused them to render obedience, the protecting shadow of the land. In the Epilogue, he lays a curse on succeeding generations of kings as much for the erasure of his name as for any alteration in the code proper. One cannot help but carry away the impression that the pagan legislator was far more interested in eclipsing the fame of all his predecessors and successors for all time to come than in insuring the welfare of his people. In the second place, the Babylonian code recognized a caste system, reduced the commoner virtually to the position of a slave, and on the whole, placed a higher value on property than on human life. Thus it distinguished between injuring a man of rank and a common man. In the case of the former the *lex talionis* was to be applied, in that of the latter monetary compensation was deemed sufficient. On the other hand, it made every form of theft punishable by death, even where the property was secured from a slave. It took cognizance of injuries inflicted on other peoples' slaves but was silent regarding those inflicted on one's own. For, within its purview it apparently made no more sense to punish a man for crippling his slave than for crippling his ox. The fact that the law allowed the slave to hold property or go free altered his status but little. During his period of service he was the owner's chattel, and woe betide him if he asked for his freedom. The law enjoined that his ear be lopped off. And more woe unto him if he escaped. The law of Hammurabi pursued him to "the four quarters of the world," promised rewards to everyone who helped in the hunt, and threatened with death anyone who aided or sheltered him.

—pages 46–47

10. *The Magna Charta of the Poor and Oppressed*

The Mosaic Code marked no distinction between man and man and put a human life far above property. It did away with the death penalty for theft and got rid of the horrible mutilations in which the Code of Hammurabi abounds. It is, of course, not the perfect or ultimate code, the code which, by the way, has never yet been compiled. It is not as impeccably humane as, let us say, the most sensitive and advanced humanitarians of our day should have liked it to be. There are still to be seen from underneath its reforms and refinements the lees and settlings of the crude civilizations of its age. Such, for example are its recognition of the existence of the witch and its acceptance of the institution of slavery. But while the as yet superstition-fettered mind consigned the miserable creature, as she was to be for many centuries to come, to death, the liberty-loving heart dealt sympathetically with the slave. If the master injured him, he went free. If he escaped he was to be abetted and aided to remain permanently free. On the other hand, if he was slow to seize a proffered opportunity to gain his freedom, he was to be publicly disgraced. One searches the other oriental codes in vain for such regulations or for the spirit that prompted them. They do not know of a day of rest (the Jew was to be mocked for a long time before the world was to acknowledge the indispensability and appreciate the beauty and sanctity of the Sabbath), of consideration for the stranger, of the prohibition of usury and of other legislation protecting and providing for the poor, of tenderness for the brute, though it should be the property of one's enemy, or of that extraordinary commandment which sought to restrain the covetousness and waywardness of the frail heart of man. No one, in a word, could speak of those codes as Herder, Matthew Arnold and Thomas Huxley did of the Mosaic as, so the last named put it, constituting the Magna Charta of the poor and oppressed.

—page 47

We do not know whether or not Lord Acton had our book

in mind when he remarked in one of his most notable essays that it was the Jewish people which laid down the lines "upon which all freedom was won." But there is no doubt as to whence Franklin, Jefferson and Adams derived their inspiration for the first design of the seal of the United States which they recommended to the liberated colonies. They recalled the delivery of Israel from Egypt, and pictured in their sketch Pharaoh, swollen with arrogance and exuding wrath, dashing furiously in his chariot through the dividing waters of the Red Sea and going down to perdition with brandished sword, as he espied on the shore Moses with his hand outstretched and resplendent in the rays of the pillar of fire. Underneath they added the motto: "Rebellion to tyrants is obedience to God." The Founding Fathers were only the most illustrious of those who have ornamented their hard-earned freedom with the rich embroidery of these undy-ing symbols.

—pages 48–49

11. *Exodus is the best proof of the election of Israel*

Most men want justice to prevail and the weak to triumph over the strong. Whether or not they believe in divine inter-vention, they certainly should like to believe that there is a something in human affairs making for the inevitable doom of tyrants. Here the cruel, arrogant, unrepentant Pharaoh encounters his destiny; the mighty, boastful oppressor is struck from heaven, by a force against which all his arms and strategy are in vain. This lesson, the way of God with a bully, was intended to be memorable. And so it is. But there is usually a sequel to the destruction of the oppressor and that is the redemption of the oppressed. The one is as significant as the other, or even more so. It certainly is considered as such in our story. God was not merely destroying the Egyp-tians. He was freeing the Israelites. He was fulfilling a prom-ise. He was electing Abraham's posterity to make of it a great people, even as the Patriarch had been assured would be the case. No other act of the Deity offered such convincing

proof of the election of Israel as did the Exodus, and more
particularly the Red Sea episode. Generations without end
were to recall that the "Lord had dried up the waters of the
Red Sea before [the Israelites] when [they] came out of
Egypt"; that He had made "the depths of the sea a way for
the redeemed to pass over"; that "He had caused His glorious
arm to go at Moses' right hand . . . cleft the waters . . . led
[His people] through the depths without their stumbling";
"that He had brought [them] up from the land of Egypt, and
led [them] through the wilderness for forty years, that [they]
might seize the land of the Amorites"; that "He had made
the waters stand like a wall"; that "He had rebuked the Red
Sea and it became dry, and he led them through the depths
as through a meadow"; that "when Israel went forth from
Egypt . . . the sea saw and fled"; that "He will [again] dry
up the tongue of the Sea of Egypt, with the glowing heat of
His breath, and . . . shake His hand over the River . . . smite
it into seven brooks, and . . . enable men to cross it with
sandals"; that "the beloved Israel shall respond to her Lord,
as in the days of her youth, as in the day when she came up
from the land of Egypt.

—pages 348–349

12. *All gods fight for their chosen—but JHWH is special*

Concomitant with the election of Israel went the glory and
the fame of and belief in the Oneness, or at least the supremacy of the God with the four-letter name. It makes no difference what our personal views are respecting the origin and
development of monotheism or the concept of a chosen people. We may reject the latter altogether, and think of Biblical
monotheism as the culmination of a long evolutionary process, and even then as being restricted, as being far more heno-
theistic or nationalistic in character than universal. The fact
remains that in this account the God of the weak is pictured
as shattering the strong, as being peerless among the gods,
and as having acquired Israel as His special possession. True,
all the gods that crowded the ancient pantheons were repre-

sented as warriors and victors and as having each a favorite people. But somehow there is no such story as this, no such disparity in power between the protagonists, no such condition of long-lasting slavery, no such battle without "arms and men," no such combat with only one warrior, no such sudden and humiliating defeat of the enemy, no such war whose soul objective was freedom rather than conquest, no such emphasis on humbling arrogance and tyranny, no such intimate and indissoluble relationship between God and people, no such predisposition on the part of a people to attribute everything to God, and no such eagerness on the part of God to claim a people and achieve universal recognition through it.

—page 349

13. *We are not sure of the author—but the Song speaks for itself*

The song itself rises above the disputations to which it has been subjected, a monument to a literary genius of high order, no matter who he was or when he lived. "Where," Herder asked, "is there a song so exciting and so elevating as this?" Sublime in thought, intense in sentiment, and masterly in style, it communicates a unified attitude towards the momentous happenings it relates. The verisimilitude of its metaphors, its lively images, its spontaneity and sudden transitions, its indifference to the symmetrical arrangement of ideas render it the very stuff of experience more than its expression.

All this, however, it should be borne in mind, the present Song has in common with all Hebrew poetry. A cursory word about the latter then should help us understand the former better. All Hebrew poetry is recalcitrant to rigid precepts, aloof to rhyme and assonance, and oblivious of meter. Its magnificent rhythm rolls carelessly, and its line knows no perceptive limit except the reader's breath. Its construction is simple, easy, organic. Its beauty is mediumless even as the God it acclaims is imageless. To seek here for iambic and anapestic rhythms or Sapphic strophes, or a strict poetic code, or anything like an accentual, metrical, or quantitative system is to labor in vain. Here meter is an illusion. Here form is veiled by the thought expressed and evoked. In a word, Hebrew poetry is forever striving, consciously or unconsciously, to shorten the distance between an experience and its expression.

In the attempt to attain this goal, Hebrew poetry developed to perfection a literary device much in vogue in Egypt, Babylonia, Phoenicia, and Ugarit, and long ago singled out by the Rabbis for high praise. It was to its exploitation, they said, that Isaiah owed his superiority over all the prophets. The device, surnamed parallelism, is basically repetition, that is, the act of repeating in new words what has already been expressed. To the ancients parallelism or repetition must have been a kind of gesturing, dancing, musical accompaniment, or aid to self-expression and communication. It was for them, as indeed it is to this day, a way of speaking eagerly, anxiously, urgently, joyously, triumphantly, under great strain, or in the grip of seething emotions, all as the case might have been. When Isaiah reported the seraphim calling to one another and saying. "Holy, holy, holy is the LORD of hosts," he was accentuating fervor, reverence, and the concept of holiness as applied to the Deity. When Jeremiah was saying, "Trust not in deceptive words, such as 'the temple of the LORD, the temple of the LORD, the temple of the LORD is this!' " he was lashing out indignantly against his people and speaking contemptuously of its national shrine. When Ezekiel cried, "A ruin, a ruin, a ruin, will I make it," he was expressing anxiety, scorn, apprehension. All three Prophets, it is obvious, resorted to repetition to make their meaning perfectly clear, lend it earnestness and add to it the greatest possible emphasis.

—pages 352–353

14. *Parallelism—the channel of the inflow of experience on expression*

It is this literary device, and above all the purpose it was intended to serve, that have helped make our Song as peculiarly sublime, as incomparably great as Herder believed it to be. True it abounds in figures of speech. Its alliterations are many, even if we consider only those that can be reproduced in transliteration: *gaoh gaah; we-rochvo . . . ramah; markevot . . . u-mivhar; qamecha . . . ka-qash . . . qaphu; neermu . . . nitzvu . . . ned nozelim . . . nora . . . nora . . . nahita . . . nehalta . . . neweh . . . nivhalu . . . namogu;* and *machon . . . miqqdash.* Its similes are perfect illustrations and perfectly in keeping with its mood; the Egyptians sink like a stone or lead in the mighty waters; the Lord's wrath consumes them like stubble; the waters stand up like a heap. Its metaphors are true and striking, as when the various people melt away out of sheer fear, or are still as stone, or when the depths congeal in the heart of the sea. Its imagery is awe-inspiring and breath-taking, as when the Lord like some cosmic discus thrower hurls horses and riders into the sea, or when He shatters the enemy with His mammoth, bare, terrifying right hand, or when the breath of His nostrils rolls back the mighty waters of the sea. Its combining in v. 9 of alliteration with the asyndeton produces one of the most striking distichs in all literature. Its brilliant framing of homonyms. Its skillful bringing together vv. 10 and 12 with v. 13, only to draw them apart and thus mark unmistakably the contrast between *nashafta beruhacha* and *natita yemincha* on the one hand and *na-hita be-hasdecha* and *ne-halta be-azcha* on the other.

All this is admittedly true. The rhetorical devices are indeed numerous. But these devices are barely perceptible. For thanks to the rapidity of movement and the brevity of the basic unit in the Song, the idea or experience leaps forward into alacrity and briskness long before the figure of speech in which it is clothed comes to possess us. Thus of the forty-one lines which make up the Song, thirty-four consist of four words each. Brief as these lines are to begin with, they each, except for the two-word line, further divide into two parts. Each of these parts expresses a complete thought, and the two

together body forth an interdependent thought. The result-
ant thought does not rest, but presses forward to pair off with
the interdependent thought of the line immediately following, with which it forms a parallelism. Little wonder that the
Song as a whole should consist almost exclusively of nouns
and verbs with rarely an adjective in sight. For in the midst
of such stir, such steady advance of ideas, and coalescence of
incidents, the mind comes by an object directly via essence
and function and not by way of its attributes, which is as
much as to say that the mind becomes aware of each thought
and its points of intersection before the eye can scan or sound
can reach the ear. And since the pauses of the mind are as
quick as thought itself, they are hardly pauses at all. In other
words, measure, pattern, rhythm, or meter are mental and not
physical. The very lines and words are illusive. Josephus was
never quite as wrong as when he was telling the Graeco-
Roman world that our Song was composed in hexameter
verse. No, its art is not so conspicuous, nor its rhetorical
devices so arresting. Rather the splendor of its diction, vividness of its imagery, and its rhythmic and musical qualities
are engulfed in the rush of parallelisms, in the inflow of
experience on expression.

—pages 355–356

15. *The Torah—the logic of reason that reasons know not of*

Right were the Rabbis when they said that Moses might
have begun the Song more appropriately with Pharaoh's boast
to the effect that he would pursue, despoil, and destroy Israel.
But they did not on that account wrench v. 9, which contains
Pharaoh's boast, out of its present position. Nor did they
presume to rearrange the other verses as if they were so many
pieces of a jig-saw puzzle. For they surmised—what so many
scholars have been slow in doing—that the Torah, as they put
it, paid little attention to logical sequence or literary coherence. If there was any logic, they conjectured rightly that it
was one of mood, purpose, or, shall we say, obsession. The
primary aim was not to compose a beautiful song. It was to

glorify God, to celebrate the fulfillment of His promise to the Patriarchs, namely, that He would redeem Israel from Egypt and establish them in Canaan. What happened to Pharaoh and his charioteers is a matter of secondary importance. There is no singing here of arms and men or revenging oneself on the enemy. The fate of the Egyptians is significant only as an attestation of God's power and what He had already done for Israel, and even more a guarantee of the wonders yet to come. The poet has no thought for order, coherence, symmetry. He let his words fall as they list, concerned only with the end in view. He is obsessed with God, with whom he begins and ends. "I will sing to the LORD . . . The LORD shall reign for ever and ever!" That is his theme, and into this theme his every word and line and image fit. And it is from the unparalleled majesty of the theme that flow the logic, beauty and sublimity of his song.

One word more. Writing of the tendency of Hebrew consciousness to escape from dualism and retain and integrate consciousness of the world, Professor MacMurray has this to say: "Jewish reflection thinks history as the act of God. Where our historians say, 'Caesar crossed the Rubicon,' or 'Nelson won the battle of Trafalgar,' the Jewish historian says, 'God brought His people up out of the land of Egypt.' This is no mere concession to religious prejudice, but the continuous form which all Hebrew reflection takes. It means that Hebrew thought is at once religious and empirical. It is religious in that it thinks history as the act of God. It is empirical in that it reflects upon history in order to discover the nature of God and the laws of divine agency." This penetrating observation of Professor MacMurray might well be regarded as a summation of our Song and indeed of all Hebrew poetry as well.

—pages 356–357

Appendix II

Correspondence

221

March 3, 1939, letter from A. Einstein to Dr. Solomon Goldman (page 254). (Original letter.)

May 17, 1939, letter from A. Einstein to Rabbi Goldman (page 255). (English translation.)

May 17, 1939, letter from A. Einstein to Rabbi Goldman (page 256). (Original letter.)

April 28, 1939, letter from Ch. Weizmann to Dr. Goldman (page 239).

February 8, 1939, memorandum of conversation between President Roosevelt, Chaim Weizmann and Stephen Wise (page 00).

February 26, 1939, letter from Louis D. Brandeis to Right Honorable Neville Chamberlain (page 245).

March 6, 1939, letter from R. C. Lindsay to Mr. Justice Brandeis (page 245).

March 24, 1939, letter from Ch. Weizmann to Prime Minister Neville Chamberlain (page 246).

May 20, 1939, letter from Frank Knox, Chicago *Daily News,* to Rabbi Solomon Goldman (page 247).

May 24, 1939, cable from Ben Gurion, Jerusalem, to Dr. Solomon Goldman (page 248).

May 29, 1939, cable from Ben Gurion, Jerusalem, to Dr. Solomon Goldman (page 249).

October 19, 1939, letter from Martin Buber, Jerusalem, to Dr. Diesendruck (page 256).

November 20, 1939, letter from Z. Diesendruck, The Hebrew Union College, Cincinnati, Ohio (page 257).

November 22, 1939, letter from Solomon Goldman to Professor Z. Diesendruck (page 258).

December 19, 1939, letter from Viscount Halifax to Dr. Weizmann (page 242).

December 29, 1939, letter from Dr. Weizmann to Lord Halifax (page 243).

February 26, 1940, letter from Mr. Lothian to Dr. Chaim Weizmann (page 244).

September 20, 1944, letter from Louis Finkelstein to Rabbi Solomon Goldman (page 259).

September 26, 1944, letter from Rabbi Goldman to Dr. Louis Finkelstein (page 264).

February 6, 1966, letter from David Hertz to Mrs. Alice Goldman (page 270).

The Marshall–Goldman Exchange

While Rabbi Goldman seems to come out second best in this round of letters, the events of the decades that have elapsed since 1925 offer grim and tragic proof that Goldman was right in distrusting the soil of Russia and the hope for a dignified human existence in the countries of the Pale. He was all too poignantly justified in pleading that the millions spent in ameliorating the plight of East European Jewry would have brought infinitely better results, if it had been used to buy the wastelands of Palestine—at the time of the Balfour Declaration when Arab anti-Zionism was still in embryo.

CORRESPONDENCE BETWEEN LOUIS MARSHALL AND SOLOMON GOLDMAN

October 24, 1925

Dear Rabbi Goldman:

Your letter of the 20th instant to Mr. David A. Brown, has been called to my attention.

You say that you cannot act with the National Committee of the United Jewish Campaign, because you are a conscientious objector. Translated into plain English, you refuse to assist the Jews of Russia, Poland and the Ukraine, first, because you "cannot make peace with the soil of Russia," and second, because you cannot give your support "to any movement or campaign that will forget Palestine for three years." You therefore ask Mr. Brown to "call upon American Israel to concentrate for the next five years" upon putting Palestine at the very heart of its endeavor.

Your words simply make me rub my eyes, because I doubt whether I have seen aright, whether I am not suffering from an optical delusion, when I find your name subscribed to this communication. Stripped of all rhetoric, you merely say that you are willing to leave the Jews of Eastern Europe to continue to agonize, to withhold from them the relief for which they are praying, to close your ears and harden your heart to them simply because in the past other Jews have suffered in those lands and the future is not certain, and for the aforesaid reasons that you do not agree with those heroic men who have objectively studied the situation on the ground and firmly believe that help is necessary.

The program against which you are now setting your personal influence was unanimously adopted at the Philadelphia Emergency

Conference. It was inaugurated by the Joint Distribution Committee, the American Jewish Relief Committee, the Central Committee and the Peoples Relief Committees. The men who constitute these committees have for ten years past devoted themselves whole-heartedly to the relief of our coreligionists in these lands, as well as in Palestine. They have raised upwards of $60,000,000, partly for palliative relief and to a considerable extent for constructive work. They unanimously decided that we had not as yet completed the work on which they had embarked, and that it was our conscientious obligation to do that work. It was expected that there would be a united Jewry behind this campaign, recognizing, of course that there are always those who are ready to find excuses to avoid their duty. We did not believe, however, that we would find any discordant voices in the rabbinate of this country. Here, at least, we felt secure of enthusiastic support and of human charity. It never dawned upon us that partisanship could be carried to such an extent among the men of God that, because they were so wedded to a particular theory, that they would be willing to put to the hazard millions of lives rather than to depart to the extent of an iota from their "ism".

Do you not see that, in dealing with the Jews of these countries, we are confronted by a condition and not a theory, to use the apt phrase of Grover Cleveland? The 8,000,000 Jews in Russia, Poland, and the Ukraine and Roumania, and their ancestors, have lived in these countries for centuries. Their homes are there. Even if it were not, what could be done to remove them en masse from their present habitations? Where could they go? How could they reach any other destination? Where are the means by which that could be accomplished? Palestine certainly could not receive them. The immigration laws of that country would make it as impossible as the immigration laws of the United States now make it. How much money do you think it would require to transplant this vast army of impoverished humanity? Take a pencil and paper and make the calculation. On the basis of five to a family, they would represent 1,600,000 families. It has been calculated that it would require $5,000 to settle a family in Palestine. Consequently $8,000,000,000 would be required to carry out your idealistic scheme. Where would you find the land in Palestine on which to settle these transplants? As I understand the facts, there are not to exceed 25,000 acres of available land in Palestine now under the control of the Government. If land is to be purchased, I am informed by the highest authority it would cost $100 per acre. Russia has offered Jews who desire to embark in agriculture 2,500,000 acres of land free of cost. That quantity of land, if available in Palestine, would cost $250,000,000.

In formulating your grandiose plan, you must have considered where this money would come from. I would like to be enlightened. But before you answer my question, will you again take pencil and paper and refer to the statistics which are available, and let me know how much money all the generous Jews of the United States, Zionists and non-Zionists, have in the past ten years contributed to the religious and philanthropic purposes for the Jews of the United States and in foreign countries. Then let me know whether you desire to discontinue the present activities of the Jews in our own country, and by that I mean the United States, and whether you believe that they would be willing to contribute even the limited aggregate to which I have referred toward the realization of your iridescent dream. There is not a scintilla of practicability to what you have in mind.

Moreover, you must recognize the fact that there is no human power which will be able to transport to Palestine more than an exceedingly small percentage of the Jews who are now in Eastern Europe, even if the one were a hell and the other a paradise. The great mass would perforce be obliged to remain where they are. Their fate must be determined in the countries where they live. That was the conclusion reached by the late Jacob H. Schiff, after the most careful and sympathetic study of the question running over many years. Even when the doors of opportunity in the United States were wide open, when the Jews of Russia were suffering from Czaristic tyranny, when America was certainly a paradise compared with any other land in the world, the number of Jews who migrated from Russia and Poland constituted an inconsiderable percentage of the natural increase of the Jews who were living in those countries. In many instances they had relatives in this country who were ready to assist them both in coming out and in finding a means of a livelihood after arriving here. I repeat, therefore, that unless we are willing to let the Jews of these countries go down to destruction, it is our bounden duty to help them where they are and where they must, as a result of inexorable necessity, remain.

When I think of my experience in Cleveland, one of the most prosperous cities in the world, and with the fine Jewish Community of your city, on an occasion when you were the chairman of the local committee to help your alma mater, the Jewish Theological Seminary of America, at the time of its financial distress, I am inclined to believe that even you would have difficulty in raising your quota of an $8,000,000,000, or even a $250,000,000, campaign for Palestine.

Let us not, however, lose sight of the fact that the Jews of the United States have been remarkably prosperous, and that they have developed a sense of brotherhood and of responsibility for their brethren during the past ten years never known before in Jewish history. I have not the slightest doubt that they will contribute to our United Jewish Campaign the $15,000,000 for which we are appealing. Nor have I the slightest doubt that they will also respond with like generosity, at the proper time, to a campaign to meet the needs of Palestine. You and your associates who, notwithstanding the decision rendered at Philadelphia, are inclining to rebellion, mistake the psychology of American Jewry. If you say that it will be impossible to raise the money for Palestine if the United Jewish Campaign proceeds, and if you ask your friends, on the grounds which you have stated in your letter, not to contribute to the United Jewish Campaign, then it is possible, nay, it is likely, that there will be many who will take you at your word, and will contribute to neither object. If, however, your Zionistic friends will carry out the Philadelphia program and will assert that the Jews of this country are in duty bound to help both causes and that they would never feel the loss of any money which they might contribute to both, they will help both, as they have before and as they can well afford to do. "Faint heart never won fair lady," and people who do not have confidence in themselves, will never inspire confidence in others for any cause in which they are interested.

In conclusion let me say that, though I would regret the fact of your denying yourself to your brethren in Eastern Europe, this campaign will proceed. The majority of the Jews in the United States still believe in Holy Writ and in its commands, that we shall not withdraw our hands from our brethren who are needy nor place a stumbling block in their path. They are unwilling to give these admonitions a narrow, parochial, partisan connotation, and I therefore feel justified in prophesying that the fund which we are seeking to collect will be subscribed.

Very truly yours,
/s/ Louis Marshall

Rabbi Solomon Goldman
1551 East Boulevard,
Cleveland, Ohio

November 5, 1925

Mr. Louis Marshall,
120 Broadway,
New York, New York

Dear Mr. Marshall:

I never suggested, and never thought of suggesting that East European Jewry be left to face its miserable plight without any assistance from American Israel. I am too near my East European brethren to forget them. To me they are not only "co-religionists" but brothers in the flesh. When the Joint two years ago decided to liquidate, a good many of us, who are now reproached with forgetting our European brethren, were amazed at such an arbitrary decision and the Yiddish press the country over protested most vigorously.

In one part of your letter you speak of my impracticability, "iridescent dream" and "grandiose scheme" (I, of course, had in mind only the number of families that Dr. Rosen maintains he could help with his plan). In another part of your letter you chide me with a lack of confidence in myself and remind me that "faint heart never won fair lady." There is, apparently, a contradiction in these two statements.

It is neither faint-heartedness that prompted me to reject Mr. Brown's invitation to serve on the National Committee, nor is it an iridescent dream that makes me want to see Jews give priority to Palestine. You speak, in your letter, of Palestine as an "ism" and as a particular theory. You tell me that "at the proper time" the Jews of America will respond generously. That is exactly where my "Zionistic friends" and you differ. Palestine to us is not a theory. It is not an "ism." Palestine is synonymous with Jewish Life. It is the embodiment of our culture, our religious ideals. It is the storehouse of the glorious memories of our Past and our sole hope for the Future.

The proper time to build Palestine is today, as it was eight years ago immediately after the Balfour Declaration was published. We lost so many golden opportunities because so many American Jews failed to realize that we were confronting a "condition and not a theory."

Sincerely,
/s/ Solomon Goldman

The Mack–Goldman Exchange

We publish this exchange between Rabbi Goldman and Judge
Julian Mack, a distinguished member of the Federal bench, a close
friend and confident of Justice Brandeis, of Stephen Wise, of Felix
Frankfurter and one of the most effective Zionist leaders ever to
come from the German Jewish community. The exchange throws
light on the reasons for the split between the Brandeis–Mack leadership and the Weizmann–Lipsky forces, a split which some historians believe set the Zionist movement back for at least a decade.
It also reveals the first groping awareness of the need to include the
East-European Jews in the heretofore closed circles of the American
Jewish Committee leadership. The exchange indicates that as a
prophet Goldman proved to be wrong in his fear that the Zionists
on the Jewish Agency would be swallowed up by the non-Zionists
and right in his insistence that the Zionist Organization would have
to take a major responsibility for Hebrew education in America, if
it was not to become a debased money-raising bureaucracy.

Dr. Stephen S. Wise   March 28, 1927
40 W. 68th Street
New York City.

Dear Dr. Wise:
   I am enclosing copies of my letter to Judge Mack and his reply.
I will be interested in your comments.
   With kindest regards,

                                                    Cordially yours,
                                                    Solomon Goldman

                          *   *   *

                                                    P. O. Box 587
                                                    Palm Beach, Fla.
Dr. S. S. Wise,   February 25, 1927
36 West 68th St.,
New York, N. Y.

Dear Wise:—
   I return you herewith Goldman's letter. I do not agree with him in
several particulars.
   Naturally we are not talking about Zionism, but about Palestine,

although in every speech that I make, I emphasize and usually tell first why I am a Zionist and second whether they be Zionists or not, why they ought to be interested in Palestine. He fails totally to catch the viewpoint of our group which ever since 1920 and even before, has been that we must concentrate on the physical upbuilding of Palestine as the basis of all of our work. He may be right that it will take at least a century, but it is our duty to endeavor to hasten the day and the only possible way to hasten it is by first laying the physical foundations strong and safe.

There are many other forces interested in the conservation of the Jews and Judaism in the United States. We must trust to them for that preservation. If we had untold forces, we could do both. Not having them, we must stick to our specific job.

I may be all wrong about it, but I do believe that more is being done for Hebrew literature and Jewish education today than ever before and that despite the fact that Habimah is having a struggle.

Of course you know how I have felt about the so called peace and indeed the whole Jewish agency, never the less, Goldman fails to take into consideration a vital element. Weizmann's diplomacy is not sure to fail because your oratory and L.D.B.'s mind failed to bring the other element in and this because neither of you nor even I is persona grata to that group because of our general viewpoint and other personal reasons. Weizmann is not thus handicapped.

Goldman's observation that these men are influential only when they sponsor movements popular with their class is extremely acute. I hope they will not turn out to be 100% correct.

In any event, Goldman's implication that *we* tried and failed, demonstrates that in our judgment at least, there is nothing in principle against trying. That is what Weizmann is doing and we can only hope that he may succeed.

Personally, while I hadn't much confidence in any great success, I do believe that no possible harm can come to our movement, that while they are not Zionists, they are not anti-Zionists.* I further have

---

* Mack refers here to the proposal to include prominent and wealthy non-Zionist Jews—like those in the leadership of the American Jewish Committee—in the Jewish Agency—the ultimate non-governmental authority in the gathering and disbursing of funds for Palestine and in the establishment of priorities in rebuilding the land.

always believed and still believe that by getting into the work they may in course of time be completely won over and that in any event even though they go into it without our ultimate aim and purpose, they are not going into it against our ultimate aim and their very going into it must in the nature of things aid in the achievement of our end.

I cannot believe that a united Zionist 50% will fail to have some support from the other 50%, especially from the European element of it which would include such men as Jimmie Rothchild. I do not believe, although I must say that L. D. B. fears it, that the Zionists will be swallowed up.

Sincerely yours,
Julian Mack

*   *   *

Judge Julian Mack   March 11, 1927
P. O. Box 567
Palm Beach, Fla.

My dear Judge:

Dr. Wise was kind enough to forward me a copy of your letter in which you discussed my letter to him, relative to the Weizmann-Marshall agreement. I have not a copy of my letter to Dr. Wise before me now. I do not recall, however, that I conveyed the impression that the Zionist Organization is to undertake educating American Israel. What I meant to convey to Dr. Wise was that the Zionist Organization has become nothing but a money-gathering agency. It is, to my mind, completely denuded at present of all idealism. I, for one, do not believe that ideals can thrive on diplomacy and compromise. For the sake of shekels the Zionist Organization has stooped to both.

Zionist leadership, in America at least, is bankrupt. Ever since the Brandeis-Mack group lost control there are no longer any personalities among the leaders that have the confidence of American Jewry. There is a strong suspicion that the Zionist Organization is one of the most corrupt bureaucracies in the world.

I did not at all fail to grasp your viewpoint in 1920 as to the importance of the physical upbuilding of Palestine. As a matter of fact, I followed your leadership, because your program was so different and the leaders high-minded and beyond reproach.

Now, as to Hebrew literature and Jewish education, you maintain that there is more being done today than ever before. I cannot agree with you on that. There is much more noise perhaps, today. Eighty per cent of the Jewish children in this country receive no Hebrew education. The Hebrew monthlies had to go out of existence. The Hadoar is struggling between life and death. The Hashiloach has been discontinued. Hebrew books have no market in this country. Most European Jews are making money, joining the reform temples, sending their children to the Sunday Schools and, in most cases, turning their backs on the Hebrew language and literature.

I never criticised Weizmann for his efforts to win the non-Zionists. I objected to his methods. I do not say that he should not try simply because the Brandeis-Wise group failed, but Weizmann, in his correspondence, has abandoned the Zionist position that Palestine must be given priority over any Jewish community in the Diaspora. It is illogical to assume that Jews who give no such priority to Palestine will ever become interested in its upbuilding. After all, there are 4,000,000 Jews in Poland, 2,000,000 Jews in Russia, and only 150,000 in Palestine. Why should the non-Zionist or the anti-Zionist give his money to relieve the needs of a Jewish community so small as compared with the larger Jewish settlements in Eastern Europe.

I believe that the formation of the agency has been postponed because Marshall realizes that he cannot get his group to support it. Marshall has thus far sponsored only movements that were popular with his group. He failed, for instance, as chairman of the million-dollar-campaign for the Seminary, to interest any of his people outside of the Schiff family. The Schiffs, of course, are loyal to the memory of Jacob A. Schiff. Marshall's efforts for Jewish education, particularly where Hebrew is emphasized, have thus far brought no results.

In the last two years, we had Marshall in Cleveland on two different occasions. Once when he came to appeal for the Seminary Campaign, Silver, Wolsey and the president of the Federation of Jewish Charities, N. W. Baker, were the only reform Jews who came to pay their respects to Marshall. His host for the day, Mr. Emil Joseph, brought Marshall to the banquet but did not remain there. Last year, Marshall was brought to Cleveland by the Bureau of Jewish Education. Silver sponsored the meeting. Every effort was made to bring a large turn-out. The hall was empty—125 men and women came to hear Marshall's message. Ninety per cent of the people were from orthodox or conservative groups. Brown, for a year, was making gestures in behalf of the Keren Hayesod. What was the net result?

You and Wise and Justice Brandeis may be persona non grata with a few of the leaders, but to the American Jew you mean much more than anyone in, let me say, the American Jewish Committee—with the possible exception of Louis Marshall. I cannot get myself to believe, much as I have tried, that Weizmann will succeed, or that Marshall will succeed, where you, Brandeis and Wise failed. Let me put it perhaps bluntly. How many members of the Free Synagogue has Wise persuaded to participate actively in Zionist or Palestinian effort? How many has Silver, in the Cleveland Temple? The wealthiest members of his congregation contributed $25, $50, $100, with but one or two exceptions, and that is not because of their interest in Zionism but because of their admiration for Silver personally. They are simply offering a bouquet of flowers to a prima donna.

The main criticism in my letter to Wise is that we are chasing shadows. We are endeavoring to reach the non-Zionist, spending so much energy on him and neglecting the inexhaustable resources in our own midst.

I wonder whether you are aware of the fact that on Eastern Parkway, President Street, etc. in Brooklyn, there are Jews of untold wealth. There are from three to five hundred men in that community who could give all the money that Palestine needs. They are nearer to the cause and more easily approached. We have never concentrated on these people. We have never put them in a position of leadership. We have never imposed responsibility upon these men. We have been trying to catch hold of the coat tails of shadows. There are a few Jews in America who have given fairly large sums to Palestine,—Sol Rosenblum, Philip Wattenberg, Peter Schweitzer. It is my conviction that many more such men can be found among the Jews of the United States.

I hope that this letter does not test your patience. With cordial greetings,

Sincerely yours,
Solomon Goldman

P. O. Box 587
Palm Beach, Florida
Rabbi Solomon Goldman   March 14, 1927.
Cleveland, Ohio.

Dear Rabbi Goldman:

I quite agree with you that our program of 1921 was something very different from what the Z. O. [Zionist Organization] has been attempting. On the other hand, to be entirely just, we must not forget that if we had remained in control we should have been confronted with the double task—that of raising funds for economic upbuilding, and also raising gift funds for the Keren Ha-yesod or whatever would have taken its place. We felt at that time, and for several years before that much as Hebrew education was needed in this country, that task could not be performed by the Z. O. but ought to be left to others.

Of course I must defer to your judgement as to what is being done for Jewish education in this country. I had thought, from the amount of talk, that more was being done than ever before.

My own views on the Agency question have not changed. Justice Brandeis' proposal in London, in 1920 offered the only hopeful solution—that is, to first get leading English non-Zionist elements—getting them into positions of responsibility for economic work in the Z. O. itself—not outside of it and not in an advisory capacity. The outlook was hopeful when it was completely ditched. That was the beginning and the basis of all the later troubles, and to my mind was the most deplorable event in the whole Zionist work. The hope was that if the British came in, men like Marshall and Warburg would follow.

Of course the present Agency scheme is entirely different. It recognizes the equality in numbers, at least, of the non-Zionists. My great difficulty is in seeing how any non-Zionist can honestly be a member of an Agency which necessarily aims to carry out the Mandate, the guiding purpose of which is to establish in Palestine "A *National* Home for the Jewish People." If anybody has this aim I should suppose that he would necessarily be a Zionist; if he has not this aim, I do not see how he can go into the Agency. Because of this belief, I have kept silent on this subject during these years. If these men believe that they can go into the Agency and in any way assist in the upbuilding of Palestine, that is a matter for their own consciences; if the only way or the best way is to secure the support of the others, I am content to let them try it and to take the responsibility for it. I do not feel a duty to oppose it because I have no fears that the non-Zionists will not honestly work for the upbuilding of Palestine and I further have no fears that those who do so work either will try to hinder or succeed in hindering the realization of the Zionist's aim, of establishing a National Home through the settlement in Palestine of the largest possible number of eventually self-supporting Jews.

We have tried to reach the Eastern Parkway wealthy men, but as you know, even Rabbi Levinthal has not succeeded. Wise, and Weizmann and I have in years past talked to them. Whether they can be influenced by those whom they may regard as real leaders— men of still greater wealth, like Warburg—I do not know. It is just groups like this, and similar groups in New York City—who are really born Zionists who because of their East European birth, ought to be among the leaders in the movement—that I hope may be attracted through the Agency. They were not attracted under our leadership into the Z. O. and they of course are not attracted under the present leadership.

Frankly, these rich Jews of East European birth are in my judgement, the most hopeless lot. The richer they grow the more ashamed they seem to become both of their birth and their orthodoxy; too many of them are ready to hide both; what they want is the honor of leadership —not the obligations of service. Personally, I feel that they are good only for the money that they can give—and, feeling that way, I am glad if any method can be devised honorably to get them to give in larger amounts. I should however, be most happy if I am doing them an injustice, and if they would, with their excellent business ability, really be induced to give time and thought in loyal service to the Cause itself.

The men that you name are the exceptions. I hope that you are right in thinking there are many others. If you can only point them out, I for one, would be willing to give a great deal of time in endeavoring to interest them in the work.

With cordial greetings,

Sincerely,
Julian W. Mack

JWM.FS

Zionist Correspondence
Weizmann Letters

The letters from and to Dr. Chaim Weizmann in Rabbi Gold-man's files have been contributed by the Goldman family to the Archives of the World Zionist Organization in Jerusalem. They reveal the qualities of mind and heart which made the first President of the State of Israel a worthy heir to Moses, the first lawgiver and statesman, who led the Children of Israel to the Promised Land. Rabbi Goldman found himself thrust into the very maelstrom of power politics during the fateful years 1938–1939—the years of the infamous White Paper. As he recalled that time, he never ceased to wonder how strange were the ways of destiny that a bookwormish rabbi of a congregation could be linked with the movers and the shakers of the world.

15th July, 1938

Rabbi S. Goldmann,
Zionist Organisation of America,
111 Fifth Avenue,
New York City.

My dear Rabbi Goldmann,

You will, I hope, have received my telegram offering you my warmest congratulations on your election to the Presidency of the Zionist Organisation of America, but I would like to take this opportunity of confirming my congratulations and good wishes in writing.

It needs no words of mine to tell you that you are taking office at a most crucial time in the history of our movement and of our people. American Jewry is now the one great Jewish community which still remains intact, and Fate has thus placed upon it, and upon you as the head of the Zionist Movement in the United States, a very heavy task, as well as a great opportunity. The coming months will no doubt bring with them momentous decisions which may influence the political situation in Palestine for years to come. But whatever those decisions may be—and I must make it clear that we are still without any grounds for prophecy in this connection, either one way or the other—independently of the work of the Commission or of the attitude of His Majesty's Government, we ourselves must see to it that our work continues under any circumstances, and continues even more intensively than hitherto.

If it is brought home to the British Government and to the British people that, undaunted by all that has happened, we are still prepared to make a greater effort than ever, this in itself will be a political factor of the first magnitude.

It is yet too early to say whether there will be a Zionist Congress this year to provide a major Zionist platform. Evian on the other hand has proved a grave disappointment, and its achievement has been almost negligible. Palestine figured hardly at all at the Conference.

On thinking over the situation I feel very strongly that we ourselves should set about calling together a Conference which shall deal exclusively with Palestine and its relation to the Jewish position in general. Such a conference would have to be fully representative in character, well thought out, and well prepared; naturally it would not be intended in any way to replace the Congress. It should take place either in England or in America. We must once and for all emancipate ourselves from the idea that we can place all our hopes in others; the classical formula of Pinsker that self-help is the only solution of the Jewish problem is more true today than it was even sixty years ago. The success of a conference such as I have in mind would depend in the first place on the support forthcoming from America, and on whether the American Organisation and the American community are prepared to throw their full weight whole-heartedly into its organisation. If this could be ensured, there could, I feel, be no more auspicious opening to your period of office.

Apart from the Jewish Agency itself, it occurs to me that, in convening such a conference, it would be well to have the support of some of our great Jewish personalities—unfortunately there are not too many of them—such as Einstein, Blum, Freud, Brandeis, and perhaps one or two more. I myself am at present in communication with M. Blum, and if my proposal commands itself to you, I would be glad if you would get into touch with Einstein and Brandeis, with a view to sounding them with regard to it.

As to the programme of the conference, I anticipate that it should be both political and practical in character. It is unnecessary for me here to enter into detail as regards the political aspect. On the practical side there are a number of economic questions with which the Conference might concern itself, and in particular there is the proposal for the raising of a large loan for development and constructive work in Palestine. This is a project on which I have now been working for some little time, and in regard to which I believe it would be possible to come to the Conference with definite proposals for consideration and approval.

My purpose in writing this letter is to ask you to think over this proposal, which I feel may be a most important one, and to consult a few of our friends in the States, like Wise and Lipsky, and a few others whom you think may be useful, and then to let me know your first reactions by telegram. It is of course essential that the whole matter should be handled with the utmost discretion, and that until we come to a definite decision, nothing should be allowed to leak out into the Press, as this would jeopardise the whole scheme.

The foregoing is, of course, only the briefest possible outline of a scheme which has yet to be worked out in detail, but I felt that before proceeding further I should like to have your advice, and that of my other friends in the States, on whom so much will depend. I shall anxiously await your reply to this letter, and should appreciate it if you would cable as soon as possible after its receipt.

With kind personal regards, and all good wishes,

> I am
> Very sincerely yours,
> Ch. Weizmann

*   *   *

Meeting between Chaim Weizmann and President Roosevelt

This is a coded memorandum of a meeting between Chaim Weizmann and President Franklin Roosevelt, arranged by Rabbi Stephen S. Wise, on February 8, 1939, to discuss the Palestine question. Y is Roosevelt; C is Weizmann; P is Wise; and F is Felix Frankfurter. Goldman, as President of the ZOA, could not be present, but was kept fully informed of the proceedings.

The appointment with Y. was arranged through P. who introduced C. and was present throughout the conversation. The talk was most friendly in character and lasted about a half hour.

Y. opened by saying that he had, of course, heard a good deal about C. and was glad to meet him. C. began by dealing with his tour.

He said that he had been traveling through the country renewing old contacts and had addressed large audiences in a number of cities. Y. remarked that there were a good many Jews here who were not exactly obstructionists so far as Palestine was concerned, but who were not too friendly. C. said, "Certainly that was so, but that on the whole sentiment for Palestine was very strong. Y. said "Yes, I agree."

Discussion then centered on developments in Palestine. C. said that in the past few years they had had a shattering time there, but they had withstood the assault. The Jews had indeed strengthened their positions in many directions and more than eighty thousand people had come into the country in that period. He was not going to attempt to harrow Y.'s feelings by a description of what was taking place to the Jews of Central and Eastern Europe. No doubt, he knew the situation well enough, but the fact was that today Palestine and the United States were the only countries which were taking substantial numbers of immigrants. Y. asked whether C. did not think that other countries too might absorb refugees and referred to Columbia. C. said that if it were possible to settle some refugees there, by all means let it be done, but none of these places could be a substitute for Palestine. He gave the example of Argentine where after sixty years of colonization under excellent conditions, only a few thousand Jewish families remained on the land. C. said that if one examined the situation in Europe today, eliminating those Jews who would have been swallowed up by the Russian system and disappeared, and those who would have perished—if the present rate of destruction continued —there would be two and a half millions to care for. Of these many would be aged or otherwise unsuitable for immigration. Some would find an outlet in other countries, while a certain number would in any case remain where they were. He believed that one million of the younger and more vigorous elements could over a period of years be drawn off to Palestine. This would be an immense contribution to the whole question. The problem was not really an unmanageable one if tackled with determination and with the object of aiming at a solution and not at palliatives. There were still great possibilities of development in Palestine which would enable the absorption of large numbers of immigrants.

C. referred to the report of Dr. Lowdermilk of the United States Department of Agriculture and said that even he (C.) could not have written a better one. Y. said that he had read the document; it was a wonderful report; the Jews had done very well. C. went on to say that the investigations of our experts had shown that, leaving out of consideration the great areas of the Negeb, there should be no difficulty in the settlement of an additional million people. Y. remarked that Chatham was sure that there was room for the settlement of at least two million people more in Palestine. C. said it all depended on the extent of development. A dense population would depend largely on industrial development.

*   *   *

April 28th, 1939

My dear Dr. Goldman,

Ben-Gurion has sent me a copy of your letter of April 6th, in which you gave details of your interview with the President. I am delighted to read it and in these times of stress it was a great comfort to feel that a man of Roosevelt's calibre is beginning to understand the importance of Palestine and the severity of the struggle through which we are passing at present. I am now three weeks in the country and cannot do better than send you a copy of a letter I am sending to our friend William Bullitt in Paris, and which gives a good picture of the situation as I see it. I have really nothing more to add to it. I shall be grateful if you will circulate this letter and the enclosures to our friends and naturally show it to Judge Brandeis. I also enclose a cutting from the Egyptian Gazette which is, as you may know, the official organ of the British in Egypt and in particular the British Embassy, which clearly indicates their attitude and methods of propaganda in the neighbouring states. With such an attitude, which completely ignores all the moral and contractual obligations of the British towards the League and us, you can clearly understand that it makes it very difficult for us to get on a footing of negotiations with the Arabs although the time seems to me at present more propitious than it was in the history of the last twenty years. Perhaps the attached short statement on our program of work among the Arabs which was drawn up by our Political Department might give you an idea of the lines along which we would like to proceed.

There is another matter of extreme importance which I would like you to bring to the notice of Justice Brandeis and that is the possibility of acquisition of a large tract of land belonging to the Druses as per enclosed map. I need hardly point out to you that if this land could be acquired, the whole problem of Upper Galilee would be definitely settled. This would give us a territory almost contiguous from the Huleh down to Rehovot, which in its size almost equals the territory allotted to us by the Peel Report. Incidentally the Druse, who are a small minority in this country are very uneasy in view of the new British policy. They are not only willing to divest themselves of the lands, but also to migrate to the Jebel Druse and join their brethren in Syria. The realization of this project would mean the emigration of 10,000 Arabs, the acquisition of 300,000 dunams and the creation of a block ranging from Huleh through the Emek down the Coastal Plain to Beer-Tuviah, with a reserve of land which would enable us to work quietly for the next five or ten years, without any fear of whatever restrictions the British Government might contemplate. In fact, it would break the attempt to crystallize the National Home. It would offer all the advantages of Partition without a single one of its disadvantages. We are actively pursuing the enquiries into this matter and understand that it will cost us something like three million pounds (on an average price of LP 10. per dunam). A certain stretch of this land is on the Eastern Carmel, as you may see on the map, so that by buying it up, the overwhelming part of the Carmel would become Jewish. I could hardly point out to you all the agricultural, economic and political implications of such a purchase. It is the greatest opportunity which has been offering itself to us during the last 50 years and can only be compared with what Baron Edmund did when he acquired the lands in the Coastal Plain. It would relieve us of a great many of our political troubles for a long time to come and by consolidating our holdings in Upper Galilee, Huleh and the Coastal Plain we would be able easily to expand further when the time comes. It would also create a significant precedent if 10,000 Arabs were to emigrate peacefully of their own volition, which no doubt would be followed by others, and I believe that the President's suggestion of a large loan for the transmigration of Arabs from Palestine to Iraq would then become a realizable project.

In the course of my meetings with the Iraquis during the London Conference I have from time to time thrown out this idea and have more than once struck a responsive cord. The suggestion would be received particularly favorably if the initiative came from America. I did not wish to go deeply into this matter because I knew that Mr.

Edward Norman was dealing with it very discretely and I believe very
ably. It would not be without value if you would go to Mr. Norman
and to Mr. Ruskin on the subject of emigration to Iraq in connection
with the President's remarks. One of the Iraqi delegates with whom I
became rather friendly indicated that he would be prepared to take
an active part in helping such a project forward. Although the
London Conference has brought us a great deal of disappointment, it
has, on the other hand, produced the effect of establishing some
personal contacts between ourselves and some Arab leaders in Iraq and
Egypt and I am trying actively to develop these relations which with
care might in time lead to some positive results. Although my visit to
Egypt was merely a courtesy visit, it strengthened the friendly relations
between us and some of the leading Egyptians. If the British were not
blinded by abject fear of phantoms they could not only help us in
settling the Palestinian difficulties but would for all times make a
substantial contribution to the friendly relations between us and the
Arabs in spite of the Mufti and his satellites. Whatever is it that has
come over the British, whether it is fear or the infection by the virus of
Hitlerism or something else, but it is certainly a bitter disappointment
and a great tragedy. Should any of our friends have the opportunity
of a further talk with your President you might point out this Druse
question to him as a typical example of the unsoundness of what
British official quarters have been saying about Upper Galilee since the
publication of the Peel Report. Their thesis was that the Peel
Commission had blundered in offering the Jews a part of Palestine
which is so thickly populated by Arabs that its colonisation would
mean a constant war with them. The heart of Upper Galilee is not
Arab, but Druse and we could acquire it peacefully with the consent
of the Druses. All the district along the Acre-Safed road as far as
Hanitah and Nahariah could become Jewish in a perfectly peaceful
manner, with the added benefit of the emigration of something like
10,000 souls. This is a typical example of the grotesque exaggeration
preached by these British officials all these years. I cannot help
feeling that this distortion of facts is intentional and malevolent.
Unfortunately, one must not breathe a word about it publicly as it
would ruin the prospects of the purchase but to our friends in
America this could be pointed out as a typical example of
mendacious anti-Zionist propaganda.

(signed) Affectionately,
Yours Ch. Weizmann

Letter from Viscount Halifax to Dr. Weizmann

December 19, 1939

Dear Dr. Weizmann:

Since we had our talk at the Foreign Office on the 30th of November, I have given further thought to the letter which you left with me, and I have taken the opportunity of discussing with others the matters at issue.

As I have already told you I have no authority to discuss the affairs of Palestine, which are outside my province, nor is my acquaintance with such questions sufficiently close and continuous to enable me to reply in detail to the various points raised in your letter. Writing, however, as a member of the Cabinet which was collectively responsible for the recent White Paper on Palestine policy I may perhaps venture to give you my opinion on the broader aspect of the question as I see it.

In the first place, may I remind you that the policy embodied in the White Paper was adopted by the Cabinet after long and anxious deliberation as the most equitable solution of a bitter controversy, and as the only course which would enable us to fulfill in equal measure our Mandatory obligations to Jews and Arabs. In the circumstances, it seems clear to me that it is not possible to modify or postpone the application of the White Paper policy in favour of one community without doing an injustice to the other. This strikes me as a governing consideration.

The policy of the White Paper became effective as soon as it had been approved by Parliament and as you know our attitude is that, as that policy does not involve any amendment of the Mandate, it does not require the prior approval of the League Council; neither before the War nor since has the Government said or done anything to justify the assumption that the implementation of the policy would be deferred either because it has not yet been approved by the League Council or on account of the war situation.

In conclusion let me assure you that I am the last to underrate the value of Jewish sympathy and co-operation with the Allied War effort. But highly as His Majesty's Government appreciated Jewish offers of assistance on the outbreak of war, it must not be overlooked that those offers were made unconditionally and were welcomed on that footing. So far as this country is concerned, we are putting our whole energy into a life-and-death struggle with Nazi Germany, the persecutor of Jewry in Central Europe, and by ridding Europe of the present German regime, we hope to render a supreme service to the Jewish people.

Yours sincerely,
Halifax

*　*　*

Letter from Dr. Weizmann to Lord Halifax

SECRET
Dec. 29/39.

Your letter of the 19th has reached me late on the same day. As I had to leave early the next day I could not answer it immediately, and had to postpone doing so until I reached here where I have to wait a day or two before taking the "Clipper."

I confess that your letter came rather as a shock. But I don't propose to trouble you with a lengthy answer.

I am not competent to judge whether the policy of the White Paper although approved by Parliament requires the consent of the League Council before it could be implemented. The House however was most anxious to hear the opinion of the League on the subject and many references were made in the Debate to the Mandates Commission whose report was awaited with the keenest interest. The outbreak of the war which has taken place a few days after the publication of the report by the Permanent Mandates Commission has removed the whole problem to a second plane and all discussion of it was suspended. But the opinion expressed in the report of the Mandates Commission leaves no room for any doubt that the White Paper is incompatible with the Mandate as interpreted hitherto by His Majesty's Government. Whatever the legal point of view adopted by the Colonial Office may be, their moral attitude is open to a very serious doubt.

We are now as before uncompromisingly opposed to the Policy of the White Paper, but I fully agree that Jewish cooperation with the Allied War-effort is and will continue to be unconditional. Nevertheless there is no reason why unnecessary and unjustified hardship should be inflicted on us at a time when every day brings in its train untold destruction of Jewish life and property.

I fervently hope that Europe will be rid of the Nazi cancer and we all realize only too well the decisive role which England is playing in this gigantic struggle for the preservation of moral values forming the very foundation of our civilization, and just because of this knowledge I had hoped that you would not like to see anything done which might prejudice the Jewish future.

After victory has been won the Jewish problem will still be there in all its ghastly nakedness as a challenge to the new world which may arise and I am deeply convinced that only in Palestine and through Palestine an equitable and lasting solution can be found.

May I be allowed to offer you my best wishes for a better and happier 1940.

* * *

DATED. 26th February 1940
BRITISH EMBASSY
WASHINGTON

My dear Dr. Weizmann:

Since I wrote to you on February 24th I have had a telegram from Lord Halifax, asking me to tell you that the Prime Minister, the Colonial Secretary and himself have received from Mr. Shertok the text of your telegram, in which you expressed concern at the intended introduction of land-sale restrictions in Palestine.

Mr. Chamberlain, Mr. MacDonald and Lord Halifax wish to assure you that, before deciding to authorize the High Commissioner to issue the regulations in question, His Majesty's Government took very full account of the considerations which you have urged. They appreciate the force of your arguments but they hope you will realize from the explanations which I gave you in my letter of the 24th February that in the opinion of His Majesty's Government the decision was necessary and indeed inevitable in the circumstances.

(Signed) Lothian

Dr. Chaim Weizmann
Hotel Ambassador
New York City

Brandeis Wire to Chamberlain

No better testimony of the desperateness of the situation created by the White Paper can be found than is in this telegram sent by a Justice of the Supreme Court who more than any of his colleagues believed that a member of the Court must not interfere in current political issues and most particularly in those affecting a foreign power.

(Secret)

Feb. 26, 1939

Right Honorable,
Neville Chamberlain, M.P.,
London.

Dear Prime Minister:

London friends advise me of the proposed intentions of His Majesty's Government with reference to Palestine. Having discussed in detail the problem of the Jewish National Home in Palestine with the late Lord Balfour prior to the publication of the Balfour Declaration and the acceptance of the mandate, I cannot believe that your Government has fully considered how gravely shattered would be the faith of the people of this troubled world in the solemn undertakings of even democratic governments if Great Britain so drastically departed from her declared policy in reference to the Jewish National Home. I wire you to consider the cruel plight of the Jews in the world today and not to crush their most cherished and sanctified hopes. In view of our own belief in direct communication I venture to address this to you personally.

Respectfully,
Louis D. Brandeis.

* * *

Brandeis personal diplomacy made impersonal

March 6th, 1939

Personal

My dear Mr. Justice,

I have been instructed to acknowledge a telegram which you sent on February 26th to the Prime Minister, protesting that the proposed

intentions of His Majesty's Government regarding Palestine are a
drastic departure from their declared policy with reference to the
Jewish National Home.

I think you may know that any opinion you may entertain on the
question of Palestine, when brought to the attention of my
Government, commands their respectful and earnest attention. In the
present instance I am to beg that whatever reports you may have heard,
you will defer forming an opinion until my Government shall have
issued an authoritative statement as to their attitude. Meanwhile you
can rest assured that they are very mindful of their obligations with
regard to the Jewish National Home under the Balfour Declaration
and the Mandate.

> Believe me,
> My dear Mr. Justice,
> Yours very sincerely,
> R. C. Lindsay.

*   *   *

24th March, 1939.

My dear Mr. Prime Minister,

Although I hesitate to add to the pressure on your time by asking
you even to read an additional letter, I cannot leave for Palestine at
this juncture without making to you a personal appeal and suggestion.
Never before have I quitted England with so heavy a heart. A cloud
hangs over the relations between the Jewish Agency and British
Ministers. Through all the ups and downs of more than twenty years,
I have found support in the thought that, to quote Lord Balfour's
words, we were "partners in the great enterprise" which means life or
death to my people.

In a week's time I shall be in Palestine. Even in present
circumstances, it will be our duty to try and keep the spirit of our
people calm and collected, and their discipline unbroken. But they
have been sorely tried, and the chances of my succeeding would be
greatly improved if the threatened blow of the new policy was not
inflicted upon them at this time. Please consider the events of the past
twelve months as they more particularly affect the Jews.

Hitler's entry into Vienna; the expulsion of Jews from Italy and from Danzig; the Nazi occupation of the Sudetenland; the November pogrom in Germany; the anti-semitic measures in Slovakia; the Nazi invasion of Bohemia and Moravia; and now Memel. It is against this background that any threat to our work and position in Palestine will be judged by Jews all over the world.

In times so deeply disturbed, could we not avoid adding to the turmoil? For such would be the result of putting forward a policy which only raises further questions and provokes further demands, and satisfies no-one. If the announcement of the decision is postponed, I do not mean to leave the time unused. Every effort will be made, and every contact used, to explore the possibility of a Jewish-Arab agreement or rapprochement. While I cannot promise any success, I would suggest that lapse of time may open possibilities in this direction.

I would like to add a word of thanks for your unfailing kindness to me throughout this difficult time. This emboldens me to believe that you may still, even at the last moment, prevent this additional sorrow from being added to our tragic lot.

> With kind regards, believe me,
> yours very sincerely,
> Sgd. . . . . CH. WEIZMANN

The Right Hon. Neville Chamberlain, P.C., M.P.,
10 Downing Street
S.W.1.

* * *

A note of counsel and consolation from Frank Knox:

May 20, 1939.

Rabbi Solomon Goldman, President
Zionist Organization of America,
3760 North Pine Grove Avenue,
Chicago, Illinois.

It is a matter of deep personal regret to me that I cannot be with you to participate in the meeting tomorrow night. However, we found an opportunity in our Saturday edition of The Chicago Daily

News to express our views very vigorously on the Palestine situation.

One of our early American Fathers warned us to always expect in dealing with foreign nations that they will act in their own selfish interests, and how emphatically and obviously the British treatment of the Jewish problem in Palestine illumines that warning.

I cannot but believe that this fresh evidence of a cynical disregard for promises made, when fulfillment of those promises seems a temporary detriment, will inure to further depletion of Britain's already depleted international prestige. In all British history, no period has seen so swift a descent in world esteem than that suffered by the British Empire since 1931 when it, callously, ran out on its pledged word to help preserve the territorial integrity of the nations bordering on the Pacific. The failure of Great Britain to support us in our demands upon Japan to preserve the terms of the Nine-Power Pact with regard to China, marked the beginning of an era in British diplomacy, the record of which future Britains will read with shame, culminating, as it does, with the undefensible violation of the British pledge to the Jews of the world with respect to Palestine.

The lesson for America, of course, is obvious: We must make as few promises as possible in dealing with other nations, and then keep those promises inviolate.

Yours sincerely,
Frank Knox

*   *   *

Confidential code cable received by Dr. Solomon Goldman, May 24, 1939 from David ben-Gurion, Jerasulem.

WE MUST AND ARE PREPARED TO BRING IN FIFTY THOUSAND JEWS THOUSAND WEEKLY THIS REQUIRES SEVEN THOUSAND POUNDS WEEKLY OUR CONTRIBUTION COST BRINGING THEM TO PALESTINE STOP CONSULT CHATHAM [Brandeis] OTHER FRIENDS DEVISE MEANS PROVIDING THESE FUNDS OUTSIDE ORDINARY KEREN YESOD KEREN KAYEMET REQUIREMENTS STOP MOST RELIABLY INFORMED GOVERNMENT WILL BE UNABLE PREVENT THIS IMMIGRATION CARRYING OUT THIS PROGRAMMING MEANS DEFEAT WHITE PAPER INFINITE STRENGTHENING JEWISH POSITION ALSO DECISIVE PREPAREDNESS EVENT WAR   BEN GURION

Cable received from Jerusalem for Dr. Solomon Goldman
on May 29, 1939:
Confidential code cable

CONSIDER CALAMITOUS IF YOU DECLINE WEIZMANN OFFER PROCEED
AMERICA STOP SITUATION SO CRITICAL TIME FACTOR SO VITAL THAT CANNOT
TREAT MATTERS ON NORMAL BASIS STOP OUR ONLY HOPE DEFEAT
GOVERNMENTS POLICY IF JEWS MAKE SUPERHUMAN EFFORT IMMEDIATELY
STOP THEREFORE URGE YOU PREVAIL COLLEAGUES INVITE WEIZMANN NOW
AM CONFIDENT WITH YOUR HELP HIS VISIT WILL BE FRUITFUL DESPITE
DRAWBACKS STOP AFTER OUR EFFORTS PMC [Permanent Mandates
Commission] GENEVA OUR POLITICAL STRUGGLE WILL CONSIST PRACTICAL
EFFORTS BY INCREASING IMMIGRATION AND LAND SETTLEMENT TO PROVE
GOVERNMENT CAN NOT IMPLEMENT POLICY THEREFORE WILL BE COMPELLED
CHANGE POLICY STOP ALSO STRENGTHENING ECONOMIC AND POLITICAL
AUTONOMY OF YISHUV AND PREPAREDNESS STOP OTHER MEASURES LIKE
NONPAYMENT TAXES HAVE DEMONSTRATIVE VALUE BUT WILL NOT MAKE
GOVERNMENT YIELD STOP YISHUV UNITED IN DETERMINATION DEFEAT POLICY
SUPPORTING OUR LINE ACTION STOP YOUTH DEMANDING MORE AGGRESSIVE
ACTION READY MAKE EVERY SACRIFICE STOP INDISPENSABLE WE DO THINGS
NOW THIS REQUIRES FUNDS PLEASE CABLE REPLY OUR TWENTY THIRD AND
TWENTY FOURTH   (Signed)   BEN GURI [on]

*   *   *

The Correspondence with Albert Einstein

It was the work of rescuing Max Brod that first brought Rabbi
Goldman in touch with Albert Einstein. When he sent the world's
greatest theoretical physicist copies of his books, Goldman never
thought that Einstein would have the time or inclination to read
them. The fact that he did and that he made such perceptive comments on their contents delighted him as did few other happenings
in his busy lifetime. He once said to me, a younger colleague: "An
active rabbinate can afford opportunities to place yourself where the
great decisions are being made and to rub shoulders with the chosen
few who make them."

I am indebted to Rabbi Joseph Asher of Temple Emanu-El in
San Francisco for the translations of the Einstein letters.

The Einstein–Goldman Correspondence

den 18. Dezember 1938

Rabbi Salomon Goldman
220 S. State Str.
Chicago, Ill.

Sehr geehrter Herr Goldman:—

Vor allem danke ich Ihnen herzlich für Ihr tiefschürfendes Buch,
das ich wegen Ueberlastung meines nicht-wissenschaftlichen Zeit-Etats
bisher nur teilweise habe lesen können. Natürlich aber konnte ich der
Neugier nicht lange widerstehen, den Aufsatz über meine Religionsität
zu lesen. Dass dabei mein armes Selbst zu gut weggekommen ist, ist
der Herzengüte des Beschauers zuzuschreiben. Vom sächlichen
Standpunkte aus aber ist es so treffend, dass ich nur sagen kann: ich
hätte nicht geglaubt, dass ein Mensch in das Innere eines andern
Menschen so tief zu blicken vermag.

Ich hätte mit diesem Briefe sicher gewartet, bis ich Ihr Buch genau
und vollständig studiert habe, wenn nicht eine dirngende
Angelegenheit jeden Aufschub verbote. Max Brod schreibt mir, dass
er in Lebensgefahr sei. Es wird in der Nazi-Presse gegen ihn gehetzt
und man weiss, was dies bedeutet. Der legale Weg der Auswanderung
dauert zu lange und kann ihn deshalb nicht retten. Er braucht eine
Einladung an eine amerikanische Universität, die ihn wenigstens
formal als Lehrer beruft. "Formal" bedeutet ohne Bezahlung von
Seiten der Universität (oder eines akademischen Institutes gleichen
Ranges). Auf diese Weise könnte er legal auswandern und den
grössten Teil seines Vermögens legal mitbringen, was von Prag aus
noch möglich ist.

Max Brod ist nicht nur ein bedeutender Schriftsteller und eine
wahrhaft verehrungswürdige Persönlichkeit, sondern ist auch im
Besitze sehr wertvoller Manuskripte des verstorbenen bedeutenden
Dichters Franz Kafka, um den sich Max Brod in selbstlosester Weise
bemüht hat. Tun Sie bitte, was Sie können, denn es handelt sich um
einen der besten lebenden Söhne unseres Volkes. Ich will mich
zusammen mit Thomas Mann auch bei der Yale-Universität bemühen,
halte mich aber nicht für berechtigt zu warten, bis wir wissen, ob sich
dort etwas machen lässt.

Wenn Sie glauben, dass Sie sich in dieser Angelegenheit oder bei
einer der vielen andern Notfälle, die aus der Verderbtheit unserer Zeit
erwachsen, meiner bedienen können, so bitte ich dies jederzeit zu tun.

Ich habe zwar keine persönlichen Beziehungen, kann aber an jeden Menschen schreiben.

Mit aller Hochachtung und freundlichen Grüssen

Ihr
A. Einstein.

TRANSLATION:

December 18, 1938

TO: Rabbi Solomon Goldman

To begin with, I want to thank you very much for your penetrating book. In view of the burden upon my time, which I set aside for matters unconnected with my scientific work, I have been able only to glance at it. However, I could not resist the curiosity to read at least the essay referring to my religious commitment. It is only because of your generosity that I come off so well. This evaluation spoke quite dispassionately. I can only say: I could not believe that one man would be able to look into the innermost recesses of another as you have done.

I would normally have waited to write this letter until I had studied your book in its entirety. However, a very pressing matter prohibits any further delay. Max Brod wrote to me that he is in great peril of his life. In the Nazi Press there is a great deal of agitation against him; and we know what that means. The legal channels to effect his immigration take too long and would, therefore, not be sufficient to save him. He needs an invitation from an American university which would invite him to serve on its faculty, at least formally. The word "formal" means with no pay from the university (or an academic institution of similar rank). In this way, he could immigrate legally and take with him the larger part of his belongings. This is still possible to do leaving from Prague. Max Brod is not only a significant author and a truly honorable personality, he has in his possession also very valuable manuscripts of the late poet Franz Kafka, about whose life he studied in a most selfless manner. Please do what you can. We are dealing here with one of the most valuable living sons of our people. I shall make an effort, together with Thomas Mann, to try at Yale University. I do not think that I shall be entitled to wait about any other efforts until we know whether anything can be done there.

If you believe that you could use me either in this connection or in any other emergencies growing out of our perilous times, I want you to feel free to do so. While I have no personal connections, I cannot fail to write to everybody. With much respect and friendly greetings, I am yours,

A. Einstein

*   *   *

den 31. Dezember 1938

Rabbi Salomon Goldman
220 S. State Str.
Chicago, Ill.

Lieber Rabbi Goldman:—

Ich habe nun Ihr Buch mit grösstem Interesse durchgelesen. Echte Prophetenglut ist darin; unerbittlich wird den Zeitgenossen der Spiegel vorgehalten, den Juden und den Gojim. Der aufrechte Mut und Optimismus tun wohl bei einem Mann, dem nichts Menschliches fremd geblieben ist, im Schrifttum und sonst in der Welt.

Fast alles ist mir aus der Seele gesprochen. Wohl hoffe ich weniger Heil von der Vereinigung des Hauptteils der Juden in einem Lande oder gar einem Staat; wie wir auch darüber denken mögen, die Notwendigkeit ernsten Strebens danach ist heute unabweislich. Man darf nicht darüber nachdenken, ob unser Volk in der Konzentration nicht jene gefährlichen und hässlichen Schwächen entwickeln wird, die wir an unsern Feinden heute verachten. Den Griechen begegnen Sie wohl nicht mit jener Wärme und Verehrung, die sie verdienen. Ich glaube, dass wir Juden von ihnen gewaltig und in gutem Sinne dauernd beeinflusst worden sind auf Grund der gemeinsamen Liebe zu dem Geistigen, zu Unabhängigkeit im Leben und im Denken.

Ihre Hymne auf "Romance of a People" ist auch gut für solche, die den Kitsch nicht auf der Bühne erlebt haben; "Eternal Road" war noch schlimmer, trotzdes feinen Textes von Werfel. Es ist gefährlich, den gewaltigen Stoff auf die Bühne zu bringen—besonders als ein Ganzes.

Köstlich fand ich besonders die polemischen Aufsätze "Jews and Christians," "The Function of the Rabbi," "Rabbis and Rabbis"; direkt bedeutend "The Goal of Judaism" und "Can Religion Change?"

Ich danke Ihnen herzlich für diese Erquickung in dieser

widerwärtigen Zeit. Sowas kommt nur von einem starken und ganzen
Menschen! Mit herzlichen Wünschen and Grüssen

Ihr
A. Einstein.

P.S. Bitte um Antwort wegen des vortrefflichen Max Brod.

TRANSLATION:

December 31, 1938

Dear Rabbi Goldman:

By now, I have read your book [Crisis and Decision, Harpers 1938]
*in its entirety with the greatest of interest. There is a genuine
phophetic glow to it; you hold up a mirror to one's contemporaries
uncompromisingly, both Jews and Gentiles. The righteous courage
and optimism is fitting to a man, to whom nothing humane is alien,
both in the literary as well as the real sense.*

*Virtually everything speaks to me most soulfully. However, I
envisage less salvation from a unification of the major portion of Jews
in one land or even a state; but, no matter how we might think about
it, the need to strive for it earnestly is unavoidable in our time. One
cannot help conjecture whether our people, concentrated in one place,
might not develop the same dangerous and hateful weaknesses which
we despise in our enemies. You do not seem to extend the kind of
warmth and honor to the Greeks which, I believe, they deserve.
I believe that we Jews have been tremendously influenced by them, in
the very best sense, since we share a love for spirituality,
independence in life and thought.*

*Your hymn on "Romance of a People" applies also to those who did
not experience the trash evident on the stage; "Eternal Road" was
even worse despite the fine text by Werfel. It is dangerous to bring this
tremendous material to the stage—especially in its entirety.*

*I found the polemic essays "Jews and Christians," "The Function of
the Rabbi," and "Rabbis and Rabbis" especially enjoyable; and most
significant the chapters "The Goal of Judaism" and "Can Religion
Change?"*

*I thank you most sincerely for the enjoyment I derived from them in
these reprehensible times. Such a work can only come from a strong
and whole man. With best wishes and regards, Yours*

P.S. Please reply regarding the outstanding Max Brod.

A. Einstein

den 3. März 1939

Dr. Solomon Goldman, President
Zionist Organization of America
111 Fifth Ave.
New York City

Sehr geehrter Dr. Goldman:

   Ich habe den Passus in meinem Telegramm "EINWANDERUNGSFRAGE NUR DURCH KOMPROMISS ZWISCHEN BEIDEN NATIONALITÄTEN LOESBAR" aus folgendem Grunde eingestzt: Was wir befürchten müssen, ist in erster Linie unsere Entrechtung und Ausplünderung der Menschen und des Besitzstandes, die das Aufbauwerk gegenwärtig repräsentieren. Diese Gefährdung muss in allererster Linie zu beseitigen gesucht werden. Dass sie sehr ernst zu nehmen ist, ist gar kein Zweifel. Wenn die Neuordnung dieser staatsrechtlichen Frage durch starre Bedingungen bezüglich der Einwanderung belastet wird, so ist nicht nur die Einwanderung, sondern auch der gesamte gegenwärtige Besitzstand in Frage gestellt. Deshalb habe ich mit schwerem Herzen den letzten Passus geschrieben. Ich persönlich halte es nicht für klug, ihn wegzulassen.

   Natürlich kann ich mir vorstellen, dass Sie die ganze Sachlage klarer übersehen mögen als ich und ich autorisiere Sie, den Passus wegzulassen, wenn Sie bereit sind, dafür die volle Verantwortung zu übernehmen.

   Ich habe nichts dagegen, wenn bei Gelegenheit meines 60. Geburtstages ein Dinner veranstaltet wird—vorausgesetzt, dass damit ein praktischer Zweck erreicht werden kann. Allerdings könnte ich selber nicht erscheinen, da ich auch in allen andern derartigen Fällen auf persönliche Beteiligung habe verzichten müssen und es ganz lächerlich wäre, gerade hier eine Ausnahme zu machen.

   Mit freundlichen Grüssen

                                                      Ihr
                                                      A. Einstein.

                    TRANSLATION:

                                                 March 3, 1939

Dear Rabbi Goldman:

   I included the passage in my telegram "IMMIGRATION QUESTION ONLY SOLUBLE THROUGH COMPROMISE BETWEEN BOTH NATIONALITIES" *for the*

*following reason: We must be very apprehensive, first of all, about the
loss of civil rights and the total confiscation of men and of property
which is being perpetrated by the current reconstruction. We must
make every effort, first and foremost, to set aside this peril. I have not
the slightest doubt that we must take it most seriously. If the
restriction of this constitutional question should influence the question
of immigration and complicate it further by way of rigid conditions,
then will both the immigration as well as the whole question of
property rights become questionable. It is for this reason that I wrote
that last passage with a heavy heart. I do not consider it wise to
omit it.*

*Naturally, I can well imagine that you have a better over-view of
the whole situation than I do and I authorize you to omit this
passage if you are prepared to assume full responsibility for doing that.*

*I have no objection if, on the occasion of my 60th birthday, a dinner
should be arranged—on condition that a practical purpose could be
achieved. However, I could not make a personal appearance, since in
all other similar events, I forfeited my own personal participation. It
would be quite ridiculous to make an exception in this case.*

With friendly greetings,   *Yours,*

                                                                  A. Einstein

Dr. Solomon Goldman   den 17. Mai 1939
Zionist Organisation of America
111 Fifth Ave.
New York City

Sehr geehrter Herr Goldmann,

Sie haben gewiss schon von dem bedeutenden Dichter Arno Nadel
gehört, der auch durch Sammlung von jüdischen Volksliedern und als
Komponist bekannt geworden ist. Er ist gegenwärtig Cantor bei der
jüdischen Gemeinde in Berlin und wird durch die Brutalitäten der
Nazis in kurzer Frist umgebracht werden, wenn es nicht gelingt, ihn zu
retten. Ich lege einige biographische Notizen über ihn bei. Glauben
Sie nicht, dass eine Möglichkeit besteht, den verdienstvollen Mann
hier, z.B. als Cantor, unterzubringen? Wenn Sie irgendeinen Weg
sehen, verfügen Sie bitte über mich.

                                                  Herzlich grüsst Sie
                                                  Ihr
                                                  A. Einstein.

TRANSLATION:

May 17, 1939

Dear Rabbi Goldman:

You have certainly already heard of the significant writer, Arno Nadel, who is also known for the collection of Jewish folksongs and as a composer. He is presently cantor for the Jewish community in Berlin and will be murdered in a short time by the brutalities of the Nazis if saving him is not successful. I enclose several biographical notices about him. Don't you believe that we stand a chance to bring this deserving man over, for example, as a cantor? If you see any kind of way, I am at your disposal.

With heartiest greetings to you,

Yours,
A. Einstein

*   *   *

Buber–Diesendruck–Goldman Correspondence

Talbiyeh, Jerusalem
October 19, 1939

Dear Doctor Diesendruck,

I want to ask you advice about an important personal question. As the publication of longer books in German is now impossible, I have been thinking for some time, whether I could publish some new books of mine in English, in America, either by translating them here in collaboration with Palestinian friends or by sending the German manuscripts to America to be translated there. All of them are books that can be understood by a wide public. Some of them are already finished, the other ones I hope to finish in the next year.

They are:

1) *The Prophetic Faith* (Outlines of a history of Hebrew religion, especially the faith of the prophets), about 250 pages, finished.
2) *Judaisn. and Christianity* (1. The Jewish and the Christian God.

2. The Jewish and the Christian Redemption), about 300 pages, drafted.

3) *Hasidism and the Religions of the World,* about 200 pages, nearly finished.

4) A Hasidic novel from the time of the wars of Napoleon, written some time ago, but needing revision.

5) *Religion and Politics,* a long book, containing a history of the relation between religion and politics, from ancient China up to our time, a systematic disquisition with examples, and practical conclusions for the main problems of actual society, civilization and state; drafted.

6) On Education, about 100 pages, finished.

As I told you, I have been thinking for some time about this matter. Now the war compels me to make haste, as besides the reduction of my regular income and besides the increasing expense in living (the families of my children are depending on me in some degree). There is not any more possibility of getting allowances from my Polish estate, which has been occupied by the Russians. For this reason I should like to ask you, if you could help me to find the necessary connections. To be able to perform this big piece of work besides my university courses, I must liberate myself of all the cares of the near future. What I must therefore strive to find is an institution, which will grant me for some time an adequate allowance, in return for which I should deliver my finished manuscripts and in a space of time to be agreed upon, the other books mentioned above. The settling of accounts would have to be made on the basis of the returns from the sale of the books in some way.

Could you assist me in this difficult enterprise of mine? I shall be very grateful for an early reply, if only temporary.

With kind regards,

yours,
Martin Buber (signed)

* * *

November 20, 1939

Dear Dr. Goldman—

I am enclosing a copy of a letter by Martin Buber which I received a few days ago and, taking for granted that you are ready to assist him in this situation, I would appreciate your advice how to go about this matter.

Unfortunately the Jewish publication business in this country is on a shamefully inadequate basis; they are all interested only in Sunday-school material where the profit is sure. The J. P. S. is very limited in its scope. There is really a crying need for a decent publishing house such as the "Schocken Verlag" or the "Jüdischer Verlag" in Germany.

Do you think some general publisher could be found who would be receptive for Buber's proposition in the last part of his letter? Or would there be a possibility of finding some private source for the financial backing of this plan, at least in the beginning?

I should be grateful for your early reply.

With cordial regards,

Sincerely yours,
Z. Diesendruck

*   *   *

November 22, 1939

Professor Z. Diesendruck
The Hebrew Union College
Clifton Avenue
Cincinnati, Ohio

Dear Dr. Disendruck:

I do not think that it will be easy at this time to find an American publisher for Buber's books. Certainly most of them would want to see the translation before signing a contract.

It would, of course, be most difficult to raise funds from private sources. I know that I couldn't do it. The Jewish Publication Society might be persuaded to undertake the publication of one or two books. If you approve, I shall be glad to write them.

With kindest regards and best wishes,

Cordially yours,

sg/erg
(Dictated but not read—
due to Dr. Goldman's hurried
departure for New York. Signed
in his absence. erg)

Goldman–Finkelstein Correspondence
THE GIST OF THE CONTROVERSY

September 20, 1944

Dear Sol:

I am very grateful and glad that you wrote me so frankly, giving your reactions to the proposed radio program. I firmly believe that if we could meet more often to talk things over with care and in detail, you would agree with me, that these outside activities, far from neutralizing the Seminary religiously, are in fact an indispensable element in building up in this country, a conservative movement worthy of the name. I tried to explain the situation at the Rabbinical Assembly meeting, and it seemed to me that virtually everybody concurred. The same was true at the meeting of the faculty when we discussed the situation.

Briefly, the facts are these. Judaism, (not only conservative Judaism, which I regard as the only type of Judaism which can survive in this country, but all forms), is losing ground every day. Last week I went over the evidence for this with Greenberg and Arzt, and they agreed that there is no doubt about it. No one is beginning to cope with the situation, outside the Seminary. At least, we have a reasonable program for achieving results, if all our men will cooperate. This program consists of (a) training a sufficient number of rabbis and teachers to man the synagogues and the religious schools; (b) establishing centers of learning, where research and study, which have always been the core of Judaism can be carried on; (c) training men who can prepare the text books and other works needed for this type of effort; and (d) training the laymen of the country, so that they will consider Judaism not a liability but a positive force for good in their lives.

It was interesting to see at the Rabbinical Assembly Convention that for the first time in history, so far as I know, all the senior Seminary professors, Ginzberg, Marx, and Kaplan, joined in urging such a program and its importance.

I think that it is generally understood that the Seminary is now doing more in each of these lines than was ever contemplated before.

But if we leave the wider problems of Jewish life, such as teaching Judaism by radio programs, entirely to secular organizations like the American Jewish Committee, or to Reform Jews, we foster the illusion that our interpretation of Judaism is unrealistic, and furthermore we help create a situation by which these extension educational systems are used to undermine Judaism. For example, recently one of our men told me that he was present at a good will meeting, at which an eminent reform rabbi announced quite coolly that "American Jews do not believe in the observance of the antiquated Mosaic ritual." The room, as is usual at such meetings, was full of children of conservative and even orthodox Jews. The rabbi told me that he was certain that they associated this rejection of Judaism with the reform rabbi's defense of the Jews, and some of them became convinced that there is no road to salvation for Jews, except through the abandonment of their religion!

That is why no responsible Jewish institution of learning can feel free to turn aside from the path which Schechter laid out when he wrote his *Aspects of Jewish Theology*. You know as well as I that that book was written in English, because it is addressed to Christians, and Jews who know as little about Judaism as Christians. Schechter rightly, I think, regarded this type of service to Judaism and the Jews, as an integral part of his effort to build up a strong, virile Judaism.

This is not neutralizing the Seminary; it is strengthening it. Curiously enough, your letter came just after Arzt told me that another one of our alumni, very well known, had complained that I was turning the Seminary too much to the right! I think he, too, is mistaken; and that he fails to understand the situation because he does not come around often enough.

I think, too, that there is a basic question which we must consider in regard to our dealing with reform and orthodox lay people. I take the view which Schechter held, that these classifications of Jews should be employed only because we have to have some way of describing one or the other. From the point of view of Jewish law, of course, a Jew, as you know, cannot by calling himself reform, free himself from any of the responsibilities which he would carry if he did not give himself that particular name. In other words, there are no "denominations" within Judaism so far as we are concerned. Everybody is a Jew, and if he is not observant, he should be called to repentance and every effort ought to be made to bring him back within the fold. For that reason, I do not believe that it would be wise to cut the bridges between the Jews who have wandered away from our synagogue and ourselves. When we meet, I should like to talk to you about this in detail. I know that I owe part of this view to Schechter; the other part to what my father tells me was the policy of Rabbi Isaac Elhanan in Kovno.

My conviction is that the Seminary, and all of us as individuals, must not only deal much more effectively than we are, with the inner problems of Judaism, but also with the general, moral problems of the country. It seems to me likewise rooted in good Jewish tradition, as well as in the teachings of Schechter and Rabbi Isaac Elhanan, whose views on the world were curiously similar. I do not have to tell you that Talmudic Judaism regards it as the duty of the Jew to observe all 613 commandments, and also, without proselytization, to get the world, generally, to accept the 7 Noachic commandments. It always has seemed to me to be the glory of Judaism that it was the first religion, and so far as I can see has remained the only religion, which on the one hand has concerned itself with the moral problems of the world, and on the other hand, did not demand that the world be converted to it in order to obtain salvation. I have heard you elucidate these points on a number of occasions far more effectively than I can, so it seems a little queer to me that I should have to stress them in writing to you.

Perhaps we disagree in regard to the significance of these extramural Seminary responsibilities for the moral regeneration of the general community. If we do, it is again because I have so little opportunity to talk to you about the whole situation. You undoubtedly have some information bearing on the subject which is not accessible to me. On the other hand, I may have some information on the subject which, because we cannot put it in print, does not become accessible outside of our limited group here.

Rome was not built in one day; and all the weaknesses in the Seminary structure cannot be overcome at one time. But I think if you were here, I could show you evidence of real progress in every direction of constructive Judaism. We have more Torah at the Seminary than we ever had before; for the first time we have in H. L. Ginzberg, Saul Lieberman, and Shalom Spiegel, a group of men, who can begin to compare to the Ginzberg, Marx, Friedlaender, and Davidson, of our student days, and who have, thank God, with them the older men, making a group of unexcelled standing and usefulness. The students are very serious, far more so than any generation that I have known during the past twenty years. Many of our alumni are doing magnificently, beginning with yourself, and continuing in lesser ways down through a score of others. It did my heart good to see what a fine influence David Aronson, for instance, exerted on our boys this summer. The Teachers Institute, which for many years was neglected, is now coming into its own. I suppose the Friedlaender Classes (or as they are now called, the Seminary School of Jewish Studies) is the only institute of adult Jewish studies in the country that has had an *increased* registration each year during the war. The laymen's institute, which Simon Greenberg and Israel M. Goldman worked out this year, was a fine experiment. (Benjamin R. Harris attended it, and will tell you his reactions to it when you meet.) We are publishing works of monumental scholarship such as Professor Ginzberg's commentary and Professor Marx's book, as well as his catalogue, the first volume of which should appear this year; and at the same time, pamphlets and booklets for soldiers and civilians, which will be most useful to them in their approach to Judaism. (I hope you will let us publish your book, too.) And so I could go on, through a long catalogue of real contributions to Judaism, which are visible and tangible. There are many which are not so visible and tangible, and yet are real, and perhaps in the long run even more significant. I could tell you of a large number of people who are beginning to understand what we are talking about, and who ten years ago would have scoffed at us.

We have to organize a better lay group about the institution. Our Board is too small for it. About two years ago, I discussed this situation with the Board itself. In their fineness of character which is real, they agreed with me, and applied to the Board of Regents for permission to increase their number to 75. This request was denied, on the ground that no educational institution in New York State—not even Columbia, has more than 25 directors. We were advised by Susan Brandeis, who is a member of the Board of Regents, to create a Board of Overseers, who would serve the purpose of the enlarged Board of Directors. This we are now trying to do. Obviously, as the Board of Directors must remain the legal corporation, there will be certain types of authority which will be reserved to it. But in essence our idea is that the Board of Overseers should act as a large Board of Directors. They will have authority over the issues you raise in your letter, the extent to which we ought to carry commitments in extension education; they will help guide the various schools and the museum; and, together with the Board of Directors itself, they will help meet the fund-raising responsibilities of the institution.

It is our thought that some members of the Board shall actually be designated by the congregations; some by the Rabbinical Assembly; and others by the Board of Directors, itself: though as a matter of form all of them will have to be elected by the present members of the Board, the legal corporation. I can assure you, however, that we will face no difficulty in regard to this situation, for the members of the Board of Directors are now as eager as I am to create a strong and representative Board of Overseers.

Obviously, in regard to the Museum and the Institute for Religious Studies it is not essential that the members of the directing committees be observant Jews. The directing and financing of these institutions can be done with the cooperatin of all Jews (and even Christians in the case of the Institute for Religious Studies) provided that the administration remains in the Seminary. Do you agree with me in this?

I naturally wrote you as I did the other alumni, asking for suggestions for these various committees, and I am sure that despite my intimate knowledge of Jewish affairs in Chicago, you can make suggestions which would not occur to me, and guide us generally. I should say that among the lay Chicago members of a Board of Overseers at the Seminary, I would expect to find B. R. Harris, A. K. Epstein, Samuel Wolberg, and whoever happened to be the president of the Chicago Council of Conservative Synagogues. There are probably others like Hyman Kohn of whom we might think, if they were available. On the Radio Committee, I should expect to include such reform Jews as James Becker, Harris Perlstein, etc., as well as a considerable number of our own people. On the Institute for Religious Studies Board, when that is developed, we could include some whom we could not otherwise influence in any manner, but who because of their association with that work might ultimately come to understand also the deeper meaning of Judaism itself.

Does all this make sense to you? If not, let us have a meeting to discuss it. I shall probably be in Chicago in the middle of November; but perhaps you will be here before then.

I still would like you to deliver the lecture you promised us, when you can come here. This is the time appropriate for it. What would be best of all would be for you to come here for some weeks or months, and give our boys a course, and let us meet at intervals for a long stretch. We need the kind of gathering both of us planned for August, and which did not work out.

I hope the coming year will be one of blessings and happiness for
you and yours. Give my love to Alice; I am sorry for her grief.

Affectionately, as ever,
Louis Finkelstein

Rabbi Solomon Goldman
The Anshe Emet Synagogue
Pine Grove at Grace
Chicago, Illinois

cu

*   *   *

Dr. Louis Finkelstein   September 26, 1944
Broadway at 122nd Street
New York, N. Y.

Dear Louis:

Thank you for your kind and gracious reply to my letter referring
to the Seminary Radio Program and the general direction in which the
Seminary has moved in the past several years. I shall attempt, for the
purpose of a rejoinder and for that of clarifying the issue, to disengage
your main argument from the assertions and *obiter dicta* with which
it is entangled and whose consideration may be deferred to another
day.

I understand you to reason as follows:

Judaism in the United States is losing ground daily. Our only hope
for its preservation is Conservative Judaism, but that has thus far
failed us because it has neglected the moral and ethical tenets of our
faith and abandoned the "wider problems of Jewish life" to
secularists and Reformists who misrepresent and misinterpret them,
and in doing so our group has "fostered the illusion" that its
formulation is "unrealistic". To correct this impression and remedy
the situation, the Seminary must engage in "outside activities" as an
"indispensable element in building in this country a conservative
movement worthy of the name". We ought to call American Israel
to repentance, and not forget the Christians either, since "there are
no 'denominations' within Judaism as far as we are concerned". Dr.
Schechter and Rabbi Isaac Elhanan were similarly minded.

Now I shall not underscore the manifest contradiction between your espousal of Conservative Judaism on the one hand and your rejection of "denominations" on the other, neither will I question your estimate of the thinking of the two illustrious teachers of whom you speak, nor will I suggest that all sincere teachers of religion, be they Christian, Reformists, Orthodox or Conservative, have ever been disturbed by the failure of humanity to rise to the highest goals of their respective religious creeds, nor will I remind you that the charge that the Jews especially have habitually paid no regard to the prophetic quality of their heritage has been made for centuries by proponents of the "new persuasion" who decried Pharisaism as intellectual myopia and spiritual petrification, nor will I recall to your mind Dr. Schechter's burning utterances on the Rabbi as a Personal Example or his eloquent pleas for *hesed,* the last of which he made with his dying breath, or the living coal of "ethical monotheism" to be found on the altar Dr. Ginzberg has erected to Israel's Students, Scholars and Saints, nor will I urge that no teacher of Judaism in the past several generations has grappled with the "wider problems of Jewish life" more assiduously and painstakingly than has Dr. Kaplan. Nor will I here and now raise the question of the acquiescence of the Seminary in the decline and disintegration of the United Synagogue and its usurpation of the functions that rightfully and properly belong to that organization, nor of that of the restraining and humbling the Rabbinical Assembly. All these are weighty matters and should be dealt with in the near future. For the present, however, I want to limit myself to your main argument.

Let me say at the outset that no matter what your personal views are with respect to "denominations" there is in the United States a Conservative Movement just as there is an Orthodox and Reform Movement, and that in this country and in our neighbor Canada there are some three hundred Conservative congregations and Rabbis who look upon the Seminary as their institution and who assume that it is and expect it to be zealously dedicated to and concentrating on Conservative Judaism. And it is on this account that they are prepared to support it. Among these people there are many laymen and Rabbis who might also be interested in calling into existence an overall institution that should seek the integration of the separatist bodies in American Israel, the harmonization of Judaism with science and philosophy, and a closer understanding with Christianity. But they do not, for various reasons, desire the Seminary to be that institution:

a. They are apprehensive lest in the attempt to be all things to all men, it adulterate and compromise its own ideology and program, an apprehension which Yabneh took seriously to heart and Tarsus held in contempt.

b. They are of the opinion that bigness is a curse, that a dispersive force is inferior to a collective, and that the squandering of energy over a multiplicity of efforts does not result in the replenishment of vitality but in its evisceration. Already it has been said that the President of the Seminary devotes his best thinking not to *res angusta domi* but to extramural business and the major portion of his time to visits to Washington, college campuses, Christian dignitaries, and Jewish plutocrats.

c. They do not want to travel under false colors and to disguise their "missionary aim". If the Seminary wants to "dedenominationize" American Israel, they insist that it be the common enterprise of all the "denominations" concerned.

d. They do not possess the means of shouldering the support of a Conservative Seminary and, in addition, an overall institution.

Even a cursory examination of what has been happening in our midst for the past several years does not fail to provide some justification for the apprehensions in the minds of an ever growing number of people. Despite the increased income of the Seminary in recent years (which, by the way, is to be attributed to skillful campaigning, the current wave of prosperity and above all, to the fact that the Seminary, deserted by its rich benefactors, has finally discovered that there are Conservative congregations in the United States), despite then the larger revenues, the "wider" or public relations activities have, in the minds of many educators, Rabbis, laymen and some of the most creative Jews in the country, (a) cast the shadow of suspicion over the institution and hurt the cause of Conservative Judaism, (b) redounded to the humiliation of the Conservative laity, and (c) further estranged from it the Jewish masses, together with the Hebrew and Yiddish intelligentsia, at a time when we were in a position to draw them nearer to us. To Elaborate:

a. On the platform of the Conference which the Seminary has called into existence, Jews have been invited to become a Protestant denomination. On the same platform, Catholics and Protestants have preached their respective creeds vigorously and aggressively,

but not so the Jews. "We understood", said many a layman, "after
attending last year's sessions of the Conference held in Chicago, we
understood what the Christian spokesmen wanted, but not what the
Jewish was after." Any wonder that rumor has it (1) that a
member of the faculty of the Seminary had given Mr. Asch his
approval of "The Nazarene"; (2) that at Cincinnati and Atlanta
the head of the Seminary had spoken with such enthusiasm of the
Apostles as to create the impression in the minds of many of his
audience that he had come near supporting the New Testament
animadversions on the Pharisees; (3) or, and this is no rumor, that
a Professor of the Seminary felt called upon to reassure the Jewish
world that the institution was not indoctrinating its students in the
tenets of the Christian faith.

Dr. Schechter, you assert, wrote his Aspects in English for the
benefit of Christians. Perhaps. But he published most of it in the
Jewish Quarterly Review, apparently expecting interested non-Jews
to seek it out there. (I remember that he felt called upon to offer an
apology for contributing the article on the Talmud to the extra
volume of Hasting's Dictionary of the Bible). What is, however,
far more to the point is this, that he called his book *Rabbinic
Theology,* disdaining to camouflage it under some universalistic
designation, and emphasizing in that work, the matchless superiority
of our faith with great candor and dignity. He did not conceal its
uniqueness in the apologetic concoction, the Judeo-Christian
tradition, which has been heard altogether too frequently from the
lips of Conservative spokesmen. I shall never forget the answer our
immortal teacher gave in his last lecture at the Seminary, when a
student asked him why it was that Jews did not engage in
proselytizing the world. Advertising, he said, was the resort of
upstart concerns, even as the airs and graces worn for fashion's sake
was the manner of the nouveau riche.

The Conference has provided a platform for a renegade Jew who
is indirectly and directly responsible for the conversion of several
young Jews to Catholicism, for a conscious and willful Jewish
assimilationist who has persistently advocated privately and publicly
intermarriage and assimilation. The Conference has already
offended traditional Judaism by having arranged a broadcast on
the Sabbath eve, adding insult to injury by presenting on that
occasion a Catholic and a Protestant who know their religions and

live by them and a Jew who neither knows it nor wants to know it nor has any interest in it. And you, Louis, are disturbed because some Reform Rabbi had said in the privacy of somebody's home that "American Jews do not believe in the observance of the antiquated Mosaic ritual." And what guarantee have you that the same Rabbi or one equally "eminent" or some dejudaized layman is not going to make over the Seminary Radio Program assertions equally damaging to Conservative Judaism? Are you going to act as the censor? By what right? The program is representative of all shades of opinion. And if it is not, why then have you put in the forefront the sponsorship that you have?

b. The persistent association of such names, names of fashion only, is humiliating and insulting to Conservative Jews. It conveys the impression that our own people are unworthy and unfit to be put forth as the leaders of the "wider activities" of the Seminary. It recreates the inferiority complex which long plagued the East European Jew and from which he had gradually begun to emancipate himself. What that does to the Conservative Synagogue and Rabbi I have indicated in my previous letter to you and I need not dilate on the matter any further.

You might argue that (1) you are seeking to lead these prominent gentlemen to repentance (you have so frequently put it that way), and (2), that you are only continuing a practice established by Dr. Schechter and Dr. Adler. As for the former, let me say in the first place quite frankly that we should like to know whether you have made repentance a condition of your dealings with these gentlemen; whether you have openly told them that you are seeking their regeneration. As far as I have had the opportunity to observe them within the Seminary precincts, they revealed none of the humility of the repentant sinner, but rather the arrogance of benefactors and potentates. In the second place, in the days of Dr. Schechter and in the early days of Dr. Adler, there were no Conservative congregations in a position to support the Seminary. I do not offer their woeful predicament as a valid alibi. I chafed in my student days under the anomalous position of our alma mater and in 1916 I declared at a dinner at which Messrs. Schiff and Warburg were present, that the time was not far off when the support of the Seminary would come from the same elements that had given it its teachers and students. Mr. Schiff, by the way, heartily commended on that occasion both my courage and hope. But why should we today, who can stand on our own feet, barter our independence and confidence in our resources for a venal puff or for a name full of sound and signifying nothing in Conservative Judaism. In the third place, Dr. Schechter and even Dr. Adler, to the best of my recollection, kept these men in the background insofar as the religious and educational program of the Seminary was concerned. Finally, Dr. Schechter and, I repeat, even Dr. Adler, knew where to draw the line. They were dealing with a Schiff in whose room at the hospital a traditional *mahzor* was found when he died two days after Yom Kippur; with a Marshal who made it his business to learn Yiddish in order to feel the pulse beat of millions of our people; with a Warburg who had an absorbing interest in the rebuilding of Palestine. Compare now these men with those whom you have chiseled into the facade of the Seminary Board, the Conference, and latterly the Seminary Radio Program.

c. The estrangement of the Jewish masses from the Seminary has grown apace. We have become anathema in the Hebrew and Yiddish press, except insofar as we have curried the favor of an editor or publisher. And even as we have grown in disfavor, the Yeshivah in New York has acquired a fresh grip on many elements in the Community. That institution and the Chicago Talmudic College have placed in positions, at least in the midwest, six men to every one of ours. Why indeed should not the masses feel estranged in view of the nature of our "wider activities", their sponsorship, and the rumors to which they have given rise. The masses put no stock in our missionary pretentions and dismiss our averment to the effect that we are out to reclaim the lost sheep of Israel as paltry artifice and idle rhodomontade. If, they have a right to ask, that was our purpose, why have we so meticulously confined our efforts to the bulls of Bashan? Why have we not reached out to them or to some of their leaders? Why have we not also felt the need of calling to repentance such men as Leiwick and Pinski, Hillman and Dubinsky, Lipsky and Hayyim Greenberg. Why is it, they should like to know, that when the Seminary does deign to give some recognition to the Orthodox community, it never steps out of the magic circle of our Spanish-Portuguese aristocracy? Are the Orthodox Rabbis among the sponsors of the Seminary Radio Program anywhere near as representative of American Orthodoxy

as some of the great Rabbinim in the country or comparable with
them in learning and prestige?
Let me in closing assure you that there is not a single item in this
letter of which educators, Rabbis, teachers or laymen have not
talked to me within or without the Seminary walls in New York or
elsewhere in the country. And now, judge for yourself whether I
could allow the high regard in which I hold you and our lifelong
friendship to restrain me any longer from expressing what is in my
heart.

With all good wishes,

                                                    Cordially yours,
SG:a

P.S.: Your letter reached me on Monday and my reply was hastily
composed. Indeed, a substantial part of it was dictated by telephone.
Had I had more leisure, I most probably would have modified a
phrase here and there, but the issue before us to my mind is what I
have indicated. And the apprehensions are recorded as I have
frequently heard them and expressed without exaggeration.

*   *   *

Letter from David Hertz to Mrs. Alice Goldman

                                                    February 6th, 1966.
Dear Allie,

. . . Morris Berick, Myron Guren and I met last Sunday and agreed
that I was to write you our reminiscences, and I have chosen to put
them in this form because it seems the most natural way to do it.

The atmosphere about the Cleveland Jewish community to which
Solomon Goldman came in 1919–1920, was quite arid. The community
was made up of families who might have been recognized as in three
strata, altho' the lines between them, on occasion, were more or less,
blurred.

At the upper level because of the prestige and status which seniority
and greater wealth frequently impose, were the German Jews, as they
were called, altho' their group included a number of families whose
origins had been Czech and Hungarian. Theirs were the two
Reformed Temples, the Excelsior Club and the Oakwood Club.

Today, if conditions in Cleveland were as they were then, we would
say that membership in the Temples or in the Clubs, were status
symbols, for such membership gave its owners a snobbish and
patronizing attitude toward the members of the other strata.

That attitude was fortified by the assimilationist values which the
earlier Reform movement had nurtured. The Jew whose conduct,
activities and associations were most nearly like that of the white
Anglo-Saxon Protestants was the one most to be given the respect
inherent in imitation.

At the next level, were the older eastern European immigrants,
Jews whose origins had been Hungarian, Galician, Slovak, Polish,
Lithuanian and Russian, but who had reached America at the close of
the Nineteenth and the beginning of the Twentieth Centuries.

Their roots in Cleveland soil not yet as deep as their German
contemporaries, they possessed fewer large fortunes and far less
elegance in behavior. But they were aggressive, industrious and
daring, and the outlines of their future acquisitions of greater
economic strength were already visible. Unlike the German Jews, they
were not conscious assimilationists and for the most part they
retained a loyalty to the Judaism and Jewishness which they had
known abroad. The result was an abundance of small congregations
organized by the various groups for the membership of "landesleute"
so that common speech referred rarely to the Beth Midrash Hagodol
or to the Anshe Emeth or to the Bnai Jeshurun, but rather to the
Litvische Shool, or the Poilische Shool or to the Hungarian Shool.
The word Orthodox was seldom used because it was a redundancy.
This stratum, however, had had nothing analogous to the social
Clubs of the German Jews. Their golf clubs were still in the future,
but they did have a small Talmud Torah, a Chesed shel Emeth, and
Bikur Cholim and a Mo'ath Chittim Society as well as a Beth Moshav
Zekinim. And in their synagogues and communal activities they had
managed to preserve some of the atmosphere of Eastern Europe's
Jewries.

However, they lived under a cloud. They were worried about their
children. Intermarriage with non-Jews altho' occasional had not yet
become frequent enough to frighten them, but intermarriage of their
sons with German Jewish daughters was becoming more frequent as
their sons distinguished themselves in medicine, law, real estate and
other businesses. Growing affluence was beginning to open doors

heretofore closed and the German Jewish daughters' social climbing was abetted by the fact that the Reformed Temples were cleaner, more orderly and their services abbreviated and more readily understood. In consequence, a migration from the second to the upper stratum had begun altho' it was just perceptible.

The elders, however, were wise enough to see the need for adaptation but not learned enough to specify what form it should take. They suggested an answer, more modern synagogues and English-speaking Rabbis.

One synagogue had experimented with a number of such rabbis and had introduced the family pew, but the migration of its younger people had continued. Another had had the benefits of unusual leadership by an English-speaking rabbi who had won the love and admiration of the community, but the membership was still uneasy. Somehow or other the traditional ways of Jewish life were not holding the affections of the pushing youngsters.

The third stratum was largely made up of newer immigrants altho' here and there among them, were to be found mavericks who altho' they had been among the earlier comers, nevertheless had stayed behind. This stratum included the artisans, the tailors, the carpenters, the building tradesmen. From the East European Jewries, they had brought their secularism and estrangement from synagogue life. They read the Vorwaerts, the Tageblatt and the local Yiddishe Welt. They had their landsmanshaften which were frequently burial insurance societies, and, of course, the Verband. For them, Isaiah, Jeremiah, Hosea and Micah had been replaced by Marx, Bakunin, Voltaire, Ingersoll, Paine, and in some cases, A. D. Gordon, Syrkin. They, too, had enough nostalgia to wish to teach their children something of Yiddishkeit and in many respects they were having a limited success. But the fluidities of the American caste system had made them realize that their success must needs be ephemeral.

The First World War had accelerated the processes of destratification. It brought a huge migration of Negroes to Cleveland with the result that the old Jewish neighborhood was soon abandoned in favor of two newer areas to the northeast and southeast. In consequence, the synagogues and temples were compelled to build new structures.

The War had also stimulated a large scale real estate boom and the profits were shared by the Jewish "real estateniks", the artisans in the building trades, and the Jewish building contractors.

The War had also enabled the Jewish dealers in salvage, in rags, in used bottles and barrels, in scrap metals, to amass fortunes. In consequence, it was no longer true that only German Jews were affluent Jews. Wealth had come to many members of the other two strata.

At the same time, Jewish overseas needs had become the chief concern of Jewish leadership in America. Large sums were needed, sums far in excess of what heretofore had been considered possible. Of necessity, in Cleveland as elsewhere, the former leaders in Jewish philanthropy felt forced to recognize elements in Jewish life never before consulted. Every potential giver had to be cultivated and cultivation compelled admitting to the councils of leadership, many who until now had been ignored. Thus, the American Jews of east European origin were beginning to participate in the status-giving activities of their groups.

Accordingly, overseas, the Jewish Agency and similarly Zionist-oriented activities began to receive support, and at home, voices began to be raised with more and more daring, in behalf of Hebrew education.

But altho' the period of gestation was being fulfilled, the embryo had not quite emerged from the womb, altho' the labor pains were being heard with more and more distinctness and regularity. This was the Cleveland that greeted him [Goldman] when as a young Schechter graduate he first came, a community historically divided along lines that had begun to disappear, a community which newer forces were driving to unity. Would it be a unity in which assimilation would triumph by making all Jews like those of the upper stratum? Or would it be a unity in which an American version of traditional Jewish life would come upon the scene? His answer was to seek the latter.

His first problem was to choose the road on which to travel. A number presented themselves.

A number of institutional activities were available. A Cleveland Bureau of Jewish Education had been created and he soon took a leading part in its efforts to live, and grow in influence and dignity. The Zionist Movement had been given new strength by the Balfour Declaration and he threw himself into the efforts to make the Hebrew University on Mount Scopus a reality. The germ of the idea to replace the Cleveland Jewish Welfare Federation with the concept of a community federation, had been born and he gave his efforts to cultivate it.

But altho' he was never apart from such activities, they did not engross him. More important to him was the world of ideas. He remained a student. When you called at his study, you were likely to find him reading William James or John Dewey or Solomon Reinach. He was inordinately fond of companionship, and when he relaxed with his friends, he tolerated gossip and personalities, but somehow, he was soon talking of Fraser's Golden Bough or some of Rappoport's writings. Without seeming to do so, he dominated every social conversation and invariably, it turned to some aspects of Judaism, or Jewish life or Jewish thinking.

He soon acknowledged his indebtedness to the elders who had built the congregation and nourished and preserved it, so that his present opportunity was possible. But his emphasis was not on their past achievements. It was rather upon the challenges of the future. To accept that challenge, he soon concentrated his energies upon the youth.

Soon word got about town among those interested, that the new Rabbi was at home in modern thinking, that he was a devotee of John Dewey and James Harvey Robinson and Morris R. Cohen and Horace Kallen; that he had a remarkable library which he kept replenished with new books as they appeared; that he was a fascinating conversationalist who seemed able to make Jewish subjects meaningful. And soon the young Jews who had returned to Cleveland from the eastern universities were making his home a gathering place for the exchange of ideas.

To his study and to his home, came young men of all shades of opinion. Assimilationists, Zionists, Paole Zionists, Mizrachi, secularists, Republicans, Democrats, Progressives, Socialists (I can recall no Communists, but those were still the days of innocence) and philosophical anarchists. Even the Single Taxers were fascinated by his delineations of the Mosaic concepts of real property tenure. But to all, it was always striking that with Goldman, all roads led not to Rome, but to Jerusalem or Pumbedita or Alexandria, or Vilna. Jewish tradition and Jewish lore had something to say of everything and to everybody.

Inevitably such informality had to become institutionalized. And soon, they found themselves members of a Saturday Night Group which met fortnightly at his home. During its first year, the group took form to study Lecky's History of European Morals, but it was not long before Goldman was discussing the Yetzer Tov.

Of course, the discussions soon revealed the need for treatment of various topics in depth and there followed a series of papers prepared by various members on limited aspects of our general topics. And when we had exhausted both Lecky and ourselves with European Morals, there were other topics that permitted the Group to continue for as long as he remained with Bnai Jeshurun and for a time after he went to the Jewish Center.

Later, the Group evolved into the Deoth Club. But by this time, his name had become known in all Cleveland. The Deoth Club was therefore a more inclusive and a more formal organization. It included not only sons and daughters of the middle stratum, but also a few souls from the Reformed Temples who were hungry and thirsty for what Goldman had to offer. It also included a number of non-Jews, among them a judge of one of our Courts. The Deoth Club was different in program in that it devoted itself largely to week-end seminars. Among those called by the Club to Cleveland for the seminars were Eustace Haydon of Chicago and Max Otto of Madison, Wisconsin.

Another of his activities away from the synagogue was, thanks to your own generosity, forbearance, patience and good nature, his making of your home a meeting-place at which we were enabled to come to know a number of personalities well-known in Jewish life. It was at your home that we met Bialik, Tchernikowsky, Stephen Wise, Haim Greenberg, Jacob Ben Ami and Bertha Kalisch; doubtless there were others, but it was forty years ago. I remember Ben Ami and Kalisch particularly, however, because we went together to see Ben Ami perform, and Marguerite and I still recall, the graceful elephant who played Consuelo opposite his He Who Gets Slapped.

We also remember his efforts to get people to attend the Yiddish theater generally, for we recall seeing with you performances of the Vilna Truppe in the Dybbuk and Jacobs Dream which we should have missed but for you.

In the synagogue, he was remarkable for his ability to relate what he said there, to our lives. He was a lecturer rather than a sermonizer. I recall his skepticism about the value of sermons and his enthusiasm

for teaching, altho' I recall that he attached little pedagogic value to
lectures, too. But he had to occupy the pulpit; it was "in the bond."
So he made himself at home by lecturing. I particularly recall his
lectures on Genesis. To him, it was not a cosmogony, but a revelation
of the soul of a primitive people. Working almost like an
archaeologist, he was able to take the fragments and shards and with
them to reconstruct the world outlook of Ancient Israel. And so he
went thru the Five Books, pointing out the beginnings of moral
concepts, the evolution of the Israelitish God, and the underpinnings
of Prophetic and Talmudic Judaism. I must confess, however, that he
never convinced me that Solomon was speaking of a beautiful woman
when he described her hair as like "a flock of goats", her temples as
"like a pomegranate split open" her neck "like a tower" on which hang
a thousand shields. But that, of course, is a matter of taste.

Thus to him, the synagogue became a center of learning which he
embellished not only with his teachings, but which he enriched by
programs which he introduced.

One was the Popular University. You will recall how he struggled
to make the synagogue school meaningful. In those days, professional
Hebrew teachers were few, and the few available had been gathered
by his friend (and our friend) A. H. Freedland for his School system.
So Goldman sought to enlist the best he could get. Under his
inspiration, Myron Guren became a student of the Prophets that he
might teach them in the Sunday School. Morris Berick lectured on
subjects within his own outstanding competency and with his
characteristic terseness. Leonard Levy lectured on his love,
Shakespeare, and I, on Ibsen.

Another was the Sunday morning Forum, which was my own pet
concern. He permitted me to bring to it some of the controversies of
the day and when members of the congregation were shocked, he was
able always to stand behind me. In consequence and without trouble,
we brought Norman Thomas, Oswald Garrison Villard, Peter Witt,
Upton Sinclair, Owen Lovejoy and others whose political views look
tame today, but were then considered wildly radical. We also brought
well-known literary names, Carl Sandberg, Louis Untermeyer, Maxwell
Bodenheim, John Erskine, and journalists like S. K. Ratcliffe, Bruce
Bliven, John Cowper Powys, and thinkers like, Alexander
Meikeljohn, Harry A. Overstreet, Will Durant (before he became
popular) and Roy W. Sellars. I can't begin to exhaust the list from

mere memory. This may be true because frequently Goldman's comments at the Forum or after it overshadowed the speakers' contributions. But to me, the clearest memories are the dinners we had with the speakers after the Forum appearances. It was then that we got to know them and Goldman as well.

This has been a long letter, but there has been much to write about. I have no doubt that the years have tinted my recollections as I frequently regard the years we had with him in Cleveland as the happiest of my life. We lived constantly with ideas, whether they were Jewish or otherwise. We were young and life still offered all its promise. What more could there have been?

Sincerely,
David Ralph Hertz

Appendix III

Memoranda to Authors, Scholars, Editors, and Publishers

NOTES

Joseph Baratz; Dr. Simon Bernstein; Chaim Bloch; Mr. Z. Broshi;Mr. A. Epstein; Jacob Fichman; Dr. Simon Ginzberg; Rabbi David Graubart; Professor Simon Halkin; Isaac Hamlin; Dr. Abraham Heschel; Isaac Lamdan; Izthak Lamdan; Professor Saul Lieberman; Dr. Ephraim E. Lisitzky; Joseph Mendelson; Henry Monsky; Mr. Daniel Persky; Dr. Simon Rawidowicz; Dr. Ch. W. Reines; Menachem Ribalow; Professor Leon Roth; Mr. H. Schauss; Professor Chaim Tchernowitz; Dr. Meyer Waxman.

These notes were dictated to Dr. Samuel Feigen, Associate Professor of Semitic Languages at the University of Chicago, from 1941 through 1953. They are but a small sample of hundreds of such notes which through the years Feigen and, after his death, other Hebraists translated and typed for Rabbi Goldman.

Professor Tchernowitz[1] letter. Answer it in a general way. Say that Rabbi Goldman regrets very much not to have been able to be at the meeting to pay him the tribute he so richly deserves, personally, that

---

1. Chaim Tchernowitz, the famous Rav Tzair; brilliant historian, teacher, orator.

Rabbi Goldman does not feel guilty of any exaggeration in his telegram, that it is only his humility which prompts him to say that. The lot of the Hebrew book in America is something to give us great concern. It is perhaps the most depressing fact in the whole of American Jewish experience, that things are so involved that the Rabbi finds himself at times unable to think matters through or to make any suggestions.

Ribalow[2]—(1) You have by this time received a check for $200. I shall in the near future send him another check. (2) I am anxious that he send Dr. Feigen's book to the press without delay. It is very important that the book appear soon. My reason for hurrying you is that I want to send it to several members of the Oriental Institute of the University of Chicago. (3) I do not know how soon I can visit the several cities for the Histadrut.[3] I have been compelled to cancel practically all of my speaking engagements for the next several months due to a chest cold that has caused me considerable trouble. (4) I read Lahover on my book. I regret exceedingly that he allowed himself to review it without having read it. That was very clear, particularly from what he quoted me as saying about Spinoza. The fact is that I say just the opposite. (5) I note from the Hadoar that you have already received a copy of the *Agadat Shlosho Vearbaah*. (6) The Maimonides is in preparation. I will send it to you soon after it is off the press. (7) I should like to give you for the *Sepher Hashanah* the last essay in Undefeated. It exists in an unusually fine Hebrew translation. (8) I have not yet received the *Tempest*.

To Jacob Fichman[4]—The story of Bialik was published here by the College of Jewish Studies of Chicago at considerable expense. It entails great hardship to put out here this type of book with the notes, vowels, and vocabulary. The reason it is done is to bring Bialik to the younger people in America. They cannot possibly turn to his works without preparation. Not only isn't there a cent of profit, the books are sold at considerable loss. At the same time I am enclosing a check for $50.00 that he may use as he sees fit. I shall some time later send him another check for *Moznayim*.[5]

To Dr. Meyer Waxman telling him that Rabbi Goldman regrets having

---

2. Menachem Ribalow, for many years editor of *Hadoar* and head of Histadrut-Ha-Ivrit, a man who almost single-handedly brought modern Hebrew journalism to America.

3. This refers to the Histadrut HaIvrit, the association for the promotion of Hebrew letters.

4. Jacob Fichman, a fine contemporary Hebrew writer.

5. A journal of letters published in Palestine, monthly or when funds permitted.

been unable to get in touch with him before; that reviews of Waxman's books will shortly appear either in *Tribune* or *News,* and that effort must be made to put the reviews in those papers; that he is enclosing check from Mr. Monsky;[6] that he understands his son already has a position; and that he will be in touch with him when he returns.

To Dr. Simon Bernstein[7]—41 E. 42nd St., New York. Express my gratitude for remembering the Congregational Library and me with its last publication, *Diwan of Solomon ben Meshulum Dapharah, Part I;* that I congratulate him that he is continuing his labors in the vineyard of Hebrew poetry. May he enjoy good health and further enrich our literature.

To Mr. Z. Broshi of Bronx, N. Y., that I am most grateful to him for sending me a copy of his book on Rabbi Saadia Gaon; that I have had time only to turn its pages; that I was happy to note that he has done an excellent piece of work. I regret that my numerous responsibilities make it impossible for me to write him at length; that if he will send me five additional copies of his book, I shall gladly distribute them among my friends; also, that he should enclose the bill.

To Professor Saul Lieberman[8] in New York City that I neglected to tell him that the money was cabled to Professor Schalit; and that if he writes to Professor Schalit, he might tell him that the money came from me.

To Mr. E. E. Lisitzky[9]—that I am most grateful to him for the interest he is taking in my book; that I beg him to write to Mr. Ribalow and to get from him a definite statement as to what it will cost to publish his book. After I receive the statement, I will know whether or not I can undertake it at this time. I have already made so many commitments to the books of others that I am very much afraid that my own book will have to wait.

Please write to *Dr. Simon Ginzberg* that the evening in honor of Dr.

---

6. Henry Monsky, at the time President of the Order of B'nai B'rith.

7. Editor of *Dos Yiddische Folk;* Director of Palestine Immigration Office in New York.

8. One of the world's ranking Talmudists; Professor of Palestinian Literature at the Jewish Theological Seminary.

9. Dr. Ephraim Lisitzky headed the Bureau of Jewish Education in New Orleans and was a prolific and distinguished poet in the Hebrew language. His friendship with Rabbi Goldman extended over many years. He was one of twelve distinguished scholars and Rabbis who were asked to contribute an article for a memorial volume to be edited by Rabbi James G. Heller.

Feigen was one of the best of its kind that Chicago has ever had. Despite a pouring rain, it was unusually well-attended. The addresses were of a high order, and the assembly really rejoiced in honoring a distinguished and worthy scholar. It would have been a great pleasure to have had him present on the occasion. Tell him that I am grateful to him for having sent me a copy of the book; that I hope I shall soon receive a substantial number of copies from him; that I shall send him a check for the balance in the very near future.

To Dr. Abraham Heschel, Hebrew Union College, Cincinnati, Ohio, expressing my gratitude for sending his reprint of the *Holy Dimension.* Please apologize for my delay in writing him.

To Mr. H. Schauss, 2922 Barnes Avenue, Bronx, N. Y. Express my gratitude for sending me a copy of his truly splendid work, *Neviim;* that I read his translation and comments with interest and benefit. I want to take this opportunity to express my regret at not having had the pleasure of seeing him on his recent visit in Chicago; that I shall be looking forward to meeting him. Also, thank him for his *Mentsch un Got.*

Please write to *Joseph Baratz* of Deganiah, Palestine,[10] and express deep gratitude for remembering me on the occasion of the New Year; that it was a delight to hear from him. I often think, with great longing, of him and Deganiah. I pray that I may be granted the privilege, soon after the war is over, to see him once again on the shore of Lake Kinnereth.

To Mr. Itzhak Lamdan—Most grateful to him for the letters which he sent me through Lisitzky and Halkin. I was happy to see his handwriting again and to hear from him directly. None of the letters which he addressed to me directly reached me. I did get several numbers of *Gilyonot*[11] I am happy and grateful that he has the courage to go on publishing *Gilyonot.* I regret only that I cannot be as helpful to him as I should like to be. By the time he receives this letter, he will undoubtedly received $100 through the Agency. I hope to send him another hundred in about three or four months. As for the article for the Jubilee issue, his letters reached me just now. We are already in the middle of Heshvon and I could not possibly write the article and have it in his hands by Kislev. I shall therefore have to wait for another occasion. I

---

10. The first collective colony (kibbutz) in Palestine founded by Joseph Baratz and a company of Halutzim near the Jordan River.

11. A journal of literary and political nature of very high standards which Rabbi Goldman helped to finance for all the years of its publication.

cannot close the letter without saying that I was shaken to my depths by the death of Saul Tchernichovski.[12]

To Dr. Ch. W. Reines—I am tremendously interested in the book of which he writes me. I hope that he will have the opportunity to publish it without delay. Several of his titles are of particular interest to me and I wish I could get to see them even in manuscript. I will contribute towards the publication $150. I am sending him $50.00 now and $100 when the book will appear.

Mr. A. Epstein, 5 Westminster Road, Brooklyn, N. Y.—Will you please express my gratitude to Mr. Epstein for his graciousness in sending me his *Mi-Karov u-me Rehuk.* It was a delight to see how beautifully the book was put out and to read his brilliant discussions. I am particularly grateful to him for his articles on my beloved and lamented friend, A. H. Friedland.[13]

Mr. Daniel Persky, 243 East 14th St., New York, N. Y.—Thank Mr. Persky for his kindness in sending me a copy of *Zemanim Tovim.* I am heartily grateful to him for remembering me and for his continued friendship. I am happy that he is continuing his literary labors and is forever creative and fruitful. Ask him to send me ten copies of the book and enclose the bill.

Professor Leon Roth at the University of Jerusalem: It is ever a delight to hear from Palestine; how much more so in these days, and particularly in the form of a translation of Aristotle's *Ethics* into the Hebrew (ha-Middot, Books 1 and 2). Will you permit me to add that the tent of Shem which he has put up matches the beauty of Japheth.

Mr. Joseph Mendelson, Buenos Aires, Argentina: (This letter is to be in Yiddish.) Please write Mr. Mendelson acknowledging his graciousness in sending me his excellent volume, rich in quality and quantity, entitled *Amol in a Halben Yovel.* I was particularly impressed with his chapters on the Talmud, Rashi, Maimonides and "Di Grindung fun Buenos Aires."

Mr. Isaac Hamlin (correspondence enclosed)—Please answer in Yiddish. Express thanks for his kind letter. Due to the condition of my health, I am writing merely an acknowledgement. I am making contact

---

12. One of the great Hebrew poets who proudly declared himself a pagan, as much the heir of the Canaanites and the Greeks as of the ancient Hebrews.

13. The head of the Bureau of Jewish Education in Cleveland, a leading Hebraist and author. He collaborated with Rabbi Goldman in the editing, translating and publishing of Hebrew classics.

with Vice President Wallace and shall use every influence I possibly can to get him to come. If I fail with him, I shall try Donald Nelson. It will not be necessary that I go to Washington. If I fail with Nelson, I shall try Secretary Knox.

To Dr. Ch. Reines: Please ask Dr. Reines to forgive me for the delay in writing. I am most grateful for the Introduction and first chapter of his book. I regret, however, to have imposed so onerous a task upon him and, under no circumstances will I allow him to send me the other chapters unless he can get them typed at my expense.

To Prof. Chaim Tchernowitz—the $200 which I sent him are for the *Toledot Halachah* and not for Bitzaron. We shall be sending our annual contribution to Bitzaron in the immediate future. I shall be glad to send him another contribution toward *Toledot Ha-halacha* immediately after Rosh Hashanah.

To Isaac Lamdan: That I have been as much surprised at not receiving my letters. The only communications that I have had from him have been indirect enclosures in letters to Lisitzky and Halkin. After hearing from him through Halkin, even before Lisitzky forwarded his letter to me, I sent him air mail an article on Brandeis for the one hundredth issue of *Gilyonot.* I hope he received it. From the letter Lisitzky forwarded to me, it would appear that he did not receive the $300 which I sent him in October, 1944, through the Jewish Agency. The Chicago bank has already cabled an inquiry, but we have as yet no answer. I follow *Gilyonot* with great interest and hope he will continue to have the enthusiasm, the energy and the means to go on with his work.

To Chaim Bloch[14]—Tell him that for the present and for some time to come, I could not possibly make any further commitments to authors. I have already assumed burdens beyond reason and I do not know how I shall be able to meet my present obligations. If the fund that I have for such purpose should be suddenly favored with unexpected contributions, I shall remember. I take great pleasure in sending him under separate cover a copy of my *Am Olam va-Aretz.*

To Rabbi David Graubart[15]—Rabbi David *hehaviv w'hanichbad:* Forgive my delay in answering your letter of last summer. I spent a trying ten weeks in which I neither read nor wrote a word.

---

14. Author of the *Golem* and various historical and sociological essays.
15. Head of the Bet-Din, the rabbinic court in Chicago. Son of a distinguished Hebrew and Talmudic scholar and a very dear friend of the Goldman family.

With respect to the *Ezrat Nashim,* I quoted our great and beloved teacher, Professor Louis Ginzberg. It was he who suggested that the Azarah was placed where the *Mehusre Kaparhh* would wait for the Kohen. Since the women were invariably in the majority there it came to be called *Ezrat Nashim.* Personally I am of the opinion that the Halachists have laboured in vain to find a basis for the separation of the sexes in the Synagogue. There is nothing in the Bible and Mishnah upon which to rest it. For two reasons. One, for a period of many centuries the sexes intermingled; two, when under whatever influences a change came about the sexes were separated, not only in the Synagogue but everywhere. Consequently, the early sources have nothing to say about an "unmixed pew." That is why the authorities have been "climbing on straight walls." The very fact that they cited Gen. 7:13 and Zech. 12:12–14 is sufficient proof of my supposition.

As to the Mishnah, Sukkah 5:2 and the Gemara *a.l.,* all they did was testify to the fact that uncritical acceptance of tradition blinds the eyes even of the learned and wise. If anything, these sources prove that normally the sexes were not separated, but precaution was at last taken when *Simhah* turned to hilarity. I should not hesitate to take *Tikkun Gadol* to mean a radical step.

To Professor Simon Halkin—Yedidi hehaviv w'hanaaleh Professor Simon Halkin. Professor should be written out and not abbreviated.

Please forgive my long silence. My handicaps weigh heavily upon me and my burdens have not eased. For ten weeks I neither read nor wrote a line. I have not forgotten you. Indeed, I think of you always. I was happy to learn from visitors from Israel to Chicago that your recovery is complete. Hardly an Israeli comes to see me but speaks with deep appreciation of the great contribution you are making, not alone in your capacity as a man of letters and teacher, but by your very presence, by the spirit that moves you and the vision that sustains you. *Lech b'chohach zeh w'hoshi'a es yisrael.*

The reports of the Jerusalem Congress and the aftermath of controversy have depressed me. To reopen at this time the old question of the Galut or to castigate American Jewry is, in my humble opinion, a great blunder. The world is far too unsettled, the air troubled, the present confused, the future uncertain, the foci of men's loyalties and interests shifty, to attempt permanent solutions of problems that are perhaps altogether insoluble. To persist in doing so might prove catastrophic.

We need, it seems to me, a decade of painful patience and heart-breaking silence.[16]

To Israel Exploration Society (list all the five names mentioned in the salutation). Express to them my deep gratitude for their very kind and gracious letter. Regarding their proposals, I recall having discussed them at length with Dr. Mazur and have agreed, without making a definite commitment because of the condition of my health, to help in the excavation of *Bet Shearim*. With that in view we have already purchased a jeep, which will shortly be shipped, together with various photographic supplies, such as cameras, tripod, films, etc. Regarding the other equipment necessary, it is difficult to get them in the United States because these instruments are not on the metric system. I therefore suggest that they order them from London and have the bills sent to us. The total amount we shall be able to make available in 1952 and 1953 will not be in excess of $5,000. We spent $1,500 on the jeep and we do not as yet have the bills for the other articles. Whatever announcement they wish to make with respect to the project they may use their own judgment.

To Dr. Simon Rawidowicz[17]—Tell him that I regret exceedingly to have delayed writing, but there are numerous interruptions, preoccupations, and the handicaps with which I do my work. I read his article in *Zukunft* with great interest and I agree with him wholeheartedly. It will interest him to know that I no longer have the bridegroom say *"Kedat Mosheh w'Yisrael"* but *Kedat Mosheh we amenu*. As a matter of fact, I suggested at one time that if the Israelis continue to use the word "Israel" we ought to perhaps adopt for world Jewry the name "Jeshurun." I did not see any article about him in *Qiryat Sepher*. In what issue did it appear?

To Professor Simon Halkin (Rabbi Goldman asked that you write to him as warmly as the Rabbi does to Ephraim Lisitzky)—Express to him my heartfelt gratitude, both for his letter as well as for the copy of Cassuto's *Shemot*. The book was delivered to me on a Friday evening after

---

16. The correspondence with Prof. Simon Halkin constitutes a volume in itself. Here there was more than a patron-beneficiary relationship, rather a true collaboration between a gifted poet and a poetic rabbi-scholar. The revival of Hebrew as the language of Israel and of the universal hopes of mankind linked with bonds of steel a reverence and affection that sprang from a rapport far deeper and wider than that which comes from the intellect alone.

17. One of the most distinguished Hebrew social historians of this century. He was for a short time on the faculty of the College of Jewish Studies (Chicago) and for a longer period on the faculty at Brandeis University.

the Services by a young couple who are very, very familiar to me but in the excitement of the crowd around me I failed to recognize who they were. If he recalls the name, he should be good enough to send it to me because I want to express my thanks to these young people.

Together with him and thinking and informed Jews everywhere, I mourn the death of the irreplacable Cassuto. It is a tragedy that he did not live long enough to finish his work on the Bible. Who knows how soon we shall have another one, combining all of the qualifications Cassuto did in himself for a modern commentary on the Bible. But death is no respecter, so instead of mourning what he might have given us, let us be grateful for what he has already given us.

Now I should like to impose upon his (Halkin's) kindness again. From time to time, there appear books on the Bible in Palestine, such as Cassuto's *Exodus*, which do not come to my attention for weeks, and sometimes for months. Unfortunately, the Hebrew scholars, even those to whom I have sent my own books, have not always reciprocated in kind. Would it then be possible for him to make contact there for me with a student of Bible who would make it his responsibility to send me the worthwhile works and reprints on the Bible.

Bibliography

NOTE: *This is not to be regarded as a full listing of all that was written by Solomon Goldman although it does include all his major pamphlets and books with as much accurate information as was procurable. In addition to this list, there are numerous papers and articles published in periodicals, but which we were unable to locate. Any information from readers that will add to the material given here will be received with appreciation. As will be apparent, the bibliography is in alphabetical order.*

Am Olam va'Aretz. Essays on Jews and Judaism from *Ha-Ogen* (New York: Shulsinger Brothers, 1944); published by the Histadrut Ivrit of America, and dedicated to Dr. Eliezer Finkelstein.

"An Address at the Opening Session of the 25th Hadassah Convention," on 24 October 1931, New York, N. Y.; 16 pp.

"An Address to Chaim Weizmann" at the Hotel Astor, 22 January 1940.

The Book of Human Destiny:

I. *The Book of Books,* introduction to the Bible. (Philadelphia: Jewish Publication Society of America, 1948); dedicated to Professor Alexander Marx on his seventieth birthday.

II. *In the Beginning,* on the Book of Genesis. (Philadelphia: Jewish Publication Society of America, 1949); dedicated to Mordecai M. Kaplan.

287

III. *From Slavery to Freedom,* on Exodus, published posthumously and edited by Harry Orlinsky (New York: Abelard-Schuman, 1958); in memory of Herman Templer.

A Challenge to American Jews, reprinted from the *Sentinel* (Chicago: n.p., n.d.), broadsheet.

Correspondence with Joseph P. Kennedy, then ambassador to Great Britain (in the Zionist Archives).

Crisis and Decision, a collection of essays dedicated to Hyman N. Kohn (New York: Harper & Brothers, 1938).

"Does Zionism Jeopardize Patriotism?"; three pamphlets (Chicago: Seven Arts Syndicate, 1931), 19 pages.

"God and Israel," reprinted from *The New Palestine,* 1929.

The Golden Chain, dedicated to Nathan D. Engelman (New York: Bloch and Co., 1937); Vol. I of *The Torah and the Earlier Prophets,* 219 pages.

Ha-Yehudi v'-haOlam, a translation into Hebrew of *The Jew and the Universe* (in Palestine: Dvir, Tel Aviv 1939); translated by Abraham Regelson.

The Hebrew Bible (with selections from the Bible), in *The Great Jewish Books and Their Influence on History,* edited by Caplan, Samuel, and Ribalow (New York: Horizon Press, 1952) pp. 19–58.

Igeret Teman of Maimonides, in Hebrew, with a vocalized text, a commentary, and vocabulary (New York: Histadrut Ivrit of America, 1950), 205 pages.

"Israel Indestructible," an address at the convention of the Zionist Organization of America, 16 July 1940 in Pittsburgh.

The Jew and the Universe, dedicated to Goldman's wife, Alice (New York: Harper & Brothers, 1936).

"Judaism for Sale," a pamphlet on Zionism, 22 pages.

"Justice Not Tolerance," an address made at the twenty-fifth convention of Hadassah and published as a pamphlet October 1939; it was later included in *Undefeated.*

L'An, story by Mordecai Ze'ev Feierberg, with a biographical essay and vocabulary aids for students of Hebrew.

"Land and Destiny," the presidential address at the forty-second convention of the Zionist Organization of America in New York; published in three pamphlets.

"The Legal Fiction in Jewish Law," presentation William Barron Stevenson, pp. 54–72.

Letters and Sayings of Achad Ha'am, in Hebrew.

"The Man of the Book" in the *Festschschrift for the Birthday of Alexander Marx,* pp. 54–72.

Memorandum on the organization and departmental structure of the Zionist Organization of America; at the forty-third convention in Pittsburgh.

"The Original Intent," in *The New Palestine,* pp. 65–67, 29 January 1943; on the Balfour Declaration and the Mandate for Palestine.

El Pensamiento Judio y el Universo, translation by Leon Dujovno of *The Jew and the Universe* into Spanish (Buenos Aires: 1940).

"The Portrait of a Teacher," in *Louis Ginzberg Jubilee Volume* (New York: American Academy for Jewish Research, 1945), pp. 1–18.

Palestine at War Preface to the book by A. J. Epstein (Washington: 1943).

Prayers and Readings, selected and arranged by Solomon Goldman (Philadelphia: Jewish Publication Society of America, c. 1938) issued with Harry Coopersmith, *Songs of My People* (Chicago: c. 1937).

The Situation in Palestine and the Middle East, pamphlet (1941).

Stories by Peretz, College of Jewish Studies, Chicago (Jewish Publication Society of America, 1938).

Stories of Bialik, in Hebrew; College of Jewish Studies (Jewish Publication Society of America, 1946).

The Ten Commandments, with an introduction by Maurice Samuel from Book III of *The Book of Human Destiny* (Chicago: University of Chicago Press, 1956).

The Text of the Book of 'amuel, in Hebrew, with commentary (London: Soncino Press, 1951).

Tradition and Change, edited by Mordecai Waxman, 1958.

Undefeated, address, published as a pamphlet, delivered before the Zionist Organization of America (Washington: 1940).

Whither?, Mordecai Zerev Feierberg, translated from the Hebrew by Ira Eisenstein with a Foreword by Solomon Goldman (New York: Abelard-Schuman, 1927).

"Why I Am A Jew," part of a colloquy with a Catholic and a Protestant, with Clarence Darrow at Orchestra Hall in Chicago, presided over by A. Eustace Haydon.

The Words of Justice Brandeis 1856–1914, edited by Solomon Goldman with a foreword by William O. Douglas (New York: Hy. Schuman, 1953); dedicated to David Jacker.

"The *Yishuv* Stands Firm," in *The Palestine Review,* 11 August 1939.

Also edited by Solomon Goldman:

Moses ben Maimon, *Letter to the Jews of Yemen* (New York: 1950), in Hebrew.

Hayyim Nahman Bialik (Chicago: 1941)

INDEX